FIRE AND ICE:

ONE AIRMAN'S ADVENTURES AND SPIRITUAL GROWTH WHILE TEACHING THE AFGHANS TO FLY

By Major Todd Andrewsen

Copyright 2012 – Todd Andrewsen

In accordance with 5 CFR 2635.807(b), as defined in §3601.102:

(a) The views presented in the following text are those of the speaker or author and do not necessarily represent the views of DoD or its components.

Table of Contents:

Acknowledgements - Pg. 5

Preface - Pg. 7

Chapter 1 – OK, I'M TIRED Pg. 13

Chapter 2 – GOOD DAY TODAY Pg. 15

Chapter 3 – NEVER A DULL MOMENT Pg. 17

Chapter 4 – ANOTHER WEEK DOWN Pg. 19

Chapter 5 – ALRIGHT, BEAUTIFUL FLY DAY Pg. 23

Chapter 6 – RUNNING, RUNNING, RUNNING Pg. 27

Chapter 7 – A LETTER TO MY WIFE Pg. 31

Chapter 8 – ANOTHER BLOG REPORT Pg. 33

Chapter 9 – BELIEVE IN GOD!!! Pg. 39

Chapter 10 – DEEP THOUGHTS BY ME Pg. 43

Chapter 11 – ONE MORE REPORT Pg. 47

Chapter 12 – OH WHAT'S IN A NAME? Pg. 51

Chapter 13 – A GLIMPSE Pg. 55

Chapter 14 – SPIRITUAL INSIGHTS AND SOME FLYING Pg. 61

Chapter 15 – QUOTES I REALLY LIKE Pg. 67

Chapter 16 – IT'S THAT TIME OF THE WEEK AGAIN Pg. 71

Chapter 17 – INSHALLAH Pg. 75

Chapter 18 – LONG, HAPPY, SPIRITUAL, FLYING EMAIL Pg. 81

Chapter 19 – FRIENDS AND FAMILY Pg. 87

Chapter 20 – NEW DAY Pg. 93

Chapter 21 – ANOTHER DAY FOR YOU/ME IN PARADISE Pg. 97

Chapter 22 – WYLD STALLIONS!!! Pg. 103

Chapter 23 – THIS IS ONLY 2,771 WORDS LONG Pg. 111

Chapter 24 – FRIENDS AND FAMILY PART 2 Pg. 119

Chapter 25 – RESPONSE TO A FRIEND'S QUESTION Pg. 125

Chapter 26 – EVERYONE NEEDS A TRUNK MONKEY Pg. 133

Chapter 27 – TRUNK MONKEY'S R US…PART TWO Pg. 141

Chapter 28 – FLIGHT, NATURE, AND THOUGHTS Pg. 149

Chapter 29 – LETTER TO LYNN Pg. 159

Chapter 30 – THIS TOO SHALL PASS Pg. 165

Chapter 31 – THIS TOO SHALL PASS TWO Pg. 175

Chapter 32 – THERE WILL BE A PART TWO Pg. 189

Chapter 33 – BE A CHAMPION IN LIFE Pg. 195

Chapter 34 – A GIFT OF THANKSGIVING Pg. 203

Chapter 35 – EXCERPTS FROM A LETTER TO A FRIEND Pg. 213

Chapter 36 – IS DESIRE ENOUGH? Pg. 223

Chapter 37 – A MUDDLE OR A MESS Pg. 237

Chapter 38 – "MY PLANE!" Pg. 245

Chapter 39 – MERRY CHRISTMAS 2010 Pg. 253

Chapter 40 – NEW YEARS DAY Pg. 263

Chapter 41 – HISTORY LESSONS Pg. 273

Chapter 42 – LIFE'S A GRAND ADVENTURE Pg. 285

Chapter 43 – HAPPINESS IS A STATE OF MIND Pg. 295

Chapter 44 – SITTING ON THE DOCK OF THE BAY Pg. 305

Chapter 45 – IN ITALY AGAIN Pg. 315

Chapter 46 – BOOM WENT THE DRUM, NOT THE PLANE Pg. 321

Chapter 47 – A LOVE STORY Pg. 331

Chapter 48 – THERE ARE DAYS I LOVE JAZZ MUSIC Pg. 337

Chapter 49 – SOME TIMES I"M A NUT, SOMETIMES NOT Pg. 347

Chapter 50 – OH, WHAT A BEAUTIFUL MORNING Pg. 357

Chapter 51 – WHAT A DIFFERENCE DOES A DAY MAKE? Pg. 365

Chapter 52 – THE VALUE OF WORK Pg. 377

Chapter 53 – FINI FLIGHT FINAL FUNCTION FINITO Pg. 385

Chapter 54 – THE BREAK ENDS Pg. 397

Epilogue Pg. 401

Bibliography

ACKNOWLEDGEMENTS

Truly no work is done in a vacuum and I must thank first and foremost, Tiffany, whose love, support, and strength has made this possible. Without her I am nothing! Throughout this book I acknowledge my Father in Heaven who has helped me to see where I needed to change and gave me the strength to do so. I want to thank my children for putting up with my constant deployments and work. I have been surely blessed with a wonderful family. This work is for them.

I'd like to dedicate this book to the men and women I served with that died senselessly soon after I returned home! To their families – Thank you for your service and sacrifice! May you find peace and happiness! My prayers are always with you!

Maj. Jeffrey O. Ausborn, 41, Maj. David L. Brodeur, 34, Master Sgt. Tara R. Brown, 33, Maj. Charles A. Ransom, 31, Maj. Raymond G. Estelle II, 40, Capt. Nathan J. Nylander, 35, Capt. Charles A. Ransom, 31, Lt. Col. Frank D. Bryant Jr., 37, and Maj. Philip D. Ambard, 44

PREFACE

When setting out on my deployment, I did not contemplate writing a book; I thought about a blog, but not a book. This is the story of my adventures and personal growth, seen through the experiences of my yearlong deployment to Kabul, Afghanistan. While there, I taught the Afghans how to fly. This provided me with ample opportunities to try not to crash into mountains. Each week I took the time to write a blog and email it to my friends and family. I experienced some profound changes this deployment and want to share my experiences and how the Gospel has changed my life and changed me. I define the Gospel as the restored teachings of Jesus Christ as revealed in these latter days through living prophets, the Book of Mormon, the Bible, and continuing revelation today. For the past 35 years I've been a member of The Church of Jesus Christ of Latter Day Saints. I served a mission, married in the temple, made many mistakes yet did not live the Gospel after the manner that I was taught. I feel that the best way to express the changes that I experienced is to let you know where I'm coming from. I'm not proud of the mistakes I've made. I'm not proud of the hurt that I caused. I am truly thankful for the gift and power of repentance. Through this gift and the opportunity to repent I found peace with myself, peace with my Savior, peace with my wonderful, supportive, and amazing wife, and I want to share this experience with you.

I completed and survived a one-year deployment in Afghanistan as an advisor to the Afghan Air Force, teaching them how to fly the C-27 Spartan cargo aircraft. I was part of the initial cadre of Air Force Instructors that were tasked with creating, from scratch, a training and operational, fixed-wing, western-style, flying program for the Afghan Air Force. This is my story, as told through my emails and blogs, in my own words and often written exactly as I think. I ramble, I conjecture, I tell stories, I embellish the insanity….that's the way I write and I hope you enjoy it. I don't claim expertise. I claim only that the everlasting Gospel of Jesus Christ saved my marriage, my family and my life. I am ever thankful to my Father in Heaven for granting me the opportunity to learn, as I could only have learned while going through this very personal trial, and while spending this time deployed. Here, I've been able to focus on what is important and it's opened my eyes to many things that I was failing to see because I asked not, saw not, and trusted not.

I'll be brief in my explanation. Between some of the stories and insights I will add additional information to help flesh out the story that you will read on the following pages. I've never been known to mince words. May my story inspire you and help you to seek your own insights, personal healing, growth, and enhance your spirit as mine has grown over these months. Technically, my deployment was one-year long. However, I was authorized to move my family for the duration of my long deployment. Thanks to the benefits of military service, I was notified of my deployment date and moved my family to be near my wife's family. Then, while at some training, had my deployment delayed four months. (Insert sarcasm here!) Additionally, the year did not begin until I actually reached Afghanistan. I spent three months training in Italy, but they did not count. However, those months counted to my family and me.

Just before leaving Italy, my wife and I had a heart-to-heart and began the healing and repentance process, which we both sorely needed. I won't go into details, but it was necessary to kick us into gear to realize what's important. What the impetus for this was doesn't matter, except to say that we've struggled and overcome some daunting issues, and are stronger and closer for it. My wife is my best friend and you'll see that throughout this story. I really couldn't be the person I'm becoming without her love and support. Together we can overcome anything and this is as much a tribute to her as it is anything.

The following pages follow me through arrival, daily studying, flight instructing and dealing with all types of people, enough to drive any man insane. The military is a difficult life that is hard for those who have never been in to understand. We're all a little nuts and there are more than a few good men and some not so good. Surrounded by profanity and filth, it's a wonder that good can be found sometimes, but it is there. If there's one thing I want to get across, it's that everything we do is a choice. You will see me refer to that idea many times. Life is a beautiful choice that we are blessed with protecting and serving. I truly try to make the most of my experiences and thoroughly enjoy the learning I'm going through, even when it's hard. Sit back, prop up your feet and enjoy the ride. There are some good stories, some self-written poetry, then mix in a lot of my learning and lessons along the way.

I said in the beginning, I write how I think. I write stories, I write lessons, I write songs, and I write things that don't always make sense…but maybe as you get to know my story through this year, you'll get to know me and understand why I live the quote from the play Rosencrantz and Guildenstern Are Dead, "There you have it, stark raving sane!" I try to live that motto to the extreme. I will come across at times as "stark raving sane" and I will always try to entertain and have fun. But, in all honesty, this is a story of growth, of learning. I will cover many Gospel topics because the Gospel has become my rock and the Savior, My Redeemer. I beg your indulgence and maybe, just maybe, you'll find the peace and joy that I'm learning to see as well.

First and foremost, there will be many war stories…though these war stories are not your typical war story. But, these are MY typical war stories. I've had a unique and interesting experience. For one thing, knock on wood, I've never been shot at, that I know of. (With no instrumentation onboard to tell me whether I've been shot at or not, I could've been shot at hundreds of times and never know. All I know is that I've never been hit.) And yet, I fly a defenseless airplane conducting training in a war torn country….makes perfect sense to me, and the kicker of it all……it's a bloody good time! The characters are unique, the story varied, the atmosphere…different than what you're used to at home, I can guarantee that. Now let's get on with it.

THE WOOD

The Wood:
At the edge of the glen, mid woods so deep
Stood a deep dark elm, with branches to weep
the fairies they trod with the softest of glean
unhurried, undaunted their wings did oft breen
with otherworldly light, with ethereal mist
as dewdrops 'pon thistles and honey leaves they kiss'd
Entering in this world of night
where magic abounds and soft looms the light
of thousands of torches, the lightning bugs glow
Magic unfurled 'neath soft drifting snow

Our hero she steps without fear and with right
for coming alone in the dead of the night
She steps o'er so softly with little elfish feet
in soft supple boots and where they do meet
the ground softly gathers, and sounds drift away
And an evening's melancholy is surely at bay
For on this night of nights when the bluebirds do sing
she lifts up her hand, with an glittering elfish ring
calls softly upon the magic therein bound
and slowly gently casts, there upon the ground
the threshes and boughs of fresh cut fern
and animals come, their trust she did earn
Elk, doe, rabbit, and fox, gathered in circle thereby to see
the magic, the music, e'en the mystery
of a child , a woman, an innocent girl
as she cast her spell to gift to the world
a moment of silence, a moment of peace
midst all the sadness and all of the grief
though tornados, and earthquakes and terrors abound
in one little corner, in one little glen
out of millions of people and millions of men
our one little hero did sit there and say
let's have peace, let's have light, if only for a day
the clouds they did part, the sun it did shine
and hearts duly hardened for a moment didn't mind

and thereby reflected on all of the good
then softly, our hero stole back to the wood
and left it all tranquil as she slowly smiled
and yawning, woke up, with her feelings so mild
the dream stayed then with her, as good dreams will do
she smiled and laughed, a children's thought too
and rising from bed she knew that today
would be a nice one...come what may!!!
-By Todd Andrewsen

C-27 on the Alenia Ramp in Naples, Italy

Chapter 1

OK, I'M TIRED

Tell you what; I've been going almost non-stop since I got here. This is going to be a short note because I'm tired. I got up at 0630 and went to work and got off at 1930 and didn't get to my room until almost 2030 (8:30 P.M. for those that don't understand military time). There's a 9.5 hour time difference from Tiffany and the kids and it's so weird sometimes to be calling as I go to bed and they are just beginning their day.

I am at Kabul International Airport and it is pretty cool because I am with the International Stabilization Force, so there are people from approximately 20-40 different countries here. Afghanistan is a dirty, brown country. It looks like Alaska without the feral beauty and it is a mess. The main thing I noticed when I went to work the first day was the smell. Our trainees have a different take on hygiene and it takes a while to get used to. I'm not even going to talk about the bathroom hole in the ground toilets so don't even ask! Nothing gets clean here, though they try, it's just dirty. Our base is divided: one half Afghan, one half NATO. I live on the NATO side and work on the Afghan.

I spoke with a soldier from Slovenia yesterday and another from the Czech Republic. I've spoken with several Italians. Funny story, I was looking for the ATM one day right after we got here and the first person I saw to ask was an Italian. Well, he immediately said he didn't speak English, not realizing I'd asked him in Italian how to find the ATM. After I repeated the request and said that he could tell me in Italian, you could see the relief in his face and he immediately gave me rapid-fire directions...that I followed easily.

I have flown twice since arriving and am flying again in the morning. It's fun and different and doesn't seem like much of a war, when we're treating Kabul like a training base...For our first several flights we're flying with our bosses and they, basically, are giving us another twenty hours in the plane to get more comfortable with it before we get sent out with Afghan students. The Afghans with whom we work are all very nice, humble people...ok most are humble. One young punk is not so humble. But then again, he was the first to finish the initial program, and since he isn't one of the in-crowd, the Afghan Air Force has sort of neglected to pay him for the last three years!!! Yeah, that's not cool!

One thing that's happened since I've been here is I'm doing a lot of scripture reading and study and becoming more spiritual than I've ever been and I like it. But, I'm busy, busy and when I'm not busy, I'm busy. So all in all, the days are long but the weeks are going to fly by. I was put in charge of all the operational scheduling for the aircraft and crews. Essentially, I'm taking a rudimentary program they've been using and trying to improve it to be a fully functioning schedule. We're trying to forecast two weeks in advance, but everything changes every day, go figure. Inshallah!!! That is Afghan for "If Allah wills it", which they use for everything. Are you going to be there on time? Inshallah! Will the passengers be there? Inshallah! Are we going to crash? Inshallah! You see how this can be a fun game. It's kind of a fatalistic attitude they have, but that is their life.

Chapter 2

GOOD DAY TODAY

Let me tell you about my flying today!!!! (Pick up bag; hold to face, breath steady, and be prepared....it won't be that bad, just warning you!) Today was an awesome day to fly. Thunderheads didn't really start popping up over the mountains until the trip back and so there were a lot of puffies, clouds that are building like towers, but aren't as turbulent as thunderstorms, but will eventually become thunderstorms. When it's like this, I play a game that I like to call cloud surfing. The trick is to dodge from cloud to cloud, banking the wings up to 45 or 60 degrees, if need be, to just brush the tip of the wing into the cloud. This is fine art and precision flying...all while trying to climb to altitude over the mountains and, sometimes, you miss and go through the top of a puffy cloud and the plane jumps. The idea is to warn your loadmaster beforehand because you know you're going to have a couple bumps when that happens. It's fun! (Ok, it is fun for us pilots, loadmasters and passengers don't always like it, but that's their fault for getting on the plane with me!!!) :)

We flew over to Herat, a small dirty little town near Iran and did a steep approach. This is where I come in from 10-12,000 feet above the airport and about 5 miles out have my gear down, flaps down, and begin, what I term, my drop like a rock approach, losing 2,000 feet of altitude per mile flown...it's fun! The nose is basically pointed straight at the ground, but we've got these big fans out there called propellers that we flatten out and the blades act like speed brakes which slow us down quickly. Then, we just plummet out of the sky!!! Afterward, at a few hundred feet, we smooth out the propeller, slow the descent rate, and have a nice smooth touchdown...all my touchdowns were super smooth today and, yes, I am bragging, because I enjoyed my flight today. However, that's how it was supposed to work, but this silly Airliner was nervous that I was 10 miles in FRONT of him. I was going to do a touch and go on the runway, but he kept at it, complaining to the controller, who then made me go around without touching down....and he let the other plane land first. But, since he was 10 miles behind me, I had to go do a couple of 360 degree turns, and FINALLY he got off the runway and I could land....gosh!!! It ended up being a really nice flight; we flew a low-level (less than 500 feet) over to another field, climbing up and around rolling hills. All in all, it was a good day of work.

I had a nice discussion at dinner with my boss, he's a practicing Roman Catholic and so we talked about our churches and how it helps us get through the days out here. I'm not going to schedule him to fly Sundays anymore, per his request, because that's when Catholic Mass is. I told him my routine and how I study every evening. He asked what, and so I told him, “religious topics.” That started our discussion on how religion needs to be a staple out here to get by, especially when you’re here for so long.

Oh, dinner was good. I'd only eaten a little bit today. (A bag of chips and a Nutri-grain bar for breakfast and a brownie for lunch) So, seven of us went to one of the two Non-Chow Halls to eat....There's an authentic Thai restaurant here on base and I had some delicious ultra-spicy Pad Thai and green curry tonight. Oh goodness, it's still burning in my intestines...I love it. That’s the only way to eat Thai. It was worth it. We've been working hard and doing a lot since we got here so it was a nice break from chow hall food.

Chapter 3

NEVER A DULL MOMENT

Life, like art, is full of swirls, eddies, changes and craziness. After all, look at a New York art exhibit...weird!!! So, why do I say this? Because the last couple days have been crazy! I'm the Current Operations Officer and Scheduler which means it's my job to figure out how to get everything planned, tracked and kept in line. That works well right up until we actually have to do anything. Today is a prime example. I only had one mission (flight) scheduled to fly today. Simple really, just go out, drop stuff off, and come back. No problem!

At least it's no problem until the aircraft blows a tire and dislocates one of its brake lines...then it's what's known as a MESS brewing and I, of course, love the fact that I'm the guy right in the middle of it all. I get information, forward plans, make plans, get the right people going where they should and eventually, five hours later, we have a rescue airplane loaded with supplies and flying off to drop off the maintenance team to rescue the problem child. Of course, this all plays havoc, possibly, with my schedule for tomorrow and the next day since everything that happens every day becomes a chain reaction decimating my carefully orchestrated two week outlook for what we're going to do.

All in all, it's an absolute blast because I get to make lots of decisions, after getting the Lt Col's permission and/or agreement and/or consent before I do some things, of course. It's crazy and fun and busy and keeps me occupied. There you have a glimpse of my daily life and it's a new adventure everyday here in Afghanistan. Tomorrow is another day. You know the usual--meet with the general, teach the Afghans, put out schedule fires, eat, run 5 miles, call the wife for hours on end just because I can, and I enjoy it and basically just have a nice relaxing normal day...

Chapter 4

ANOTHER WEEK DOWN

Far be it from me to decide when to write…Ok, I do decide when to write and I enjoy the whole writing thing. I've been super busy lately. It makes time go very quickly. All of a sudden it's another weekend. Okay, weekend for us because Friday is the one day a week we don't work, because it's the Muslim version of Sunday. It's been a busy week. I've done a lot of work, spent long days and had a blast…I'd like to point out that I always have a blast because that's my nature so it is important to note that. What have I done this week you ask? Let me tell you! I know I'm so predictable.

First off, I got a roommate. Sad, but true! I have a roommate now and it was so nice when I was by myself and could just talk to Tiffany whenever, which I still do, I just have to be careful what I say because I don't really want to have a fun, frivolous, flirtatious discussion--ok a lovey dovey sappy conversation--with my wife with my roommate sitting there possibly listening.

Second, I've been very busy massaging schedules on a daily basis, teaching ground school – especially when, on one day I was supposed to teach, I forgot I was teaching, and had to grab the instruction book and refresh my memory very quickly!!! It went well. I enjoy teaching the Afghans ground school. They're very nice and polite and interested in learning, though one of them doesn't like to study, thinking he can learn everything by osmosis. My schedule is more of a fluid rather than a solid. It changes on a daily basis and requires lots of maneuvering. It's been nice though having enough airplanes to actually get everything on the schedule completed.

Then there's the flying. I flew my fourth mission this week and am now certified to instruct in the C-27 on my own. This will be fun. I much prefer doing things on my own rather than having someone watching over my shoulder, but that's because I like to be in charge.

My "Certification" flight was awesome. We took off out of here and began flying west and shut down an engine due to what we thought was a fuel leak, because there was fluid pouring out of the engine. We turned around and came back. I wasn't actually in the pilot seat because there were two of us being certified. I was in the back watching the fluid flow out....it was interesting. We shut down and the pilot came in high and fast and ended up smoking the brakes and we had to evacuate the aircraft after we parked. (Brakes get hot, smoke and if they get too hot, catch on fire-these didn't catch on fire) So, where was I? Oh yes, luckily we had a spare airplane and we were able to change out and begin again, just a couple hours delayed. We flew down and began to fly a low-level through the mountains. Now, low-level is fun. Low-level is a blast. Low-level through the mountains is really fun and really a blast.

But, we made our Afghan loadmaster sick, I'm pretty sure he puked in the trash. He was done after that. In his defense, it was bumpy, swirly, bumpy, we went up and down and turned and back around and hit turbulence and descended and climbed and basically played around going a couple hundred miles low level through beautiful mountains. We saw the Tower of Jaam, which is a 2,000 year old minaret or Muslim prayer tower. It was pretty cool. Then, I got in the seat and did steep descents for landing, my favorite. Drop like a rock….absolutely fun! You should try it sometime. It's just fun to make the airplane do what you want it to, feel the speed when you're flying low-level, and be able to set the plane down on a short airstrip. It's a beautiful plane to fly.

I also had a great week studying a book with Tiffany, we read every night together and it sure brings us closer together and helps us open up and talk about a lot of things. When I'm not working, I ran 3-5 times in the week a minimum of 3.7 miles and studied a lot of scriptures, and gospel subjects. Additionally, I relaxed for a couple minutes reading the old 1980 version of Battlestar Galactica...Love it.

All in all, as usual in my life, I'm completely busy, totally sane, insanely happy, except when I'm not and just enjoying life, especially talking to Tip so much. Life is good, except there are suicidal flies in this office that are about to die because they keep trying to fly in my ears, mate in my hair and lick the fluid from my eyes....obviously we have a slight fly problem in the office, but no matter how many we destroy,....there's always more. It's quite disgusting because they feed off the stink that is the air here.

Chapter 5

ALRIGHT, BEAUTIFUL FLY DAY

Here we go a caroling among the clouds so green, la di da di da da di da di da da di....or something like that. Never in my wildest dreams did I expect to be a blogger, but I really enjoy writing this email, blog whatever, however you receive it, because it's really fun to write. This week has been a week of craziness and it's not even over. Let me give some of the highlights: Pulled into a meeting with several Afghan Generals and Colonels who act like 5 year olds that don't get what they want; pulled into multiple meetings with my boss (helps that my desk is right in front of his door) to plan multiple different things; kicked-off of one flight since my planning skills for international missions were invaluable and too valuable to have me fly; cancelled said international mission right after getting off the phone with the Embassy; Afghan airliner crashed in the mountains....organized, prepped, and scheduled a new flight to go fly Search and Rescue operations...they didn't find it; flew first by myself operational mission with an Afghan copilot and delivered passengers around the country.

Enjoyed every minute of flying today...I'll give the airsick details shortly of my approach into Kandahar, since I love to provide said details; spent many days at work until 1830. or later, ran several miles; today ran 5 miles and basically, I am trying to lose weight; spoke with the beautiful, wonderful woman that is my wife for hours every day; studied Italian, Dari, and Serbian/Croatian while also beginning to study my professional development classes. All in all....I don't' have, or want, much free time. I enjoy studying and have never enjoyed video games. Tiffany and I have been reading a book together over Skype and it's just awesome. She's such a strength to me and a wonderful wife and mother that can handle pretty much anything. The Lord blessed me with a wonderful woman. I've been immersing myself in the gospel and it is an amazing feeling to study and know the Lord loves me...if you can't get close to the Lord during war, where can you get close to Him....But, mostly I'm just enjoying life, and all the craziness that surrounds it. Every day is a new adventure, everyday an opportunity to choose to live a happy productive one or to choose a blahhhh one. I choose happy go lucky.

Now as promised....we were flying into Kandahar...it's in the desert of Afghanistan, cross the mountain range and there you are, but they, air traffic control, likes to keep you high at altitude until you're pretty close, none of these silly airliner 100 miles to descend so you barely notice you're descending games like in the USA. Oh no, we wait until we are 25 miles or less and then power out of the sky at maximum rate of descent with the vertical velocity meter pegged down, the airspeed pegged up, and the airplane screaming across the ground. I know, screaming across the ground in a C-27 is not quite the same as say, in an F-16, but still fun!

We drop and maneuver to set up for a straight in. Now, normal procedure would have me slow down about 12 miles out or so and begin a nice leisurely descent at 130 MPH or so down to the runway...Well, that's all well and good, but it's much more fun to descend and come in at 220 MPH at 4,000 feet and push in to four miles. Then, rip the power back to idle and as the plane starts to slow, throw down flaps which slows it more and then, with the gear and additional flaps we approach about two miles away from the runway still at 4,000 feet. Shove the nose over almost twenty degrees below the horizon and ride the elevator down for a nice smooth-as-a-baby's-butt touchdown....kiss the ground....or not, but sometimes yes! I flew that leg and then let him fly the plane back on the second leg. That's my story and I'm sticking to it!! Hope you have a nice day!

Thank you for riding Andrewsen Airlines, and thank you for keeping your arms and legs inside the ride at all times, should at any time during the ride you feel nauseous or sick…Well, either grab a bag or puke in your helmet....and you're taking it with you no leaving it on the plane, so...good luck!!!!

Chapter 6

RUNNING, RUNNING, RUNNING

Dust clouds billow as the trucks drive along the paved and dirt road. Choking exhaust and gagging dust as my body strives to haul air into my lungs through the filter of my nose, which immediately makes me feel the inner lining of my sinuses crack and dry out! Running, getting in shape, losing weight…that's what I'm doing, I remind myself, left foot, right foot, left foot….breathe in breathe out, etc…ankle wrapped, check, knee a little sore, check, gasping for breath…not as much anymore. I'm getting used to it and able to run further and longer. Love it! How far today, you ask? Three and three quarters are the minimum…the other day I ran six and a quarter. I'm really enjoying running. Only problem, I tell myself, is that I get off work, tired, worn out and don't want to do anything…..so I sit on my chair, remove my boots, change my uniform to PT (physical training) gear, put on my tennis shoes and the whole time I'm saying, "I don't want to run, I don't want to run"….and I grab my headphones and IPod, and walk out the door. I enjoy running, I do. It hurts and my body doesn't like it, but I do, so I do it, and I'm less sore and my body likes it better every day.

This week has been an interesting one. The last couple weeks since I last wrote have been busy, busy, and busy. I've gotten to do all sorts of interesting things and have even gotten to fly a couple times. I had the opportunity to take an airplane and go on a three day off-station mission teaching some Afghans how to fly. Then, the other day I took a plane and we went to Herat, a place on the far west side of Afghanistan and went in search of pizza....I mean, if you're going to go to an Italian-run base, you need to go look for pizza. We finally found it, but the pizza shop was closed. We had to settle for some left-over sandwiches. Got gas, flew back, and had a nice day.

I'm involved in all sorts of enterprises here. I'm working on my Master's degree, ACSC (Air Command and Staff College-a required program for Majors and Major selects); I'm scheduling all the flying for our planes and sit in on meetings with Generals and Colonels almost every day. I pretend that it's because I'm nosy, but really it's because I enjoy being involved; it makes the time pass quickly. I speak with Tiffany twice a day and it's awesome to be able to feel a part of the family life even though I'm here. Additionally, I get to plan some big events that we are looking forward to use with for the Afghans for the future.

I'm working on getting an assignment to Europe following this deployment and my Wing Commander is 100% in agreement with me to try to get me that assignment. So, hopefully, I'll be taking the family to Europe for a few years when I get back....again more to follow. This is my life...always busy, with more to follow. There is no stability....except at home...Tiffany is my rock and my stable lover, friend and wife...I love it.

I've had very little time to do things other than work, exercise, study both religious and school studies, call Tiffany, and sleep. But Fridays are always nice because I get to go to church, sleep and watch conference talks and good movies....In other words, I don't really have time to waste. I'm reading a couple of books and enjoying them while I do everything else: Anita Stansfield, Battle Star Galactica, The Book of Mormon, Between Husbands and Wives (a book Tiffany and I are reading together and it is cool to do every day since I have to be so far apart). If you haven't figured it out, I love to study. I love reading. I worked on Serbian today along with some Dari. I'm crazy. I'm studying Dari, Italian, Russian, and Serbian right now along with everything else (only little bits at a time), but, it is fun! Life is fun, it's an adventure. Life is to be lived and lived in the right way. Doing good things and learning new things are AWESOME!!!! I love challenges. And there are lots of those here. I'm going on another three day trip soon too.

Now, this is very much an email of me bragging about all the things I'm doing and in reality, I don't mean to brag. I'm just excited about all the things I AM doing. I love listening to W. Cleon Skousen talk about the pre-mortal existence and the Atonement. I love his depth of understanding about the need and reason of Christ's coming. I've listened to his talk at least 4 times. It's amazing.

Anyways, I think I've rambled on enough. I love it. I enjoy life and enjoy what I'm doing. I miss my family and I miss being at home, but I love what I'm doing. I love helping the Afghans; the people I work with are some amazing people in difficult circumstances. The flying is fun and I tend to think I'm pretty good at it. :) Life is good. I'm in a good place and am perpetually happy...go figure!

Remember to enjoy whatever you do!!! Life is a choice, it always is!!!

Chapter 7

A LETTER TO MY WIFE

I enjoy Irish songs! They're rollicking and frolicking and full of fun. Aye, they're joyful rollicking tales; unfortunately they're usually talking about drinking, but not all. My favorite, The Green Man, has nothing to do with drinking.

A silly and fun life is good. I might even get to send this eventually if the internet comes up. I've been listening to a book about being happy regardless and it's really good….I think so because the author is stating things that I've said and believed forever and that is that you need to be doing what you love and she adds a lot more depth to that. She talks about soul fulfilling work.

Oh my, what a day. This day is so cool. The internet died at 0830 this morning and that means that I've done a lot of reading and listening to my IPod to accomplish something today. I actually pulled out my Dash-1 and studied emergency procedures. Crazy, I know. Oh well, such is life. Life is crazy fun. The wind blows, the dust storms, the world sighs and continues! The ACSC stuff I've been studying has been really interesting because it's been all about cultural awareness and cultural training and learning. Also, about all the stuff I've been saying about the need of the American culture and military to study others and not keep ourselves isolated and force others to do things OUR way because sometimes there are other different ways that are just as effective if not more effective because they deal specifically with another culture.

You know the interesting thing I've seen while studying is that although the military prides itself on a couple things the foundation that we are supposed to strive to emulate is not always there. First, Integrity – the cornerstone for building trust, saying what we mean and do what we say…what's interesting about that is how that relates to one of the CD talks by Dr. John Lund that I'm sending you. It's about love language and all that….and one of the first rules is that the author challenges couples is to OWN their words. Meaning, mean what you say 100%...I think I mentioned this before and when you listen to the talk….you'll understand! The second that I like from my ACSC study that applies to the spiritual as well, is the need, requirement, desire to have moral courage…this means the willingness to stand up for what one believes to be right even if that stand is unpopular, or contrary to conventional wisdom. The rest of that subject is obvious now in our current process of change.

So I'm about done with this. I need to run today. I need to get something for Savannah. Ahh, life is good.

5 June 2010

Chapter 8

ANOTHER BLOG REPORT

Well, my eyes are about full to bursting. How do you change a heart? How do you touch a soul? One peaceful experience at a time! I can't believe or imagine the last twenty-four hours. It's been a whirlwind of emotion. Why? Because a good writer with a gift of touching the Spirit and letting others feel has touched my life in an amazing way. I don't think I've cried this much in my entire life. It's not just the story though. It's the feelings, the Spirit, the knowing and seeing my life and the paths I've taken and recognizing that while they haven't been the right ones all the time, my life is guided by my Father in Heaven, who knows me and loves me and knows the different choices I would make. He knows me and loves me and provides the way for healing and change and repentance and love. What an amazing gift. There were so many things in these last two books that have just reached out and squeezed my heart and my eyes; they have been flowing constantly for hours. I couldn't put the book down last night and as I finished one I moved on to the next. There are so many things; especially the music. You see, I hear music, in my heart and in my head. I may not write music, but I write poetry and it flows and the poetry of the song written stirred my soul. The changes in the character's lives, especially as the Gospel was brought into their life melted my heart, burned in my bosom, etched my soul with desire to be better, to do better, to sing and dance and swing Tiffany around and hold her for all eternity.

Wow, what a deluge of passion, pain, grief, hope, sustainment, love, loss, healing, family....there's a frame on my desk that says, "We live, we laugh, we love." The saying is so true. We do live and laugh and love. This life is amazing. This world that our Father created for us is beautiful, full of gifts, yet also full of strife and pain. Life is a time when we prepare to meet God. I've known that my entire life. I've grown up in the Church of Jesus Christ of Latter Day Saints, I've made covenants, I've served a two-year Church mission to Guatemala, and I've broken promises, and had a split personality, a divided person. Unhappiness settles upon one's soul when they're not following the commandments. 'Wickedness never was happiness' and all that. I look back on my life and I see all the good times and the bad. I see, as Jayson did in these books, the good, the bad, the choices I've made, the wonderful woman I married and am looking forward to spending eternity with. It's not going to be an easy road, in fact the closer Tiffany and I have come to working on doing what's right and becoming closer to each other the more the devil has worked on us. Opposition in all things! Why, would the devil not work very hard when we were not living as we should? Because, he didn't have to! Now he wants to make sure that we fall back into old patterns so that changes don't stick. Well, my opinion of Ol' Scratch is that he can stuff it! I love the fact that as I've been reading these stories I've, "had a high water table". What's the point of feeling the Spirit if you can't have an outlet for it? It's been amazing.

The Sound of the Rain, A Distant Thunder, Winds of Hope, awesome books by Anita Stansfield! I've read many books, thousands, actually. There hasn't been a story that has touched me to the core as these. Tiffany was inspired to send them. Do I have issues? You bet I do. Am I working on them? Absolutely! This is amazing. I can't stop saying this is amazing. I think about how judgmental I've been of Utahans and others, to include my parents. I've always accused them of being judgmental of me and others and in some respects that is true, but their love never faileth. They love me in spite of my weaknesses. The unconditional love is there. Life is full of changes. Life is full of mayhem. Life is full of weakness. Life is also full of beauty. Life is full of love. Life is full of happiness, if we reach out and grab it. This life, as I said earlier is a time to prepare to meet God. There's a part I want to quote from Anita Stansfield's book.

This is one of the songs, "You stood tonight…beneath the light of Heaven's narrow moon. And on your face…I saw the trace of a love that waned too soon….When love bleeds red, the words you said, pierced me to the core. When all is said and done, the battles fought, the victory's won, what could I do more, to show you that I love you? Oh, how I love you….A trace of love gleamed in your tears and trickled down your face. A glimmer of the hope we shared in another time and place. I reached for you, you reached for me, and the glow burst into flame. My lips met yours, your tears met mine, and I knew that we could have it all again…?"

I know we can have it all again!

This is my own version:

I've been lost in a wilderness,

Missing you and missing time.

My world is fraught with difference

Recompense and a sense of emptiness

When you're not there,

When we are far apart

When we will stand

And hold each other's hearts

"Love bleeds red,

The words you said

Pierced me to the core"

Together we will overcome

And hold each other forevermore.

This sandy world, of wasted youth

This gritty place, wherein it's hard to see the truth

So many lost, so few are found

Lord bless all those who are turning round

Searching in and searching out

Looking lost and turned about

But seeking all and seeking right

Seeking to accompany us to the light

The world bleeds red, with the words you said

They pierced me to the core, I'll love you evermore

Now the world would have us lose

No one's patient, all must choose

Do we grow or do we die

With our sins inside

We must now partake today

Of the choices that we make

Every day of every life, we stumble and we strive

Looking in and looking out

World within and world without

Spirit whispers do you mind

Will you choose to walk the line?

The world bleeds red, with the words you said

They pierced me to the core, I'll love you evermore

Now as I am far away, searching always night and day

For the peace I left alone, in my soul a long time ago

Evermore and ever loved, you are spirit from above

Loving you takes no more time, than eternalness inside

For with choices that we make

We can will or lose or stay

We can be and live and grow

We can love and we will know

Love bleeds red with words you said

They pierce me to the core, I'll love you evermore

Love bleeds red no words unsaid

You pierce me to the core and I WILL Love you ever more

I love you ever more…

Ok there's my rendition. I can actually hear the music in my head. I always have, when I write it's like I hear it and it just flows on paper. I'm not saying I'm as good as Jayson in the story, but I do believe I have several gifts from the Lord for which I am absolutely thankful. The world outside is chaos. The world we live in is full of sin and recriminations. But for now, in this moment, all is peace! Oh holy night, the stars are brightly shining, it is the night of the dear Savior's birth. … Oh my Father, though that dwellest, en el celestial hogar, cuando volvere a verte, I haz tu lado mi altar…

For Tip, I must add this other song in Anita Stansfield's book, because it made me cry, "I've heard it said that true romance only comes once in a lifetime. And for fools who miss their chance, fools who pay the fiddler but miss the dance, they'll spend their days with only memories to keep them warm. But, memories grow faint with time, and the years become a stale companion, and with each passing day, I only missed you more. But, I'm a man who believes in miracles, and lady you're the one…who turned around and took my hand and said, 'we've paid the price. The fiddler's tired, the band's expired, but we still have time to dance.' I'm a man that knows beyond a doubt that God smiles on fools like me. I'm a man who got a second chance….You are my music, you are my song. You are the right that counteracts my every wrong. You are the rhythm in my heartbeat; you are the breath beneath my voice. You are the light dispelling dark in every choice….And, I'm a man who believes in miracles, and lady you're the one…who turned around and took my hand and said, 'we've paid the price. The fiddler's tired, the band's expired, but we still have time to dance.' I'm a man that knows beyond a doubt that God smiles on fools like me. I'm a man who got a second chance."

That's exactly how I feel. I love you. I love our family. I love our life. I love our love. I miss you and want you to know that I'm a man who believes in miracles, and Lady you're the one, who turned around and took my hand and gave me a second chance. I love you. I love you. I love you.

Chapter 9

BELIEVE IN GOD!!!

"Believe in God; Believe that he is; believe that He created all things both in heaven and in earth; believe that He has all wisdom and all power, both in heaven and in earth; believe that man doth not comprehend all things which the Lord can comprehend." – Mosiah 4:9

Today is a good day. Today is a day of rest and reflection like all good Fridays are these days. Today is a day of listening, to the wind, the Spirit, the Gospel, life….as I said a day of reflection. Especially considering the last few days where I've been immersed somewhat in a humble existence, a humble people with very little but a desire to please and apologetic that things are not up to our "American" standard. What am I talking about you ask? I'm talking about the fact that the last three days I spent in Mazar I Sharif with the Afghan Air Force on their side of the base. On one side of the airport you have ISAF (NATO International Security Force) built up with buildings and power and roads and vehicles and tents and internet and phones and all the amenities that modern militaries bring with them when they're deployed. On the other side you have the Afghan Air Force, where we stayed. They have no buildings except for a couple decrepit buildings that were built by the Taliban. There is no power, no air conditioning. There is nothing in the way of luxury--running water….non-existent.

So where did we stay? We stayed in the building built by the Taliban, next to an old Taliban mosque. Out the window was a great view of a rundown building and a grass hut. The soldiers we became familiar with lived here. They fed us, prepared a room as best they could for us. But, most of them slept on the ground outside or on the roof of the building because it was 113 degrees Fahrenheit and in the building with no A/C it was at least 120. Sweating was a constant and we blew through water like crazy. We had to walk across the dirt road to the control tower to use the shower/bathroom (it was the general's personal bathroom) and even that was reminiscent of some of the holes I stayed in Guatemala. Very sad, very poor, and yet very humbling! The people were very nice and bent over backwards to help us and to get to know us. The young soldiers were very interested in sitting and chatting over broken English/Dari to just communicate as we would sit on the porch of the tower at night and watch the other crew fly. Our whole reason for being there was so we could get some night training in. It was sad and special and wonderful at the same time. The room was elegantly furnished with woven carpets that looked fairly new.

The one thing that we realized was that they don't go by watches very well. They go by the sun for the most part. The sun came up just before 0500 and they were in our room setting up breakfast for us…..yeah after going to sleep at midnight we were really, really excited to see that. We gave up on sleep around 0600 and sat relaxing, then napped again. It was almost surreal. It's sad, but their heart is in the right place. The people there are striving to do right by their country, serving their country. They are the builders of a new world for themselves and I'm excited that I have the opportunity to assist in this. The day we left the general wanted to have a big luncheon with us so we sat and broke bread and ate kebab and lamb and spicy soup and rice with raisins in it and it was delicious. We didn't ask how the food was prepared, we just ate and enjoyed. They're a very giving people and the ones I've worked with are very humble and proud to be serving their country. They just are in a tight spot. We're doing well helping them and I'm proud to do so.

The flying for night training was excellent because we got to spend the whole time concentrating on training and not on transiting from one location to another so we stayed in the pattern each night and did lots of takeoffs and landings with multiple practice emergency procedures. After all, if they're going to be doing this on their own they need to learn to think ahead of the airplane and "what if" things. Really, because they are so humble, I want them to become more decisive when they're at the controls. I try to play the dumb copilot sometimes and it is interesting to see the befuddlement on their face as I try to get them to be decisive, without me telling them what to do. It's a unique experience. Actually this whole experience is unique.

I started this out with scripture because I'm feeling so close to the Lord today. It's a good day. I've watched General Conference (semi-annual conference of the LDS church), The Testaments – a film by the LDS church, and it is just a good day. I love being able to study and spend time that in my opinion is not wasted. I'm learning and growing spiritually. There are so many people that just pass one day to the next without goals, without knowledge, without hope of a better life. I'm happy to have the Gospel in my life. Anyways, that's my week in review. It's been a good week, a crazy week, and an amazingly unique week. Enjoy all and have a great day.

View from the room we stayed in…and the room we slept in…

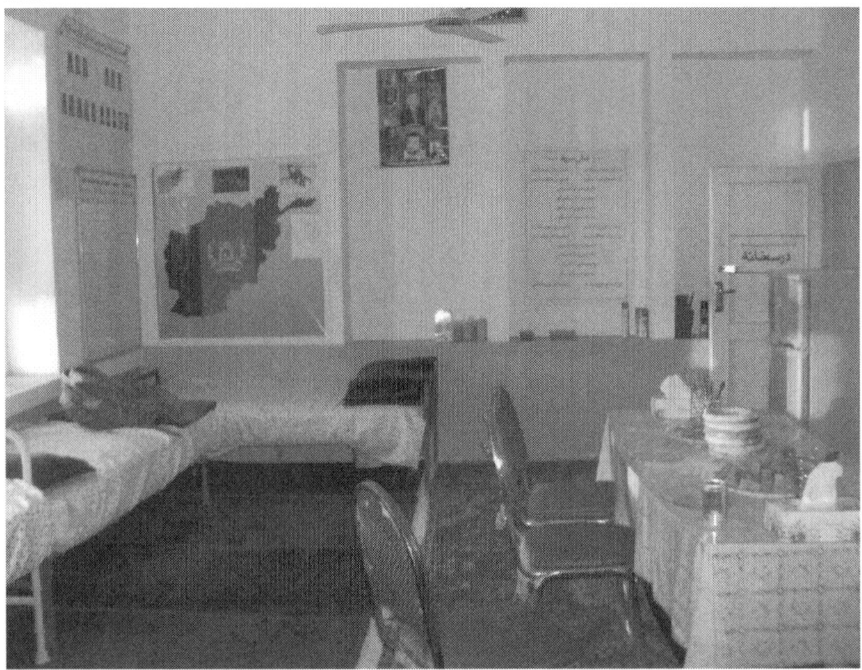

Chapter 10

DEEP THOUGHTS BY ME

"To my mind, the idea that doing dishes is unpleasant can occur only when you aren't doing them. I enjoy taking my time with each dish, being fully aware of the dish, the water, and each movement of my hands. I know that if I hurry in order to go and have a cup of tea, the time will be unpleasant, and not worth living. That would be a pity, for each minute, each second of life is a miracle. Each bowl I wash; each poem I compose; each time I invite a bell to sound is a miracle, and each has exactly the same value. If I am incapable of washing dishes joyfully, if I want to finish them quickly so I can go and have a cup of tea, I will be equally incapable of drinking the tea joyfully. With the cup in my hands I will be thinking about what to do next, and the fragrance and the flavor of the tea, together with the pleasure of drinking it, will be lost. I will always be dragged into the future, never able to live in the present moment." — Thich Nhat Hanh

Now as I sit here, in Afghanistan, contemplating another day, another hour, another minute I reflect on these things I'm learning. This life is an experience unlike anything that we could devise on our own…except that we do. Our life is known, but not planned out. Our paths are ours to choose, but do we choose to do as the previous author wrote, "the dishes joyfully", or do we choose to live a life full of unpleasantness or looking only to the future and not the present. I personally believe that it is imperative that we choose to enjoy every minute of every day. True, there will be days when that will be near impossible, but I've found that I can take joy in, or have fun, in spite of all but the most extreme stressful situations. Then, I may still laugh like a madman and really enjoy myself. We only have one life. The ubiquitous 'they' always say, "Live each day as if it was your last." We look at that and say, yeah that's a good idea, but do we embrace it. Do we live in the moment? Do we live, make our choices and stick with them? Do we constantly try to embrace life as a child, full of wonder at all the new things, or do we let other people live, such as through TV or by not DOING things ourselves? Or, have we ever sat and pondered on where we are, what we're doing and are we LIVING? Or, are we passing through life? If we're just passing through life, we have a long way to go. Another quote! This time from a very famous figure!

"It is better to conquer yourself than to win a thousand battles. Then the victory is yours. It cannot be taken from you, not by angels or by demons, heaven or hell." – Buddha

Think about that. I've been doing a lot of religious study as I've been here. Especially since there've been aspects of my life where I haven't conquered self. That is one of my goals out here, to conquer self and be complete master of me. Life is full of things that happen TO us. We don't have control. We don't know if this is our last day on earth. We don't know if we'll live to be a hundred and thirty. We don't control that, we control ourselves. This has been interesting these last two months being here. I'm learning all about control, of our selves, of our minds, of our place in life. The Afghans are on a completely different realm, time means almost nothing to them. This is due to the fact that their lives have changed relatively little in two thousand years. The work here is immense; the challenge intriguing; the difficulties many; the fun.....legion. This is the pleasure and pain of living and working in Afghanistan. It is intense and lackadaisical at the same time. It is contrary and funny, it is yin and yang. Life is full of joy and frustration...and through it all, an absolute blast. I've been reading a lot and realizing the best way to enjoy ANYTHING you do in life is to just live it. It's a choice. I am really learning that lesson. EVERYTHING is a choice. How we deal with everything is our own personal choice. I love it and am enjoying it. Another quote or two:

"Always do more than is required of you." — George S. Patton

"Love what you do, and you'll do it more and you'll do it better. Love, laugh, learn. It is no surprise that Peter Pan—the boy who never grew old—could fly" – J.M. Barry

I throw this in because I fly. I'm a pilot. I love flying. I love soaring among the clouds, playing games with the clouds, making the attempt to have the perfect landing – greasing it in so you can hardly feel the wheels touch, viewing all of God's creations from 20,000 feet and seeing all the beauty that is there. The dirt, the trash, the cares of the world fall away as I soar among the clouds. Flying is almost a religion, and those who fly understand this. There are few pilots that don't believe in God or a supreme being because you can't soar among the beauty of the clouds and the wind without feeling and acknowledging there is something greater than you out there. I know, I believe, and I love being able to experience that even though I'm a world away from family and friends….I'm close to God every time I strap on an airplane. I am the eternal Peter Pan and always will be, because I want to be. And as Tiffany will acknowledge, "I do believe in fairies," – she is my Tinker bell. (Hey don't knock Tinker bell. She rocks!) Anyways, flying breeds wonder and flying around here it is amazing every time I get to take the plane and train someone else. I've never been a numbers guy. I love the feel of the air, the embodiment as I strap on the airplane and try to "BE" the airplane. It's a state of mind that is intrinsic in its good feelings. Now another:

"You have to love dancing to stick to it. It gives you nothing back, no manuscripts to store away, no paintings to show on walls and maybe hang in museums, no poems to be printed and sold, nothing but that single fleeting moment when you feel alive." — Merce Cunningham

Living life! Loving life! Living each moment! In the movie The Last Samurai, they state…"Life in every breath." This is a true state of living. This is realizing each moment that this is your life. You don't get younger. Every moment gives you experience. Life in every breath! Emotion, feeling, learning, living, loving…..they make up life.

"There are two ways to live your life. One is as though nothing is a miracle. The other is as though everything is a miracle."

— Albert Einstein

Amen!

"Most people are just trying to get through the day. Be committed to learn to get from the day. Don't just get through it; get from it. Learn from it. Let the day teach you. Join the University of Life. What a difference that will make in your future. Commit yourself to learning. Commit yourself to absorbing. Be like a sponge. Get it. Don't miss it." — Jim Rohn

Yes, I'm a student of philosophy. I'm a student of life. I'm a student of my religion. I'd say truthfully that I'm just a student. I love to learn and grow. Here, in the desert, I learn each day. I'm getting more out of each day I'm here than I did in a month back at home station….why? Priorities! My priorities have shifted. I'm not the same man I was several months ago. I have a higher purpose. I love my life, my family and especially my wife…and therefore, want to become the best person I can possibly be. As you read this, don't take it as my preaching to anyone, because it's not meant that way. It's a message about life, a message about how we look at our lives, a message about what we do…In truth it's a thought about introspection. Look at yourself and ask…..Am I happy? If not…why not? Most often the problem is not external. That's the biggest thing I've learned. Our problems are ALWAYS internal. Always! Why? Because only we can choose how we respond to external stimuli. I love all of you and hope for your happiness and joy in this life as we choose our methods of living.

Chapter 11

ONE MORE REPORT

Let's talk for a minute. Let's think about the time I spend and the time I've spent since my last post. There are many, many things I've been doing. I'm interested in the way life is constantly flowing from one point to another, from one minute to another. Day in day out we flow with the river of time through daily chores and daily tasks. We have the opportunity to watch our own life pass and do many things. My last blog was a statement of thought and a thoughtful iteration of the passage of life and time in my mind. Introspection is a wonderful way to take stock of your life.

Now, my last flight was interesting. Let's set the scene. I had to get up out of bed at o dark thirty….actually that's not true because for some reason the sun enjoys beginning to come up at 0500 so it was just a little before that, namely at 0430, a time that angels don't even choose to get up because it's too stinking early, that I got up. Got ready and went in to fly at 0500. The reason for the early morning takeoff was due to the fact that we were carrying a super heavy truck in the plane and it's a wasteland desert here and our altitude at the airport is 6,000 ft. above sea level so the airplane performance is not quite what it could be. Needless to say, we were heavy. In fact, it's the heaviest I think we've taken off in this plane because people wanted rides and we kept saying OK…I know we're silly but it's all good, we were within our departure limits, even if at the low end. To make it more fun, I flew with the Group Commander, an F-16 guy that's been trained in our airplane...he's actually a pretty good pilot, for a fighter guy, and an Afghan copilot that pretty much isn't well equipped for flying. Now I don't say that lightly, he really is not good, how he passed his check ride, I don't know, but my job as instructor was to ensure everyone was safe so I did. I was quiet except when I had to coach the copilot or make comments of aspects of the flight that needed to be improved. We flew!

We landed and dropped off the truck, then returned....But alas, our day wasn't over. We then took a bunch of passengers down to a location that we have to tanker gas to get to so we were very heavy for an afternoon takeoff when it was furnace HOT!!!! So I hopped in the seat due to our performance data and I flew the takeoff and landing then gave the seat back to my Afghan copilot. I could actually see the Colonel cringe because he was getting a FULL instructor appreciation ride with the Afghan in the seat. The copilot was in lala land most of the day and it was like pulling teeth to get him to know what to do. It was funny at the same time it was sad. I had fun at the Group Commanders expense because he got a WORKOUT and I let him. I felt that our leadership needed to understand what it is like for us every day so I purposefully let him handle most things and only stepped in when I thought things needed to be done that weren't getting done. It was a long day. Seven hours of flying and an 11 and a half hour day total. The Group Commander looked worn out at the end of the day, and while I was tired too, it was funny.

I've really been enjoying listening to books on tape by John Bytheway while running or sitting at work. He makes a lot of pointers that I really like. Lately his talks about opposition and getting rid of TV and video games have been really good and making a lot of sense to me.

I picked up a guitar at the bazaar and have practiced a little bit every day since I got it. Slowly I'm working on my goals as I outlined them earlier this last month. I've got a lot of things I want to accomplish and little by little I'm making headway. It's a joy to finish, or even begin things that I want to do. In fact, just since I rarely if ever watch TV I have plenty of time to study and desarrollar (develop) my talents. I love the Gospel and am enjoying learning more every day and being able to answer questions that the kids pose.

I've spent a lot of time recently studying a website that is all about aviation. It is called the Inner Art of Aviation and is a psychological study of meditation and Zen and how we can improve not only our flying skills but our life through developing the six inches between our ears. I've sent many a quote to Tiffany and the kids. In fact, one of the most astonishing and wonderful facts was that I could make the information I was learning apply not only to flying but to life as well. The things I learned had spiritual qualities that were intrinsic in their beauty. The joy of learning, the joy of living and living each moment of every day is a quality that we can always learn. Life is a beautiful crazy game.

As scheduler the many facets of my job make for a multiplicitude of changes every day. They are numerous and daily; they are insidious and outlandish; they are a pain in my neck at times and at times no bother.

So, the final jest of this gift of gab is the question….how am I doing? Aside from being tired from staying up too late I am doing very well. I'm happy and full of life.
Life in a nutshell is life
Life with meaning
Life with strife

Beautiful Afghan Mountains

Chapter 12

OH WHAT'S IN A NAME?

Oh what's in a name? I think I started writing with this one in mind already. Philosophy, romance, gospel instruction, all are things that are primary parts of my daily life. I've spent a lot of time on philosophy of late, as can be seen in previous posts. There's a joy of learning that fills me with excitement and fills me with joy at creating, examining, growing and pursuing my talents. I know I talk a lot about me, but then again this is a blog about my life and the daily adventures or misadventures as they may be, and so I take poetic license in the art that is my life...

Life flows through a looking glass and the sands of time draw on. We grow and live and learn each moment...Have you learned something today?

I really haven't been flying as much as I'd like. In fact none of us have, because we all would like to fly 3-4 times a week, but as an example, I'm averaging only once. Yup! Once per week, but they're usually interesting and fun with a little chaos and adventure mixed in. I wrote about my last flight in my last post. I haven't flown since then but my scheduling position in the squadron has definitely kept me occupied. Maintenance threatened to mutiny on us, as is their right because we have contracted maintenance with a set utilization rate for the airplanes and the last couple months we've been blowing the contracted hours out of the water....so needless to say they were going to close us down for a couple days, right when we had some important flights planned...so we negotiated and gave them a couple days with no flying next week and we'll take those days as flying safety training days and the 4th of July holiday, we'll still be working of course, but we'll actually let them work on the airplanes.

The problem stems from the fact that we've been flying 150% of our contracted hours.....that's not exactly good when the parts supply system is still not that great. Planes like to fly. But when they break they like parts too, otherwise they sit and get cranky.....Maintenance has done an amazing job considering the stress they've been under. I mean, I've got a great relationship with them because I meet with them all the time. I've got a good relationship with our contractors and they've done an outstanding job keeping these planes running especially when the maintenance manuals are translated directly from the Italian and sometimes it comes out as gibberish. :) Got to love poor translations! But such is life. In six months we've only cancelled 3 missions for maintenance....that's like 99% effective. Back in NC, we maintained a 50 % effective rate over the last couple years I was there. So, in spite of very big hurdles, it's a great group to work with.

My latest craze, changing topics as I'm wont to do, is reading LDS General Conference talks. I read the same talk 3 times and have done this for 4 days in a row. I read it first in Spanish, then in Cyrillic in Serbian, then in Italian. In this way I'm getting my gospel study and my language study in at the same time. I love it. I love studying the gospel every day and it's funny but I watch my roommate and others spend so much time playing video games or watching TV and I have no desire to participate. It's just too much fun to learn and grow. I've also really been enjoying reading *LES MISERABLES*. The long extended translation of the original. There are so many good lessons in there as well. I've underlined parts that are just very helpful. I know most people don't like to read 1,300 page books, but for the history alone, along with the lessons about trials, and justice and mercy, and God's love and infinite atonement make it worth it. You really can't go wrong by seeking "out of the best books words of wisdom..." (D&C 88:118)

I know I haven't added more flying stories, but I haven't flown. We're starting some new students and I get to fly with them on Thursday for their first time in the copilot seat. I'll definitely have a post in a couple days regarding how that went. I hate to say it but it'll be full of heroism, insanity and "Oh-I-saved-the-day-isms". After all, this is my story and since this is my forum and it's not a book...yet...then you can enjoy! I love my life, my wife, my kids, my job, my life, the Book of Mormon, the gospel, Jesus Christ, writing (I've written twenty pages of poetry and will fill a book by the time I return) and all in all life is good and I wish all who read these things herewith a pleasant evening and a beautiful life (good movie by the way - A Beautiful Life...it's in Italian but has subtitles! Well worth the watch, but you'll cry)

Working hard on schedules and email…

Chapter 13

A GLIMPSE

Now I wasn't planning on writing at the moment but feel it imperative to put thoughts down while they're still fresh and before I've distorted the story with my usual happy exaggerations!!! So, here's a glimpse of training Afghans in the air...

Me, "Turn right."
"Turn right."
"No your other right"
"NO, TURN RIGHT!"... (Me yelling at the student and…)

At this point I take the yoke (steering wheel of the plane) and force it in my student's hands into a right turn. We're at 14,000 feet practicing turns and when I tell him to turn right he tries to go left....ay yay yay this is going to be an interesting day. Steep turns coming up; let's see how he handles them.

"Ok, good! Move controls to 45 degrees of bank, now you've got to pull. Feel how the nose wants to drop, pull to keep it from dropping, no don't increase bank, pull...no roll out some of your bank, no Roll out, less bank," and again I tap the yoke to get him to understand. So, instead of rolling out only a few degrees of bank he rolls almost straight and level, but he hasn't released back pressure on the yoke so we suddenly climb 500 feet. I'm actually really enjoying this. This is what I do; this is what I live for. It's a challenge and is fun. Well, time to work on stalls. Yep, for those not in the know, a stall is not like a car engine stall where the engine stops. An airplane stall is where you put the power at idle and then pull the nose up to hold your altitude...you slow down and keep holding the nose up...until the airplane can't fly anymore and tries to fall out of the sky...hence doing it at 14,000 feet. We don't actually go all the way to a stall in this plane, we just get to the beginning of it and then we recover by adding power and leveling off. I demonstrate and notice an odd engine action when I recover. So, I let my student try it. This time the engine action is much more noticeable...one engine recovers quickly, the other waits a couple seconds....that is not the best situation. We only did straight ahead stalls, no turning stalls with this plane since it would try to flip over on its back with the delay in that engine. After the fun, we went to the airport for landing practice. Their landings were actually pretty good, except that they were lining up on the dirt in between the taxi ways and the runway and just letting the wind blow them to the runway. Again, not the best method for lining up to land! All in all, it was a really fun flight, a challenging flight, and rewarding too. I found out that one of my students did really well with English; the other couldn't understand English over the interphone or radio. Ahh, the joys, so now we returned...I must admit though that in their defense it was their first flight in the right seat of the airplane....

That's my flying experiences lately. I'm only flying about once a week and I thoroughly enjoy it every time. I've been practicing guitar every day, even though it's only for a few minutes, I'm trying every day. Knowledge is a wonderful thing. I study in all my free time and it's amazing.

Faith, that's an interesting word. So many people wonder and search, or don't have faith, or don't know what to believe. I am so thankful for the knowledge and faith that I've gained, especially through study and prayer. Am I becoming a religious nut?

Absolutely! I'm finding that the Gospel is a major part of my life. Let me share a personal note: today, I had an epiphany. As I was on the stair machine at the gym, reading of all things a science fiction book, written by a Christian author, I had another of the many aha moments I've had lately. I was flooded with warmth and light and love for my Savior and also my Father in Heaven. I was on the machine for 65 minutes and from minute 15 to minute 57 I didn't even register the passage of time. True, the story was very good, but it was when I read about the unbeliever being given a glimpse of heaven and being filled with heavenly music, it hit me. Music! My entire life, I've been a lover of music, I love to play it, to write it, to sing it (off key of course if you ask Tiffany), and especially, lately to listen to good music. I can't believe how much BAD music is out there, music that corrupts the soul and angers the mind. But, as I read about the music in the book, I thought of my recent experiences with the Anita Stansfield books, and my reaction to the music in them. I feel the spirit through music. I FEEL through music. I love music. See, I'm one of those odd guys (it's more of a feminine trait I believe, that's what makes me odd) that needs to share his feelings with others, especially family and friends. It makes me happy to do so. I'm writing a book of music and poems while I'm out here and have written over thirty pages of music and poetry. But I feel like sharing the one I wrote tonight. So indulge me or delete me....

A touch
Just a brief touch on my mind
It swelled
Music filled me all inside
I asked
Was this meant only for me?
Do I share?
That's the way it's meant to be
The music of the soul, that comes from God above
It makes my spirit glow, fills me with my father's love
Inside me to abide me, he cleanses from within
The music scours me out, removing stain and sin
I love the feel of Heavenly hand

Lifts me up

When my legs are dead as sand
I cry
As the music enters in
I try
To gain his strength inside, within
The music in my soul, inspired from high up above
It makes my spirit glow, fills me with my father's love
Inside me to abide me, he cleanses from within
The music scours me out, sundering all my sin
The world
Takes music, draws it down
Brings out
All the evilness around
It tries
to mask it all so well
Holds a hand
out to you to lead you down to hell
but,
The music in my soul, inspired from high above
It makes my spirit glow, fills me with my father's love
Inside me to abide me, he cleanses from within
The music scours me out, I surrender desire for sin...
The music in my soul

It grows.....

Ok that's my latest composition...coming to a stage near you...only missing the melody, the background, the guitar parts, the drum beat, the orchestral arrangement and the bass, but other than that..... :o) Thank you for listening. It means a lot to me to share my spiritual experiences with those that I know care to listen to me. I love the Lord, I love the Book of Mormon, I love my Savior, and I love my wife and my family. I love all that I am becoming and am trying to let my studies and my mind be open so the Lord can mold me into whom and what he wants me to be. They say there are no atheists at war. I'm glad that I'm not only NOT an atheist, but I am becoming firmer in the faith than I have ever been in my entire life, even more so than when I was a missionary. I fear not, though I walk through the valley of the shadow of death I will fear no evil....for the Lord walks with me. Afghanistan is an interesting place. We each should take stock of our lives. After all, we have this life to learn and grow. I love you all, especially Tiffany because after all she's my wife and I love her with all my heart.

Initial cadre for the C-27; on the ground in Kandahar (below)

Chapter 14

A WEEK'S SPIRITUAL INSIGHTS AND SOME FLYING

I have been enjoying the ability to write and create and share. Below is a religious song I wrote today. I'm working on putting this one to music that who knows, maybe I'll actually play for you someday, but for now I hope you read and enjoy...The idea came to me as we studied the scriptures today in church. Jokingly our teacher said that eventually we'd read through osmosis, since we have so many different ways of accessing them nowadays, i.e. online, on I-phones, on computer programs, and traditional hard copy. Someone then commented on the fact that that wouldn't happen because, as we read, certain passages of scripture mean different things to us at different times and it's the struggle we go through of learning that helps the Lord answer our questions and prayers. That got me thinking and I challenged that we already do learn through Osmosis. Osmosis requires liquid and at times when we read, or have had struggled with a question or problem, as we read the scriptures an answer suddenly hits us, and we cry...through our tears our spirits are touched and we learn...someone then pointed out that in those instances we can learn something instantaneously that would then take an hour to explain if we can even explain it...to me that's osmosis right there. So, I liken the learning through osmosis through the spirit with the rain and our tears that fall like rain, happy tears, joyful tears....

BRING ON THE RAIN - by Todd Andrewsen
Science will say that osmosis is a method
That something is passed through liquid inside
Now I'm not sure that science has proven
But I know that my spirit's inside,
It has a touch of feeling, a touch of mystery
Science can't tell but I can surmise
That someday soon the lord will provide the answer
And through my tears give me knowledge that's why
I say

Bring on the rain, that's what my heart is saying
Bring on the rain, as my tears they fall down
Bring on the rain, when for the spirit I'm praying
The word will filter into my brain
So bring on the rain

Now time has passed and time is a given
Time will challenge everything you know
time is a catalyst for all things written
Time will help you save things in your soul
Now
Bring on the rain, that's what my heart is saying
Bring on the rain, as my tears they fall down
Bring on the rain, when for the spirit I'm praying
The word will filter into my brain
So bring on the rain

I'm not saying that life is easy
I'm not saying that I get it right
I'm not saying that I walk without leaning
I'm just saying that I'll look to the Light
So
Bring on the rain, that's what my heart is saying
Bring on the rain, as my tears they fall down

Bring on the rain, when the spirit is pressing
The word will filter into my brain
So bring on the rain
Life then is full of chaos and struggle
Life then is full of challenge and pain
But sometimes the lord will peek through the muddle
And pour his spirit into our brain
And then our tears will fall like rain
Bring on the rain

Bring on the rain, my heart is aching
Bring on the rain, my tears will fall
Bring on the rain, as the spirit is saying
Through my tears he answers all my pain
My tears they fall like rain

Bring on the rain, when the spirit is talking
Bring on the rain, he shelters me
Bring on the rain, in silent answer
He heals me from all my strain
He knows me, he loves me – I'm sane
Bring on the rain…
Bring on the rain…
Bring on the rain…

That's my poetry, song, spiritual discussion for the week. I've said it before that I've found out that the lord talks to me often through music and poetry. I love it. I feel so close to it. I don't apologize for discussing it because the Gospel (again for those not members of the LDS church it is the entire teachings of Jesus, and his holy prophets) is a prominent fixture in my life. It hasn't always been I'm sad to say, but it is now and I'm glad of that. Especially as I fly around Afghanistan in an airplane, doing training in a war zone. As the strippling warriors stated in The Book of Mormon, "I fear not, my mother knew it". This has been an interesting week. I got to fly yesterday and it was a great day for flying. It was hot of course, but that goes without saying.

I flew with an Afghan Major this week. We're clearing up some discrepancies he had on his check ride, namely single-engine work....poor, poor guy, because I'm sadistic when it comes to stuff like this. Therefore, after dropping some pallets off in Jalalabad, which has a nice small runway and small ramp, we flew to Mazar I Sharif, and got gas, then proceeded to do some pattern work. I warned him that I suspected maintenance had been messing with the airplane, because darned if that plane didn't have engine problems (simulated) from the moment we took off. He thought he was going to get it nice and easy and at least get one normal landing.....nope....I failed (simulated) his engine on his first time around the pattern, and continued to fail it every time, and we kept having to do low approaches because of helicopters and bears on the runway (ok no real bears but simulated bears anyways)...his legs got a workout. But that's my job; teach him to handle all sorts of situations. You never know when your engine is going to fail for real, so you've got to know what to do.

Now, I'm constantly noticing things, at least all week and month I have, that are applicable to the Gospel and to life. You never know when things are going to go wrong. Life is full of problems, questions, stress, ups and downs, financial difficulties, sickness, unknowns, and crazy people...whatever. We don't always choose what problems or trials we will face in life...it could be a neighbor that speaks badly about you to other neighbors, or it could be a child getting sick, or an engine flaming out when you don't have anywhere nearby to land. Whatever it is, we can always turn to the Lord to help us and to be prepared for whatever comes our way. The Bible says, "The Lord is my shepherd I shall not want"(Psalm 23:1)...Do we take Him at His word? Or do we just read the words? I'm learning to trust the Lord. That's my biggest takeaway so far from my deployment and my life changes. I'm learning to lean on the Lord, because I can't solve all my problems, but He can.

With that in mind, my Afghan Major got an earful of advice such as, “More power”, “Descend! No! Descend!” “I know you think you're descending but look at the altimeter.” “Still climbing, look at your instruments they'll guide you!” “Keep the nose down to accelerate!” “No, you can't turn early you'll overshoot!” “Wing up”, “wing down”, “Careful, watch your airspeed, watch your airspeed, MY AIRPLANE!!!!!” Speed is life when you're single engine....and other such things as that. But it's true. We always need to listen to our instructor (the Lord) as He gives us advice about what to do, and how to steer, and how to correct, and sometimes we just need to give Him the controls of the airplane (our life) and let Him steer us when we're unable to make headway.

Chapter 15

QUOTES I REALLY LIKE THAT SPOKE TO ME WHILE I WAS STUDYING

I was studying about flying and spirituality and these really stuck out to me.

http://www.pilotpsy.com/flights/3.html (This is the website I pulled them off of.)

"Jim Fannin, a performance coach to many superstar athletes, says you should, 'go on a mental diet and think about what you think about, the intended result being a clear mind with less thought.' He claims that, 'the average person has between 2,000 to 3,000 thoughts a day,' of which some 60 percent are chaotic and not really useful. However after learning to train the inner voice, 'The superstar has 1,200 and every one of them has a purpose'" (*Ketcham, 2005*).

"Mario Andretti, one of the most successful automobile racers we've ever seen, a driver with 109 wins on major circuits and the only person ever to win races over five decades, told a sports psychologist that:"

> 'Before a race, I need my space to collect my thoughts and weed out distractions. I set out to control my mind around a single objective. I become possesses with being excellent that day. Only one objective and all my thoughts are on it. When I am in 'the zone,' I am in a trance and time does not exist.'

"The experience of flying tends to focus the mind anyway, it's something people love as the worries of the world get left on the ground, but we should work on our inner voice on the ground as well. Pay little attention to impatience, gossip, prejudices, anger, jealousy, envy and other negative thoughts that crowd our heads. All whining, negative thinking and excuses need to be ignored and eliminated. You have one voice; let it be positive and useful."

"Meditation has been practiced for thousands of years as a way to focus, as a way to silence the yap yap yap of the babbling inner voice. In his 2002 keynote address to the American Psychological Association in Chicago Herbert Benson, PhD, of Harvard Medical School declared that mediation has been shown beyond any reasonable doubt to quiet the central nervous system. You don't need to be a Buddhist for this. You don't need a robe or a shaved head. You don't need to believe anything more or less than you do now. And you don't need a mat or an incense stick."

"You do need to sit in silence for 15 minutes."

"It sounds the cheapest, simplest, quickest and easiest thing in the world. However cheap, quick and simple it is, it is not easy. Turns out that doing nothing, thinking about nothing, is one of the hardest things in the world."

"In some loose comfortable clothes find a reasonably peaceful private place. Set a timer for 15 minutes or so. Sit down on a cushion or rolled up towel in stable cross-legged manner, with good upright posture, hands rested on the knees. Rest your eyes a few feet in front of you, not really looking at anything but not closed (we don't want to fall asleep). You don't chant (although some practices do: it's called a mantra) and you don't have to try the most pure Zen meditation, which is to empty the mind. Try counting breaths, deeply and slowly to ten. Then start at one again."

"Slowly now. Breathe, one, breathe, two, why am I doing this. Aha! The yap yap yap of the inner voice intrudes almost immediately. Learn to let it come, acknowledge it, and then let it go. Bye bye. One, breathe, two, breathe, three, my leg hurts. Let it go. Quiet. Peace. Breathe, one, breathe, two, I think I'll have pizza tonight. Boy this is hard. One, breathe, two . . ."

“Soon the time will be up. Now try doing this every day for a few weeks. See if your concentration improves. See if you can find a little inner peace and calm. Studies, only recently made possible due to brain imaging technology, show that people that meditate regularly are calmer, have more focus, and can concentrate during intense activities better than those that can never silence the voice in their head. If it is true that 'performance equals potential minus interference'—then mediation may be a way to remove the limiting part of the human equation.”

“Sam reminded me that although events may be beyond my control, my reactions to those events are entirely controlled by me and me alone. He stayed positive. He stayed focused.”

“You cannot hit and think at the same time.” — Yogi Berra

“Inner peace is the key: if you have inner peace, the external problems do not affect your deep sense of peace and tranquility”. — Dalai Lama

“Make it thy business to know thyself, which is the most difficult lesson in the world.” — Miguel De Cervantes

“If a man is called to be a street sweeper, he should sweep streets even as Michelangelo painted, or Beethoven played music, or Shakespeare wrote poetry. He should sweep streets so well that all the hosts of heaven and earth will pause to say, here lived a great street sweeper who did his job well.” — Martin Luther King, Jr.

“Showing off is the fool's idea of glory.” — Bruce Lee

“I count him braver who overcomes his desires than him who conquers his enemies; the hardest victory is over self.” —Aristotle

Afghan Major

Chapter 16

IT'S THAT TIME OF THE WEEK AGAIN

It's that time of the week when I pour out my heart and soul, write the words that coalesce in my being throughout the week and give a little bit of me to everyone. It's one of my favorite things to do and I'm proud to be able to share my adventures, witticisms, anecdotes, stupid jokes, life lessons, religious revival, facts and anything else that pops into my head for that matter. Since my last writing I've flown a couple times. My goal in flying (since I flew with the same student to clear up some problems he had on his check ride) was to challenge him, definitely not to make it easy, after all if I can't be a sadistic instructor….I can at least have fun with my students. I mean, I'm in a war zone doing training and flying with guys that for the most part have been pilots before, but …there's a lag in understanding and acting and a complete lack of situational awareness (That's the genius required when flying to know what's going on around you, with the airplane, with your crew members, with the radio, with the sky, with the ground….to prevent minor things like crashing into one of the 18,000 feet tall mountains around here.)

I flew and immediately started in when we got to our training base by giving him the airplane and failing his engine…he wasn't happy. But, to be nice I only failed it about 8 times that day. It was hot, and windy and it was NOT an easy day for my student….I only took the airplane away from him a couple times when he was getting too slow, or too high, basically losing track of where he was and what he was doing. At those times, I'd take the plane, put it back where it belonged, explain why I took it and then give it back to him. I can honestly say he improved over the two flights. They weren't easy, they weren't meant to be. The crosswinds were challenging, the outside temperature made it difficult to accelerate. On the second flight, I decided to take the airplane from him when he couldn't make a MINOR little decision of whether to turn right or left. See, the problem was that there were some hills coming up in the direction of the shallow turn we were in. We were slow and not accelerating. He had several options, and he let the situation deteriorate until he was quickly running out of options. Since he wasn't making a decision, we finally reached the point where I was uncomfortable and I took the airplane, brought in the other engine, accelerated a little bit, popped up and over the terrain and then gave the airplane back to him.

We had a LOOOOOnnnnnggg discussion after that about him making decisions, because when I first recognized the problem he had many, many options, but by the time I took the airplane, he was down to only 1 or 2 options. He'd squandered away his options to NOT crash the airplane into a hill. I thought about that as we flew along because he really seemed like he would just keep going on in that direction until we crashed or until I took over.

Now, I'm going to get religious for a second. How like life is that? Often we make choices, or don't as the case may be, and at the beginning of a situation if we would just look, we could see all the escape routes from that bad situation that is forming. But, so often we blind our eyes, we close our minds to what is in front of us and press on until either we're forced by circumstance to change or we crash headlong into the mountain in front of us. The Spirit, the Holy Ghost, conscience, inspiration (whatever you want to call it based on your religious affiliation) talks to us, just like I talked to my student, asking what we should do, giving us options to prevent problems…I thought of all that just now, but it's so true. The key is our need to listen when we get those promptings of what to do or not do as the case may be.

I've been trying to listen to promptings and have been writing a lot of songs lately. But one thing with that is I finally got my staff paper and with my guitar have begun to compose music. Tonight at church I was finally able to play what I'd written and while it still needs some work, I like it. I'm trying to make the most of my time out here. I hope I don't sound like I'm bragging about everything I'm doing, learning, studying etc. After all, if I'm not at work I've got nothing but time on my hands which I could waste doing things that don't matter, or I can improve my life and myself and that's what I'm trying to do. Some of my favorite things out here that I'm involved in and doing, especially this last two weeks: Writing music, writing period, playing guitar, studying the scriptures, reading Anita Stansfield (church fiction author) novels, reading good books that teach good lessons, studying a couple languages on Rosetta stone, writing in my journal daily, reading and praying with my family via Skype, just learning and studying the gospel such as I haven't done since my mission to Guatemala so long ago. Those are some of my "hobbies" out here.

They all kind of relate because my reading is all church oriented. I've developed a love for my Savior, I've developed a dislike for most worldly things (i.e. crappy music, crappy TV, and crap in general) and I'm continuously trying to improve and learn how my Father in Heaven talks to me so that I may become an instrument in His hand. I want to be what He wants me to be, regardless of what anyone else thinks of me. I'm not only working on the spiritual me, but I'm also working on the physical, working out five times a week and killing myself on the stair machine and doing 100+ pushups, 100+ sit-ups and 25 pull-ups each workout, (and yes I'm bragging about this.) because I want to be physically, mentally and spiritually reborn by the time I leave here. It's not easy, but it's worth it.

Life is good, it's meant to be good and to be a "refiner's fire"! How we respond to challenges determines the quality of our life. I'm well acquainted with the fact that everyone will have challenges, and it's how we meet those challenges that define us. As always, another long story from Afghanistan, some flying, some religious, some internal thinking of my sometimes rational, sometimes irrational, sometimes just plain crazy brain, but if I weren't stark raving sane then I'd be mad….So there you have it, stark raving lunatic full of complete sanity! That's me, yin and yang, shallow and deep, but happy. Actually I'm not shallow, I'm normally just deep, but don't tell anyone.

Life lived in an instant
Infinity and eternity
At one breath
Golden sun and dark moon
Challenges faced
And conquered
Begets
hope

Life is one conglomeration of events that shape us....live it don't be lived by it.

One thing is always constant.....if you dance in the rain like an idiot, it doesn't matter what anyone says, you'll be happy!!!

Chapter 17

INSHALLAH

Inshallah...What a phrase! It brings apathy to new heights, it makes rational decisions irrational. It makes people who otherwise might think ahead to what they're doing....not. But you ask, what does this mean? Why would I go off on a phrase? Why does Inshallah bother me so? Well, since you ask, and even if you didn't ask I'll tell anyways. :) Inshallah means "if Allah wills it" or in our terms "if God wills it". Now on the whole that's a good way of thinking. After all Christ said, "Not My will but Thine be done" right? But I don't think it means that. Basically, here in Afghanistan it is a recipe for apathy; a recipe for laziness; a recipe for nothing getting done, because they use it to mean, I might do it, or I might not. I might study, or I might not. I might crash the airplane, or I might not, it is not in my hands but Allah's...a fatalistic style of thinking if there ever was one. Why do I bring this up? Well, I bring it up because I spent four days flying with students this week, at night, at a different base and it was everything I expected it to be. Ohh, the joys of flying! I love flying and I'm thankful that I get the opportunity to do what I do.

I love being in the sky floating on air...It makes me think of the words to the old Greatest American Hero TV show theme...."Believe it or not, I'm walking on air, I never thought I could feel so free e e, flying away on a wing and a prayer, who could it be...believe it or not it's just me!" Now, why do I bring that up...well let's analyze the words. I do walk on air when I fly. I love it and before I began flying I never thought I COULD feel so free. When flying away, it requires lots of prayer to be flying on the wing (after all these students are interesting to fly with) who could it be? It's just me. Even though I often still feel like a kid, I'm not really a kid, just a kid at heart, I'm surprised often by the fact that I'm doing what I'm doing. I'm an instructor pilot teaching Afghans to fly....and it's a challenging business.

Here's my latest experience. Two nights of flying, both times flying with an older Afghan pilot that is fun, has somewhat limited English and who's favorite term is....you guessed it...INSHALLAH. Inshallah, he studied (actually very little actual study) Inshallah he won't try to land on the control tower (it doesn't help that he points the airplane at it instead of the runway). Out of 15 touch and go's I assisted his landings with heavy inputs to the controls....normally to keep the airplane on the runway and not to:

1. Land on the approach lights, since he kept trying to do that.

2. Land on the tower...made him go around a couple times for that.

3. When I say pull power off, that does not translate to ADD power....

4. When I say lower the nose, that doesn't translate to raise the nose.

5. When I say the runway's over there, point and show you, that means....go that direction.

In order to experiment on what his control inputs were like, I told him to let go of the controls and I let go of the controls as well...and the plane shot up and to the left. That, my friends, means that the trim was way out of whack. I fixed the trim and showed him how to point the airplane where you want it to go and trim off the pressures. All in all, an interesting couple of nights. He's going to need a number of extra rides, mainly because I don't trust him and also because he doesn't put A and B together to reach C.

It was a long day today. Started out very slowly, having to go and sit through meetings. Then, I managed to get myself locked out of my room for two and a half hours. I sat and did nothing but people watch from the side of our building. My arms sunburned though, so that's a plus. ;) I was feeling blah. Then I went to church. I actually went an hour early. I was going to practice guitar with another guy but he had to work. I figured since I was there, I'd play and sing so I played loudly and sang, "Viva La Vida, 21 Guns, Sweet Home Alabama, and Home" It was awesome. It felt so good to play and sing. I can't sing in my room but it was cool to just sing loudly and play, if I do say so myself, I actually sounded pretty good. Then, church was really nice. I actually was able to use my story that I sent last week, along with the insights during the lesson since our lesson was about agency.

It's amazing how often this topic comes up lately. Agency, choices...Life is a choice, everything we do is a choice. If we are happy or sad or angry or mad, it's a choice. We have our agency to choose what we do every day of our life. As the scripture says, "we are free to choose life eternal through the great mediator or to choose captivity and death..." I'm grateful that I'm seeing these lessons on a daily basis. It reaffirms my testimony of the divinity of this work. Every day I see people, Americans and Afghans alike, making choices, letting their agency deprive them of options or using Inshallah to not have to make choices, which in and of itself is a choice.

We are the masters of our destiny. As the old church rock group used to sing, "I am the master of my soul" I am the one who makes the choices. I will continue to choose to follow my Lord and

Savior. I will share of my knowledge and testimony with you all. I love the Gospel, I love the Lord, I love the church, and I love my wife and family. Make choices! And, to quote The Fast and the Furious Tokyo Drift, "We make choices and we don't look back." Look to the Lord and live. Live happy, choose to live happy. Choose to be happy. Choose to let hardships roll off and learn from experiences.

I wrote this one day after working out and feeling really good.

My peace I give unto thee

Not peace as the world giveth

But peace as to the spirit

For in the house

You set aside

My spirit therein dwells

For in the house

Apart from the world

A calming presence lies

To hearts that need

For friends in deed

For help and comfort give

For knowledge passed and present day

Revelations, personal and sweet

All things are known

To I the lord

Before ye ask of me

So in this house

Which ye prepare

Wherein I can set foot

I'll bless thee, calm thee

Soothe thy cares

Within the wall, without

Without the walls

Of this dear house

My spirit will linger on

And bless thy soul

Till that next day

Wherein you come again!

Chapter 18

LONG, HAPPY, SPIRITUAL, FLYING EMAIL

This has been an eventful week in several aspects. Will there be adventure? Absolutely! Will there be lessons learned? Definitely! Will there be spiritual insights? Would I be me if I didn't throw what I'd learned spiritually this week into the email? Exactly! Will I talk about my wife? Duh!!! Does that even need to be asked? The best benefit that I can say from my spiritual awakening over the last few months is the fact that Tiffany and I have become better bestest friends than we ever have been in our lives and as we approach our 14th wedding anniversary in a couple weeks I look back and see the growth we've accomplished and I look forward to the next…oh I don't know, let's say next 300 years to start. That's a nice round number (I would say eternity because that's what I mean, but putting an actual number like 300 sounds so much more fun…think how much fun we'll have together in 300 years…it'll be awesome) I know, ya'll think I'm nuts and to that I say…thanks for the compliment.

In case you were wondering, NO! I haven't been shot at as far as I know. Sure, there are probably a few people out there that take potshots at the airplane but I haven't seen anything and I haven't had any holes in the airplane so it's all good. After all, I know some of you must wonder if I'm really in a war zone based on the stories that I send out, but yes there is a war going on. Sadly, people are still dying every day, and I'm sure there is a little bit of danger out there, but I say if you can't figure out how to have fun in a war, where can you figure out how to have fun!!!! So, since every good story starts out with adventure, I'll tell about my flying adventure this week.

This week I had a long flight. I spent almost five hours in the seat with two students, and it was HOT, and sweaty and humid and an absolute blast. We flew up to our normal training base and the fun began. It was fun for me!

Maybe it was a little sadistic of me, but it definitely was not much fun for the students…they got worked and well too because they need it. The first student was put through his paces…and except for the times when he'd zone out and have zero control over where the plane was headed…he did a great job. I jest, but there's truth to my jesting. He really does zone out, and he really did do a good job. I had fun killing his engine over and over and while he didn't know what to brief, his control of the airplane was sooooooo much better than last week. I even showed him how to look for opportunities to get around problems…since we were doing left-hand patterns again, aiming for that same pesky hill that everyone wants to try and run me into…I don't get it, but I showed him how he could lower the nose (not descend, but not climb either) accelerate and then make a harder turn in spite of the dead engine…Plus after making him suffer through something like 14 touch and go landings I took one and on takeoff, leveled off at about 50 feet, got my gear and flaps up and accelerated, climbed to 300 feet and made a hard G left turn, feeling the plane push my butt into the seat, rolling to 60+ degrees of bank and pulling around on downwind, going 200 miles an hour and then pulling the power back, configuring the airplane for landing with flaps, gear and then a nice turn to final and a soft kiss of the wheels on the ground…ok except the wheels didn't exactly kiss the ground it was more of a smack and a twist….but it was my first landing and hey I can laugh at my first one. The next time it was a nice soft touchdown!!! I can laugh at myself if I want!

The lessons went well, we returned to Kabul without dying so it was a good flight! I've decided if I ever return to Kabul dead, that would be a bad flight and I'd write it up in their training folders…don't kill the instructor. That is rule number one for students!!!! I'm morbid I know, but se la vie!

I wanted to comment on a book I read this week. I am an avowed readaholic. I especially am reading a lot of church related books, church fiction and non-fiction, and writing music. But, that's beside the point. In one day, I read this book and it's what got me thinking about what I wanted to write today. I know that about half of you that will read this are female and the other half male, obviously. I started this out talking about how my relationship has changed with Tiffany such that we've become closer than ever before. I want to share some insights. The book, called "Brianna, My Brother and The Blog" by Jack Weyland, was very good. But what jumped out at me was the description about the need that we as men have to take care of, nurture, respect and care for the women (wives) in our lives.

There are a couple of quotes I'd like to input from the book, "Guys, this isn't about doing something just so you can show a girl what a great guy you are. First, become a great guy, care about others, look for opportunities to serve your neighbors, and then after that, whatever else you want is more likely to come your way." This is interesting because the truth is, until I worked on BECOMING A GREAT GUY first (I was always a good guy, but had my own issues, now though I'm working on becoming a really great guy if that makes any sense.) The author talks about how Joseph Smith and his wife, Emma referred to each other as true and faithful friends. What does that mean to be a true and faithful friend? To me, being a true and faithful friend means you can be completely trusted. It means you care about and think about your friends, you hold confidences, don't gossip, are there when they need you, and as the author says, "someone who will be there for her when she's going through a hard time, someone who will do his share of the work around the house, it means that your hobbies, or sports, or TV don't trump whatever she needs from you." I'm trying to take my own advice. Tiffany and I are growing closer and its' the most amazing thing. I challenge my guy friends to do the same. Spend some time communicating, helping and learning your spouse's needs and be a true and faithful friend.

That's really just the tip of the iceberg for my week. I love studying as I said and I had the most awesome spiritual experience today. I know, I know, I have these every week, but I'm finding that the more I put my life in tune with gospel teachings and seek the Lord, the more I have these awesome experiences, even if they do come from books! For those of you who like to read, I recommend picking up the books by H.B. Moore. She's written LDS Church historical fiction about Book of Mormon characters. I know this is gibberish to some, but the book I read is about the prophet Abinadi and includes Alma as well. Now this story in the Book of Mormon comprises only a few chapters. Abinadi comes on the scene from out of nowhere preaching repentance to a wicked people, teaches, is arrested, and burned to death, sacrificing his life for his testimony of Jesus Christ, sealing his testimony in his blood. In all that time, and really, his are some awesome scriptures with some of the deepest teachings, he didn't know if he affected anybody. He didn't know if anybody believed is words, until Alma, but I'll get back to him.

Abinadi, it doesn't give his age, or tell us much about him. The author, HB Moore, chose to bring him to life. It's quite possible that he was a young man, not old, but quite possibly had a wife and children. We know from reading the Book of Mormon that the prophets all seemed to be called young, married and had children…the book brings him to life. I've never thought about him as a man other than as a story in the scriptures. But he lived. He had friends and family, he had hopes and dreams and was called to bring a message to a wicked people that had forgotten God. And regardless of his own life, he fulfilled his mission. What a man! What an inspiration! I mean, how often do we take things for granted just because we can? Yet this man gave up everything because the lord told him to teach repentance to a wicked people. Did he fear? Maybe, but he didn't take counsel from his fears. Did he know he would be killed? Probably! Yet he went anyways. What courage! I don't cry, but lately when the Spirit has touched me strongly I do and I cried during the end of this book. I'm not ashamed to admit it. I'm currently in a situation where I put my trust in the Lord, because there's too many ways to fail in this life. Especially in a war zone…too many ways to die, so I put my trust in the Lord and then….do everything I can to make sure my students don't run me into mountains…silly things.

Now before I close this dissertation, I said I wanted to talk about Alma. I suddenly have a new respect and admiration for this man too. Again, when we read the Book of Mormon we always read about Alma the prophet and how he converted thousands, teaching near the waters of Mormon, and we gloss over the first part of his life. We know that he was raised up in a family that knew the teachings of God. Then, when he was a young man he became a high priest of King Noah, a wicked king. We tend to forget that this entailed his being a drunkard, a worshiper of idols, a liar, a cheat, a philanderer…Ok really just about anything wicked you can think of, they were doing it! He'd been raised differently, but succumbed to the king's court…why do I bring this up? Because it's another story, like Paul's in the Bible, of what the Gospel does to those who listen. It's a story of change. A lost soul became one of the strong prophets of the Book of Mormon.

I want to be like Alma, strong in the Gospel. I've had my own shadowed days, as we all suffer through at times, but I know especially as I go through it now, that change and spiritual rebirth is an amazing thing. I'm not trying to be holier than thou. I just am so excited by the changes for the better that have occurred in my life. The Lord has blessed me abundantly. Helen Keller says that, "life is either a great adventure or nothing". I'm going to go with adventure. May each of you be blessed and protected and find your own life adventure guided by the hand of the Lord!

Kandahar is flat, dry, dusty and dirty.

Chapter 19

FRIENDS AND FAMILY

I love the opportunity to take time each week and share my experiences in a war zone, my testimony, and my elements of learning that have taken place in my life in the last week. I am in a war zone, not that my war stories are all that exciting. But they're interesting and I don't get shot at, knock on wood, but flying with Afghans brings with it its own inherent challenges.

To start off, I dub the first part of this, "How to make a 3.5 hour day stretch to 11 hours." Ah yes, the joys of Murphy's Law coming into play. I only have one flying story this week and that's due to the fact that I only flew once, but it did give me good fodder for at least a short story. We had a simple mission planned, the first flight with only Afghan Loadmasters, and in fact I was going to be the only American on the plane. And then people started up with the, "Hey can you drop in here to pick up some cargo" and "we've got a pallet out of Kabul for you." No problem! I always like getting things done, so we accepted. On the day of the flight, no cargo! Frustrated I asked, "Where's my cargo? Who knows where my cargo is?" Finally they located the pallet, someone had decided to lock it in a shed and the person with the key was not around.

I was about to leave the cargo and just go, when they came running up saying they'd found the person with the key, and were getting the cargo out. I agreed to wait and saw that time passed and still no cargo...."Where's my cargo?" again became my question. Turns out the forklift drivers had all decided to take a break, all of them at the same time. One of our loadmasters was working the issue for me. He went and yelled at them all until they brought the cargo out to the plane, 5 minutes before our scheduled takeoff. Needless to say, it was a little frustrating, but I wanted our Afghan loadmasters to do well and work it out, so they brought the forklift with the pallet behind the plane. Now, I don't load pallets that often, but even I could see it wasn't going to work. The forklift driver tried to come at the airplane at an angle…

FINALLY, we got the pallet on the ramp, sort of, and it got stuck....it wouldn't fit. We banged on it, fussed at it, and finally pushed it off the plane and said we weren't taking it. We had very little time left to try to get to our next location during our allotted time and so we gave up on that pallet....ahh, but the fun wasn't over yet my friends, it gets better.

We started engines and things went quickly because I had the copilot with me that is more American than Afghan. He curses like a sailor, but he's as good as any normal American copilot. He just hadn't flown in 7 weeks because he'd quit for his 6th time. Anyways, I digress. We took off and flew to Bagram...fast; we were on the ground 10 minutes after takeoff, straight shot, only got in one other aircraft's way and it was their fault anyways...so they moved. :) Got on the ground, shutdown and waited for them to bring our two pallets from Bagram...That's when I had to laugh at the absurdity of my day and how I knew it was going to continue.

They brought out a married pallet...this means that two standard size pallets are linked together to hold a bigger than normal item. No problem, except for the minor difficulty that they'd built it wide side for loading, and we couldn't take them that way. See a pallet has a wide side and a skinny side. While C-130s and C-17s take pallets wide side, C-27s take pallets skinny side forward. Yup, you guessed it...PROBLEM! I knew they needed the parts on the pallet because it was to fix a helicopter that had been shot up a couple days before. I told them I'd wait, if they could get it fixed in an hour. I was only supposed to be on the ground for another 15 minutes, but I was already late so "whatever"! I sent my guys to lunch and watched as the ground crews didn't bother working on the pallet for 50 minutes. Then, I called and they got someone to hurry up and do it. Finally, two hours after I arrived, the pallet was back behind the airplane, but the K-loader, a big vehicle used to move married pallets, couldn't get close enough to the airplane and I had to stop my Afghan loadmaster from running it into the side of the plane. That wasn't something I wanted to happen. You gotta watch these characters sometimes.

We got it close enough to push the pallets onboard, but there was a 3-4 foot hole in between the loader and the airplane. Well, as luck would have it, the pallet got stuck in the same spot, but we forced it on, half of us pulling from the front and half pushing from the back. That worked well, except that the two guys pushing, including one of my Afghans, fell through the hole and got all bruised up...Ahhhh what a day. So, pallet loaded, we finally flew to Mazar I Sharif and delivered it. We worked hard in reverse and the helicopter guys were very appreciative. Finally, finally we were able to begin our pattern work, our flying, to get my copilot back in the swing. And here is where I start making my spiritual comparisons. He hadn't forgotten anything, but being away from flying for 7 weeks made his flying, in a word, sloppy. Off-airspeed by 10-20 knots, off-altitude 200 feet, nice landings, but drug in and low, floating for 1,500 feet down the runway...in other words, sloppy...and how often does that correspond with our lives.

How often do we start getting comfortable and maybe not studying or reading or praying quite like we should and our faith and adherence to the Gospel becomes "sloppy". That comparison played in my head as we flew and I critiqued him hard. I specifically told him that I expect more of him, because he always claims he's American trained and better than the others. I told him that because of that specific reason, I EXPECT more from him. As members (those of you that are members of the LDS church) the Lord also expects more of us.

That's my flying story for the day...he didn't try to kill me, but our day lasted 11 hours and we only logged 3.5 hours of flight time. That's not that good. And now I want to move on to the second part of my story. This is a subject that's been of great interest to me this week due to experiences I've had this week. To begin, have you asked yourself, what is revelation? And further, what is personal revelation? Revelation is information given from our Heavenly Father to people on earth to help them in many aspects of life, to help bring them back to him. Personal revelation is just that, specific information for an individual to help them in their life, to know what to do, etc., personal guidance from God to help us.

Now you're probably asking why I'm talking about this. Even if you're not asking, I'm telling! :) It's my prerogative. I'm talking about it because for the first time in my life, I've had extremely clear directions, midst direct answers to prayer and I'm amazed and blessed by it. Now I've had promptings before, such as when Tiffany and I were directed to join the Air Force. Another time when I was 15 and learning to fly, I did the walk around of the Cessna, getting it ready to fly. I started to walk back in and "felt" the need to look at the plane again and saw the braces of the nose wheel snapped off. It was close to the frame and difficult to see which explained why I missed it the first time. That could've killed me.

I've had promptings over years, but I don't think, until I started putting my life in order, putting my life in the Lord's hands, and spending all my free time studying Gospel principles and becoming closer to my Heavenly Father, that I've had as direct or quick answers to prayers. But, the truth is, this week has been amazing. I've been working out at the gym and while listening to classical religious music and with my mind blank, I've heard the Lord talking to me. I'm not kidding. For a change I was listening. I'd said several prayers in which I was asking specific things and I heard words, scriptures in my head, in my voice, but flowing one to another with the answer I'd been looking for. The next day I asked another question and the same thing happened. And the next day as well! I know for a fact that the Lord loves me and is giving me direction for me and my family. I'm sure He's talked to me before, but I haven't been in a position to listen very well.

The scriptures talk about a still small voice and that's exactly what it was. I've only heard it that clearly once before, and that was when I asked in faith if I should ask Tiffany to marry me right then, or if I should wait until the end of summer. I was clearly told to ask her then, and that she was my soul mate and I needed to ask for her hand. What I'm saying is that I just wanted to share how blessed I feel that since I've been studying the Gospel and living the Gospel and doing what I should, I've been able to ask and receive, seek and find and knock and have the windows of Heaven opened. I love my Savior and I'm thankful that He's mindful of us. I don't want to go into the details of what He told me because they're personal for my family and me and are helping us know what to do this year that I'm gone. Thank you for listening and I want all of you to know that it's true....Heavenly Father is there to answer us, we just have to ask and ask in faith, expecting to receive and answer and we will.

Again, I’m not trying to be holier than thou; I'm not trying to brag about receiving revelations. I just am so thankful and want to share my joy and thanks with you my family and friends, because you are the ones I can share this with, without fear of ridicule or incredulity, but knowing that you understand my joy and happiness.

Now, as I conclude, I'll just say that the Lord has promised us that as the signs of the times of the second coming of Christ are shown forth, as they are being shown in our day, we need not fear if we are striving to live the Gospel. I recognize that there will be a lot of chaos, contentions, wars, calamities and fear during these days; after all, everything seems to escalate doesn't it. But, I share with you my testimony of the joy and peace of living the Gospel.

Training, training with an Afghan student (above), AN-32 below

Chapter 20

NEW DAY

More interesting things today…I sat in a meeting that went on for two hours and meant nothing. What a pain to realize the wasted time, due to the fact that people are not used to making decisions, always wanting someone to make them for them, or to rule over them…Sounds familiar doesn't it, kind of like Satan's plan--the easy way, and the way that relieves man of his agency. People are so fickle sometimes and want someone else to do the work or the worrying or the deciding for them, not wanting the reward or the consequence to be brought on them. Interesting, but duly noted. My eyes truly are opened to the way the world is succumbing to the chains of the devil as he wraps men up, ties their hands and they thank him all the while…how wrong!

Another event today that I found interesting, I found an interesting fact to be true, the Afghans admire strength. In what way you ask? I'll tell you. As I walked back to work, there was this cement truck coming toward me on the road. They purposely swerved toward me to pass close by me. There were five guys in the cab of the truck. I think they were expecting me to jump out of the way so they could have a laugh. However, I saw that they weren't close enough to hit me so I just stared them down and kept walking. The driver started clapping and the others in the truck nodded their heads to me in respect. I found it an interesting experience. I do need to add that they were going slow enough that if they had tried to really turn into me I easily would have avoided them by stepping into the dirt off the road. Just an interesting note so stop my worrying mom!!

Now something I've been speculating and thinking about and studying about the last couple days.

Faith, what is faith? Faith is believing in, and hoping for something not seen that is true. My faith has been growing daily. It's amazing. I love studying the Gospel and learning all the things I'm learning. Take Helaman's 2,000 stripling warriors for instance. They had faith from their mother's teachings that if they did not doubt the lord would preserve them. And he did. When thousands of their brethren, the Nephites, were killed in battle, they survived. They survived when their army was surrounded, three to one, and they WON the battle. Not only that but most Book of Mormon historians agree they were between the ages of 13-18..they were young and they fought against men many years their senior, battle hardened and they were inexperienced. But they had faith. How can I, or we, develop that faith? We learn that things happen in our lives such as challenges, disappointments, disasters, or whatever to help us develop faith. They are not caused by the Lord, but He lets things happen to try our faith and help us grow stronger.

There are many evil and wicked things that happen in the world that the Lord does not cause, but He permits, to help men grow in faith. Our faith grows through our challenges and I've been seeing that first hand. My own challenges have made me dependent on the lord at all times throughout the days, every day. I love the Lord, my Savior, and my Father in Heaven. They challenge me to grow and be strong. I hope to someday be like unto Helaman who helped his young men develop the faith their mothers instilled in them so that although they fought many battles…they were all preserved. I hope to become someday like Captain Moroni, a man of such strong faith that if all men were like him the very powers of hell would be shaken…That is my desire. I don't boast of my own strength because I am weak, I am human and I am dependent on the Lord. He helps me daily.

OK, I know some of you really don't know who these people are or know the stories that I'm describing, but that's ok. I'm sorry if I confuse some of you, but I can't help but enjoy my fresh outlook on life and my fresh take of experiences. I am truly blessed of the Lord.

Mountains around Afghanistan

On the Afghan base; (below) Watermelons grow well here

Chapter 21

JUST ANOTHER DAY FOR YOU AND ME IN PARADISE

My chair broke this week making it a precarious perch from which to write, but it keeps things interesting. :) This week has been a week of Chaos.

Chaos: What is chaos? Chaos is defined as something orderly moving into disorder. Definitely an apt description for my flying schedule this week! My schedule has fallen apart, been put back together, taken early morning turns, expected late night turns next week, and ultimately slid into the same pattern of the previous week because it's been a pain in the neck to adjust. Right now we've entered the twilight zone...otherwise known to the Afghans as Ramazan (Ramadan in the rest of the Muslim world). For basically 45 days Afghans don't eat or drink during daylight hours, fasting and giving up many bad habits, kind of like lent for the Catholics. So, it's 35 degrees Celsius (95 degrees Fahrenheit) in the middle of the afternoon, we tried to adjust the schedule to accommodate their beliefs so that we don't have them flying dehydrated and not learning anything. But as luck would have it...it's a pain to get them on base super early in the morning and it's more hassle than it's worth so they asked to just use our original flying schedule. Se la vie.

OK, doesn't seem like too much chaos yet does it....well, I flew once this week. And it was a spectacular display of chaos if I do say so myself. I consider myself a patient guy and very relaxed....I snapped at my copilot trainee by the time we were done...you'll understand in a minute. My original plan was to takeoff, after a 0400 show time, at 0700 and fly to Herat, do an hour worth of Touch and Go's and return, making it back to Kabul by noon or just after....Ahhh, how the plans we make fall like dominoes. First, an airplane needed a new battery in Kandahar. Then my boss decided to go with us to deliver the battery. Not too bad so far. We flew down to Herat and I had two students with me. Because we added a trip to Kandahar for the way back, I skipped the area work that meant no steep turns, stalls, slow flight...you know all the fun stuff, but that was ok, I was going to get some good training in. Well, we got to Herat, made a low approach and came around for our first touch and go....and tower told us to LAND.

We landed, thinking it was a fluke. I told them that we wanted to do an hour worth of pattern work and then leave. I dropped my boss off for an errand and we went to take off. I thought the tower said that we were good for pattern work....what they actually said was "You're not cleared for pattern work". So, we were coming around to land and do a touch and go and they said..... “NO!!! You can leave!” Not exactly what I wanted to hear. I queried them and was told our training was DENIED. How annoying was that? Without further ado we landed, picked up the Lt Col and left, since we couldn't do anything else. I put my other student in the seat and off we went to Kandahar. Now, Kandahar is NOT a base to do training at. It is WAY too busy. Too many planes, too much static on the radio, too much chaos! The place is a dirt hole in a desert brown plain with dirty brown sky and dust clouds all around.

And I had a student....ON HIS FIRST FLIGHT IN THE PLANE with me. Yeah, you can begin to picture this now can't you? We get all these twists and turns and finally were cleared to fly an instrument approach and our instruments weren't working right and so, I was taking the plane from my student, talking on the radio, trying to configure to land and basically flying almost like a single-seat pilot. At times I was fighting over the controls with my student who didn't understand when I said it was "MY airplane"! It was a bit stressful, then we were on short final...less than two miles from the end of the runway...and they denied my landing clearance and told me to go away. Not technically, but they put me on radar vectors until they could get things straightened out. I let my student fly to follow the Radar vectors while I talked on the radio. They kept us low so I was also watching out for hills that my student wasn't exactly watching out for during turns....ay yay yay! I was sweating!

What a workout! Finally, they gave us clearance to land and we got on the ground, taxied next to the other plane, kicked off the Lt Col with the battery and left. I made my commander go on the other plane, I wasn't waiting around. I was probably in the chocks, in parking, for about 3 minutes. Then we pulled out, finished our checklists, got to the end of the taxiway by the runway and were given almost immediate clearance to takeoff...I took the takeoff from my student and as I got onto the runway, instead of stopping, I did a rolling takeoff. I was probably going 50 miles an hour by the time I was even on the runway.....I just wanted to GOOOOOOO! It was fun. After the takeoff, I gave the plane to my copilot again and proceeded to fight with the radio again. We got out of there and back to Kabul....and then.....while letting my student do the approach, a visual descent, he wasn't paying attention to his speed and we got going FAST.

I killed his power and told him to bring up the nose to slow down...he raised it approximately one degree, then let it drop again. This happened about 5 times when I finally grabbed the controls out of his hands, pulled backward and snapped at him to "PULL the NOSE UP!!!!" He got the point that time and did just fine on his landing with my help. I was in a grumpy, stressed out mood for the rest of the day and into the next day...all because of the chaos that ensued that day. It's amazing how chaos is the antithesis to order, how it saps the strength and takes us away from the calm enticing of the Spirit. Yep you guessed it, now I wax poetic and spiritual! My entire life revolves around the Spirit, the Gospel, my family and my work. There is no separating them. I learn from every experience in my life and apply a spiritual lesson to it.

I actually have a very good reason for my next comments. I took the question to the Lord about what message to share with you, my friends and family, and he quickly answered me that I needed to talk about the Plan of Salvation. After all, my whole discussion on chaos is centered on it being the opposite of the Plan of Salvation. First, what is this Plan of Salvation that I speak of? Well, I'll start at the beginning, and yes, this is going to be a little long, but If you're still reading you know that I share these thoughts in sincere desire and because you are a major part of the Plan of Salvation, though some of you know it not...

In the beginning, before this world was created, we all lived with our Heavenly Father, we're His spirit sons and daughters that he created, giving life to our spirits. We progressed in learning and knowledge as far as we could go. Our Father in Heaven is a being, God, with a body of flesh and bone, a perfect glorified being. We were spirits. He presented a plan to create a world for us to come to where we would receive a body of flesh and bone and be tried and tempted and have the opportunity to obey his rules and make choices. Our Agency was the main point of the plan. He told us that many would fall and not choose to obey and that as humans we'd come short. For that purpose we would need a Savior, someone that could pay the price of our sins, to assuage the demands of justice with mercy and if we repent and come unto Him, then we'd be able to return to live with God. Now, Christ came forth and stated that He would sacrifice himself as our Savior and would give the glory to God the Father. Another stood, Satan, Lucifer, he has many names, and he was an angel of God. He stood, and said he had a different plan. He would force everyone to obey and bring everyone back to the Father and therefore, he thought he should receive the Father's glory and power.

For his rebellion, in trying to steal the throne of God, he and a third of the host of heaven were kicked out, never to receive a body, and sent to earth to tempt and try men. Now, Satan is the Master of Chaos. He seeks to usurp the power of God, and destroy the plans of the Father. He wants order destroyed; he loves chaos and all the pains it brings. But he'll lose...Because Christ did come, he overcame the bonds of death, allowing all men the opportunity to become immortal when we're resurrected, and giving me and you the opportunity to repent and strive to become like God and return to live with Him. So, there is constantly a war between good and evil being waged on the earth. We are either the victims, or the heroes, but nobody is immune.

The Plan of Salvation is simple. It started in the pre-mortal existence where we lived as friends and family. Then, we chose to come here to earth to learn, get a body, be tried and tested, and return. When we die we will go to the Spirit World, where those who received the Gospel will have the opportunity to teach it to those who never had the opportunity to receive it in this life. Everyone will have the opportunity to accept or reject the Gospel of Jesus Christ before the end comes and we're judged. "Now this life is the time to prepare to meet God". It really is. We go through struggles and problems, which sometimes we don't understand. One of the Lord's Apostles said, "Just when all seems to be going right, challenges often come in multiple doses applied simultaneously. When those trials are not consequences of your disobedience, they are evidence that the Lord feels you are prepared to grow more (see Proverbs 3:11-12). He therefore gives you experiences that stimulate growth, understanding and compassion, which polish you for your everlasting benefit. To get you from where you are to where He wants you to be, requires a lot of stretching, and that generally entails discomfort and pain."

This life is a challenge; chaos comes at us from every side. Personally, I'm at a point where I've relinquished myself to Heavenly Father's will for me. I have to. I lived too many years just going day to day and living, but without goals, without peace, without purpose. I know my purpose. I know that I am a son of God, that He loves me and wants me to become like Him. I know that He lives, that He wants all of us to return to live with Him. There is much more information available about the Plan of Salvation. It is a gift from Him to us. We each will go through trials of various sorts. Satan thinks that he is destroying the plan when he tempts and tries us. But Heavenly Father knows the end from the beginning and His plans will not be thwarted.

Now, I want to end on this note. I am a husband. I am a soldier. I am a father. I am a pilot. I am many things, but the thing I'm most proud to say, is I am a Son of God. Now that I understand that and am living the Gospel like I should many things are so much better. Let me tell you what is better. My wonderful wife and I have become better friends than we've been our entire marriage. (This will be 14 years in two days!) She has become not just my wife, but my best friend and confidant, my better half, my soul mate. Our relationship has improved; our children are eating up the Gospel like starving people want water. Our confidence has improved, we're working forward, getting out of debt, we're happier, stronger and more in tune. We've been able to get revelation from Heavenly Father for our family and together we can do anything...these are things that are coming to us from the changes in our life we've made. I share this with you my friends because I know that Jesus Christ suffered in the Garden of Gethsemane and was lifted on the cross for me. He took upon Himself all my sins, my pains, my sickness, my sufferings, my sadness etc. All so that He will know how to succor us when we are sick, or afflicted and He'll be able to have compassion on us when we repent.

Chapter 22

WYLD STALLIONS!!!

Owwwwww, that's how I'm feeling, owwwww, my body and legs are sore right down to my toes and my back creaks like an old lady!!!! I'll explain my pain in a minute. Needless to say, I'm fine and in excellent spirits, but my body is sore. This has been an interesting week. Like all weeks go, I've stayed busy, worked a lot and made a ton of changes to the schedule. Now the joy of all this is that I've got a lot of fodder for my blog email, but at the same time...I'm sore!!!

So without further ado, I give to you...the reason for my pain...Yesterday, in a grand feat of excellence and gallantry and effort that would be sung by bards both far and near if that practice were still around, I participated in the grand excellent experience of an Amazing Race...Set up somewhat like the TV show but without the benefit of travelling all over the world, or the use of vehicles...when my friend signed us up as a team for the Amazing Race, I didn't realize it was a bloody RACE!!!!!! This delusion was quickly put to bed when they pointed out that the opening portion of the race was two laps around the perimeter of the Base...equating to 2.5 miles...ugh, and I hadn't eaten.

In fact, I'd rolled out of bed, called my beautiful wife and after a quick prayer slipped out to go participate in the race. Oh, the pain....when they stated the first event...I cried (not literally, but I wasn't thrilled, I was in my old shoes, didn't wrap my ankles and hadn't eaten, let the games begin) So we started. My partner and I quickly took to the lead, (there were ten teams of two) and I was running pretty well, but fast for me (I didn't want to be the dead weight or the handicap for my partner even though I was because he runs MARATHONS at a 6 minute mile pace for the whole thing...me...not so much) But, we stayed in the lead until the last half of the second lap when another team passed us, and when we finished, I was pretty tuckered out. I thought that was going to be the longest portion of it....I was wrong.

We got our clue and ran another couple hundred yards to an outdoor pull-up bar and dip bar and one of us had to do the challenge. JR (my partner) elected to do it and the other team that was ahead of us was already there working on it. He had a choice to do either, 20 pull ups, 40 dips or 80 pushups (the other team was doing pushups)...Now JR weighs about 100 pounds wet and he jumped on the pull up bar and cranked out 20 pull-ups and we were back in the lead. We ran to a small outdoor soccer field and I got to take a shot at a small goal with a keeper in the way. It took two shots, but I scored on my second shot and we increased our lead. We pressed on. Each place we had to run to was a couple hundred yards away. There was a simple task, finding a clue in movie cases and then, a quarter mile run to the passenger terminal for the finish of the first leg of the race. We came in first there and earned a 15 minute rest.

Once all the teams were there, they gave everyone a ten minute break and then read the next clue....a run from our compound over to the Afghan compound, the Afghan gym...which was about a mile and a half away. My body just cried and screamed at me. JR and I took off again in the lead. My body really didn't like me at that point but, we ran and were passed by the same team again and they got to the next location first. Unlike the TV show which lets you compete at the same time, we had to wait and when they finally finished we got to go in. There was a volleyball net set up and we had to return service, making sure to hit the ball three times before sending it over the net. They weren't being nice either, so it took several turns before we finally got it. Then, we took off running to the Afghan dining facility and had to answer five words in DARI, the Afghan language. We nailed the first four and couldn't remember the fifth...the Afghan worker tried to tell us, but was stopped and so we had to wipe down 20 tables... (We found out later that every team after us was allowed to ask the Afghan worker for help...aaarrrrghhh) :)

Oh well, we ended up in third at that point and had to run to the far side of the Afghan compound and go through a big shipping container. We had to fill up 5 bags of school supplies. We heard them wrong and thought we EACH had to fill five bags...NOPE! It was five per team so we wasted time trying to do double the work. We finished and started running again, going to the Afghan Air Force Wing building, another several hundred yard run. We ended up there in 4th place....Lucky us, at that point we'd run over 5 miles. Only the top 4 teams continued on at this point and we had to run to the opposite side of the Afghan base and put camouflage paint on our faces. Then, we had to throw tennis balls over a HUMVEE into a basket with our partner coaching us which direction to throw. We finished that and had to run back halfway across the base to the American gym and make three free throws with a basketball. I shagged the balls, JR shot and kept missing, but we got them in and then moved on to the final test, we thought! We had to shoot water balloons at a Humvee with a sling shot.

We had NO luck with that stinking sling shot. It kept twisting and our balloons would pop halfway there. The one girl team showed up, fired about three water balloons, hit the vehicle and took off running. We finally hit it after about twenty balloons and received the final clue—to run back the mile and a half to our building. UGH! My body protested, my mind protested, my brain protested, even my pinky toes protested, but we ran. We could see the other team a couple hundred yards ahead of us and we ran and ran and finally caught them. (I was pretty well wasted by that point!) All I could think of was, "I've just got to pass them, I've just got to pass them..." We passed them on the last quarter mile and while I couldn't breathe, and couldn't lift my legs. We finally got to the building and saw that we had to apply a tourniquet, lay a patient down on a stretcher and carry them to the end of the building. They caught us while we were doing this and we were neck and neck, but JR and I grabbed the stretcher and fast-walked to the end of the building, coming in third place, having run over 7 miles and done everything else. I gave it my all and I was satisfied. What a day! We won two free meals at the Thai restaurant on base too. I hurt, I was dead to the world, but I felt great for having done it and done my best. It was a lot of fun.

Now to switch gears, the whole story above is about a race and how I gave my all, and at times it wasn't good enough. I was helped and supported by my partner who was much better suited to it than I was, but together we came through and won a prize. That was pretty cool. How nice is it to think about the fact that this life is nothing more than a race, a test, one through which we are asked to give our all, and the Lord makes up the difference. I read in my studies this week a saying I've heard many times over the years and really like. Martin Luther said, "Pray as though everything depends on God, then work as though everything depends on you." That is so true. I know that the more effort I put into solving my problems, while asking Heavenly Father to help me out, that's when I find it easier to receive answers, because He always answers, and He makes things go smoother.

Part of my study this week dealt with problems in life. Pain, which my body feels because of the effort I just put forth, and suffering are central to parts of this life. I want to quote a good message. I highlighted it because I liked the way it explained things. I'm learning a lot from church fiction and nonfiction books, and the principles taught are true regardless of whether it is from fiction or non-fiction. Here's the quote:

"...I believe in a longer period of existence than most, a life before this one, a life after. In the one before, I made decisions that impacted this one. In the one coming up, my decisions here will have an effect. God sees me in all of them and bases his decisions to interfere in my life on his view of that wider perspective. So, when I scream for help because of pain while I'm here, his answer--and he always answers--is based on what he sees. Lots of people have very short mortal lives, or very miserable ones devoid of anything but pain, but that's far from all there is for them. When they die their mortal experience is valuable to what is yet to come. They learn, grow, experience things in a different sphere, in ways I never will because of what pain they suffered. Good things, blessings, if you want to give them a name."

"God could prevent death, pain, sorrow, and suffering. He could interfere in everything we do. But He won't because in our former life we committed ourselves to accept those things as a part of the larger picture, the future opportunities. We understood it wouldn't be easy, but we accepted it as a necessary part of the experience by which we can return to live with Him and ... even to become like Him."

"There it was; the doctrine that set us apart from other beliefs. The doctrine that made all the difference, really! If you didn't believe you could become like God, then you looked at Him as a kindly father who should always come to your rescue instead of a God who is schooling you for the opportunity to be all that you can be, even as He is.......It's not His will that we suffer, or that anyone suffers. It was our choice to experience this life, because we knew that without that experience we could never learn compassion, and pure love, and sacrifice. And all the things it takes to become like Him. If, now that the experience was hard, He interfered, what would that do to both of us?"

OK, enough quotes. I really liked these, because this life really is a test, a time to prepare, a time to see what we are going to do. This life is a time to choose. We all will be tested and tried. We all will fail and have problems, some big, some small, but He's always there to strengthen us and help us...but not remove the test from us. We learn the most from our trials and our struggles. I am living proof of that and I thank my Father in Heaven for watching out for me and caring enough for me to guide me even when I didn't know what I wanted or if I wanted to be guided. But, I stand before you and tell you that I KNOW this life is for our learning and growth. We need to learn all that we can, all that we have the opportunity to, knowledge of spiritual things as well as knowledge of everything good in the world. We are told that "whatever knowledge we attain to in this life will be that much more beneficial to us in the life to come." Life is so strange and wonderful. We meet friends and have family and many people pass through our lives, yet the ones that stay, or become friends instantly, or through random seeming events, I know that we knew each other before this world was. I strive to listen to the Spirit to guide me now, much more so than I did in the past and I love feeling the voice of the Spirit guiding me, in my studies, in my flying, keeping me safe and teaching me things to help me become a better person. I'm still the person I've always been, slightly nuts, carefree, happy go-lucky, childlike, and weird at times, but now I've added, I hope, a much deeper spiritual dimension that I've been missing. I don't know how I always lived without it. I'm me, and yet becoming an even better me. I hope you all understand this.

I didn't have an Afghan flight this week so no crazy Afghan flying stories. I flew on a newly configured airplane, but I rode in the back and basically took a nap. I was supposed to fly it but sat in the back. We climbed to about 16,000 feet and the plane started to depressurize. The guys flying worked on it, got the pressure to come back, then it failed again...and meanwhile they began disturbing my dreams of my wonderful wife and companion. To continue...they rudely interrupted my dreams by returning to Kabul with my ears popping as the cabin altitude increased. I had a nice 45 minute nap and then was done with my scheduled flying for the week.

I get to fly twice this week though, so I feel vindicated. Lastly, other things I did this week. I called and had a nice conversation with some Spanish controllers at a field I plan on flying into this week. I made a thousand changes and micromanaged the last couple days flying schedule so we can have a special flight go tomorrow, but I'll talk about that next week, because I don't think it should happen, but I've been directed to make it happen so I'm making it happen....(that's my teaser for next week) I need to mention that I have the most wonderful wife that puts up with a lot, is home alone with 4 rambunctious but awesome children, and is growing with me spiritually and emotionally, and deeply and truly is my best friend. I just want you all to know that. She's the best and I'm so thankful that the Lord led me to her...because I never would've suspected I'd marry a gorgeous redheaded southern belle....but I did and I'm so thankful that I did. She's my soul mate and my better half.

Flying around Kandahar – see the distinct desert/cultivation line

Chapter 23

THIS IS ONLY 2,771 WORDS LONG

Do I start at the end, or the beginning, the last, or the first? That's a question to ponder. This week has been a week of ups and downs....kind of like a yo-yo, but in a good way. Each day seems to muddle and run together at times, in a never ending groundhog day...and yet each day is different, yet the same. How to explain this, to people that aren't over here. It's not something you can easily explain. It's not something that makes sense, and yet it does. Such is the incongruence of my life....which makes perfect sense. :) Yin and yang...balance and opposites, good and evil, light and dark, Taliban and regular Afghan, airplanes flying and trying not to crash!!!! Always a symmetry and a beautiful kaleidoscope of chaos ... such is my life and I'll expound on this week's adventures and lessons learned.

Number one: four day old pizza kept at room temperature tastes funny when reheated!!!! Probably shouldn't eat.

Number two: The more I try the less I do, the more I know, the harder I try, the more I study the more I learn....don't know where I'm going with that, but it's there....

Number three: Confucius says, "man with cold in nose sleep all day and feel like crap all night....but get better anyway!!!"

Number four: Quoting Anita Stansfield, "Good music can be made by bad people and bad music can be made by good people and it's important to pay attention to how a song makes you feel." (Tiffany sent me this series, the Jayson and Elizabeth series, and this is the second time I'm reading it. I feel such an affinity for Jayson the main character and Tiffany, my wonderful wife and lover, understood that I'd have this connection...how awesome to have a wife so in tune…now we just need to start a band)

OK, on to my adventures; I only flew once this week and that was sad. I was scheduled to fly twice and as scheduler I have control of my destiny, but I didn't have control of the sniffles and they brought me down. I gave up a day of flying for a day of sleeping in bed. Oh, it was soooooooooo worth it; a day without working; a day without anyone bothering me; a day without anything except my head on a pillow. True, I didn't feel that great, and I didn't sleep well, but I stayed in bed until two o'clock in the afternoon and felt soooo much better. Instead of getting really sick, I managed to thwart it at the pass and sleep it off, thereby feeling better quickly so I can fly this week. Yeah me!!!

I flew an operational mission this week. I haven't done that in a while and it was nice to get out and do a simple mission, not involving people trying to kill me (at least as far as I know) and with qualified copilots. Now I use the term qualified loosely...they're qualified on paper, but they still try to kill you or land you on towers or other such things, so you have to always be on guard. We flew a nice simple passenger mission. I had two copilots with me. I hadn't flown with them in a while and they had always had some issues, but I was pleasantly surprised. Their radio skills have improved, though they're not where they should be yet, but they're getting there, and they didn't try to land me on a mountain so that's a plus in their favor. My first copilot got to make the landing to the unimproved field we were going to. This was a fun location to go to because it's unique and the runway is skinny and made of dirt. You basically have to put the airplane down on the ground in the first 500 feet of the runway. I let the copilot have the landing but I was on the controls...I didn't have to help TOO much; a little rudder here, a bit of power pull or input there, a pull on the yoke to get the nose up so we don't nose dive in over here....good... We landed and were able to taxi in and pick up our passengers, no problem! Then we took off again, after switching out copilots.

The new copilot seemed to have not realized that when the wings are tilted way over on your ground roll, that's bad and you need to move the ailerons to level the wings (propellers striking the ground is considered bad juju). We got the plane straightened out and took off, then had a nice uneventful flight back to Kabul...All in all a nice relaxing flying day, with only those minor inconveniences....But what happened this week was very interesting, even though I wasn't on the plane.

We, as the C-27 squadron, hit 1,000 hours flying in country this week…yeah, and there was much rejoicing in the land. I had to adjust to make the schedule work just right to be able to fly a special crew on Sunday to be the 1,000 hour crew...It had an Afghan Pilot, Afghan Copilot, a Standing American Instructor and two Afghan Loadmasters. It's what we're looking to accomplish, but most of us instructors don't think all the Afghan pilots are ready for it. The crew that flew, they're mostly ready, but just them...we can't do this with others, because they're not anywhere near ready.

Anyways, I digress--which I'm really good at. We made this big hullabaloo about it and turned a simple nice event into a circus and everybody and their dog got involved (I think we ate the dog, but that's ok) and I guess they did a great job....except for some minor inconveniences when they were loading passengers on the airplane...apparently, since the ground personnel at the location they went to were told it was an all Afghan crew...they figured they'd load the plane the way they do with the other Afghan planes. They cram as many people in as they can without regard to climb or takeoff performance. This is what we are trying to change. While the crew was talking to medical personnel about some patients that had to come on the flight, the ground personnel started loading a ton of people on the airplane.

Now, we actually run performance data, and know how many people we can take, etc. and we release that many seats...If we release 25 seats, the Afghans ALWAYS try to get thirty people on the plane. They also claim women and children don't count, but that's beside the point. To make a long story longer, as the crew started trying to get people off the plane, an Afghan Commander brought his family out and started handing kids up and forcing wives onto the airplane. Meanwhile, the crew was trying to get people off the airplane. I guess the hot-headed Afghan Lieutenant started pushing people and it turned into fisticuffs and a brawl broke out on the back of the plane. Our Squadron Commander was the Instructor and he got hit in the face.....craziness!

Finally, they forced everyone off the plane, only took the injured, and told everyone else emphatically that, "No, they weren't getting a ride!" They closed up the ramp and still, some guy with a broken foot climbed over the ramp (probably 6 feet in the air) to get on the plane....So yeah...they're not REALLY ready to do things on their own. I don't know that they would've handled the situation the same if they didn't have an American Instructor with them. They probably would have just overloaded the airplane and been unsafe like the other planes do. But, we're trying to teach them to do things differently with the C-27 and not do things the haphazard, dangerous way they've done them for years. There's a reason they used to have 400-600 planes and now only have 12... That includes the 6 we've brought. I guess I should mention that we bombed a lot of them out of existence in 2001 and 2002.

Why do I share this crazy story? Because it's the same as life; if we go at life in a haphazard manner, without safety nets, safety precautions, rules to live by, and spiritual guidance to follow, we'll be left in the lurch just as the Afghans are when it comes to moving people and cargo....disorganized and dysfunctional... Tiffany and I lived quite disorganized and dysfunctional for a long time and we're now developing our abilities and gifts that the Lord promises us, when we live His Gospel. I'm so thankful that she's my partner in this race of life.

I want to talk about my studies this week, because I've had a lot of opportunity to study and rest and pray and study some more this week, especially the last couple days and I continue to change and grow and live and learn and laugh and enjoy life to the fullest. This life is a time to learn joy, to learn to live free from sin, to learn to make mistakes, repent and grow. This life is the time to prepare to meet God. This life, this moment, this day, this hour, this minute, this is when we need to be doing all we can. Because we don't know when our moment could end; when I was in high school, a car full of guys and girls from my school were playing around and rolled the vehicle, killing the driver, who was only 17 at the time...We don't know when our moment is up, so we need to be preparing every day. I used to hear the phrase; live each day as if it was your last, but it didn't sink in. Now, I'm fully aware of that. I'm fully aware of the sanctity of life, of the beauty of it, and the tenuousness of it. We think we are in control, but we are not. We are subject to all sorts of possibilities in this life.

But, we should not be afraid. Fear is one of Satan's greatest tools. He uses it at all times to get us to stop doing what's right, be it fear of ridicule, fear of dying, fear of not knowing enough, it doesn't matter. He uses fear to enslave us, to keep us from progressing. I read some really good quotes about fear this week. Fear is the opposite of the Spirit. When we seek to have the Lord's spirit with us, we are not afraid. "Yea, though I walk through the valley of the shadow of death, I will fear no evil."(Psalms 23:4) This is a scripture that we've heard quoted I don't know how many times. But, when we are striving to do what's right...we have no need to fear. Fear makes us weak. Fear takes away our choices. Fear makes us give in to wrong impulses. In short, fear....keeps us from progressing.

Have I been afraid? Have I been scared? Absolutely! Although there are really only two things that scare me; One, would be going backwards in a back handspring or back flip (even though I can do it...I've landed on my head too many times to not be afraid...I think that explains a few things.) And two: I'm scared of not progressing or not doing everything in my power to follow the Lord's commandments.

There's a difference between being scared and fear. Being scared or afraid...you have control, you know what's bothering you and you know how to overcome...Fear is intangible and prevents you from acting....I want to act, and I am acting....I'm doing what I should, I'm learning and growing. Tiffany received good council from a friend and counselor to not take counsel from our fears. (Tiffany and I are working together on becoming spiritual giants...amazing what working together as a couple can do to help us learn and grow...no wonder the Lord instituted marriage...I wouldn't have anyone else...she's my best friend, my wife, my lover, my soul mate...)

You ask, is that why I always speak of spiritual things now? Absolutely! I am learning and growing by leaps and bounds, because I'm making immense effort, on a daily basis, to grow and be a better person than I've ever been. I'm changing to become the person my Heavenly Father wants me to be....I couldn't say that before, and I definitely didn't share as many spiritual experiences then either. Now, though, I hunger for the Spirit. I feast upon it. It keeps me sane in an insane world. I'm surrounded by people all the time that are worldly, vulgar, twisted at times...par for the course in war sometimes, and in changing as I'm working on changing, it keeps me centered on what's important...to be a light in the darkness. If I can help one person, be it through my studies, or my messages, or my talking with people about things of God, then I'll consider myself blessed. It's too easy to succumb to the world. Look at the high schools these days; they're ten times worse than in my day. The things kids are doing would shock even the hardest of people and it causes grief all around. I wish I could warn everyone about how much evil is out there and help all my friends and family to find their center. Find their center in Jesus Christ and learn how He can help us withstand everything, if we ask, if we seek, and if we knock...

I've started my music again. I took a couple weeks off, as I was working on other things. I've finished most of my Bring on the Rain song and have been writing more. I love music. Good music brings the Spirit, opens my mind to hear personal revelation, to hear the still small voice and to keep my thoughts centered on the things that are most important. Bad music does the opposite. It drives people to sex, drugs and rock and roll. There are many good songs, and there are many bad. Like I started this out with, Anita Stansfield's quote that we must sift the good from the bad, we must learn to distinguish the difference, we must learn....See, we've come full circle.

Skip to the end and you're at the beginning. This whole life, all that we are doing....is about learning. What will you learn, what will I learn this week? I always welcome emails, letting me know what you've learned. But that's what I've learned this week.

I leave this with this statement. Music is the gift that can bring us closer to God, or further away. What are we going to choose? All life is a choice. The longer I live, the more I study; I realize that life is a choice. That's why I'm usually in such a good mood. I know it drives some people nuts (moody people) but life really is a choice, I can choose to waste my life in an angry state at the problems, or whatever, that I see...or I can enjoy life and try to get closer to God. Choose ye this day!!!! It's all a choice.

Time
As a winter's friend,
It slips warily from day to night,
and endlessly ticks the notes of life.
For life and death, friend and foe,
Are all made manifest and answered;
All are brought to this point,
For wherever you are,
Whatever you do,
You are always
In the moment known as
NOW!

I get so carried away in my spiritual insights I forget to write how wonderful Tiffany is...But she is, and I can't wait to be back in her arms. Sadly this week makes a year ago that the family moved from North Carolina, thinking I'd be deploying immediately. Then that got shifted four months so I've been gone for a year, but have 7.5 months left....ouch!

So in the end we skip to the beginning and all is made sense of the senselessness of the chaos...and so be it!

Chapter 24

FRIENDS AND FAMILY

I come before thee humbled that you would take the time to read my ramblings. I love sharing my thoughts and my adventures with you. I love being able to inspire, amaze, scare, and provoke a laugh. I love being able to make you consider, think and ponder on life's necessary details. Without knowledge where are we? We are in a gall of bitterness and without hope if we succumb to that. Since my last email, there have been many occurrences that have taken place. Life is always an insane rush to hurry up and wait! You realize when you're around the military, and even in aviation that life is a kaleidoscope of events that are punctuated by rushing around and waiting. We have a saying in the aviation community that flying is hours of boredom punctuated by moments of sheer terror. I've had those occurrences in the past and I'm sure I'll have them again in the future. That's the nature of the beast, especially in aviation.

You've all read my flying stories and this week is no exception. I flew with two students again this week and was both impressed and disappointed in them. It really is like teaching children how to fly. In some ways, they did better than expected.

One student, who we always thinks suffers from English de-comprehension as soon as you put a headset on him, was able to answer radio calls (simple ones) and did a very good job at that...But, was unable to brief what he wanted to do in the traffic pattern to save his life. He no longer was diving at the approach lights at the beginning of the runway, but instead would shift his aim and float halfway down the runway before finally touching down. The other student, while doing very well at briefing, would then have the problem of not being able to push the nose down at his aim point and I actually had to shove the stick in his hands to point the plane at the runway. I find it intriguing how one week they're diving at the ground; the next they are clinging to the sky like it's going out of style. In fact, last week I believe I was complaining about having to yell at them to pull the nose up. This week I was yelling to push the nose down. (I know! I'm never satisfied!!! I just want them to learn to do well)

There were other things that went on this week. We went through a change of command. The General in charge of the wing finished his deployment and was replaced by another General. Now I'm not going to knock fighter pilots, but they really don't understand airlift sometimes and this general was a fighter pilot. I had an interesting insight during the change of command.

The outgoing General's replacement demanded immediate respect from the Afghans present. He gave his short speech in English, then a prepared speech in Dari....perfectly pronounced and he sounded like he'd spent the time necessary to learn it! The difference for me is amazing. I respect the effort! Personal effort! That's something I respect and admire. Work and attempting--that is also respectable.

Why am I not asleep? I should be. After all it's almost one o'clock in the morning. But, I felt I needed to write tonight, so I'm writing tonight. An artist is slave to his muse after all and when I feel the spirit indicate to me that it's time to write, I write. I hope I can finish writing what he would have me say in this the spiritual portion of my email. I try on a daily basis to feel the Spirit, to talk with the Lord, and to communicate with him to learn what He wants me to do.

One of the main lessons I learned this week had to do with faith. What is faith? We talk about it; we hear about it; we write about it; we read about it; but what is it? Faith is a gift. Faith is the result of a desire to believe, or a hope for something to be true. Faith is a gift given when we ask with sincerity. Faith is a gift that we are given when with only the desire to believe in something that we can't see but which is true, we act on it. Faith is a gift that comes from the verb, to do. We act and receive acknowledgement. We desire to believe and we fan the flames of that belief through our actions and see the results. We're told that every good thing cometh of the Lord and every evil thing cometh of the devil. That is one way that we can know if something is worthy of our faith. Faith and the desire to believe beget actions which beget answers to questions, which in turn give us experience and opportunities for knowledge to grow. Once we gain knowledge, it is no longer faith. But it is not the end, it is but the beginning. Faith is a constant growing seed that after it flowers once, then we have a flower, but not a garden. We are working to cultivate a garden.

Life is full of mystery. Life is full of adversity. Adversity is there to help us grow, to strengthen our faith, to see if we'll grow or falter. What choices are we making this week? Today? This minute? This week my study on faith came because of inspiration to read the epistle of Helaman. Here he was, a prophet of God, writing to his brother and fellow soldier, Captain Moroni, who I consider a personal friend, especially when I read about his convictions and why he fought, telling a story about these two thousand warriors.

He refers to them as the stripling warriors because they were young and full of vigor. They WERE young, probably just teenagers, never having fought, but they told him that they didn't fear death. They didn't fear. Fear and Faith.....don't mix. Their mothers had taught them that if they had faith in the Lord, they would be preserved. Throughout the couple chapters that this story talks about, they fought in some intense battles. These armies fought with sword and spear, bow and arrow, slings, scimitars, maces and all manner of weapons, meant to kill and maim. They fought hand to hand combat, not like we fight today in airplanes from far away, or at the far end of a rifle scope. No, these boys fought MEN...BUT, these boys, these teenagers, fought with the ferociousness unseen before in all the battles ever fought by the people.

They fought with the Spirit of the Lord and entire ARMIES surrendered to them. When they were in a losing battle and the rest of their army was retreating, they stood firm and resolutely "OBEYED…WITH EXACTNESS" all the commands of their leader Helaman. (Alma 57:21) Their faith was such that they were firm in their belief that, if they did what they were supposed to, they would be spared. Now the account is not long, but over the many, many battles they fought against an innumerable enemy, not one of them perished. Think about that. Thousands of their fellow soldiers died, yet not one of them did. This was an extreme example of faith, but they'd been taught, they believed and they were given the gift of faith to be protected, and they were.

Why share this story? Because we are like those stripling warriors! We are in a battle. True, I'm literally at war. I'm in a war torn country, but so are you. All of us are in a battle for our souls. The devil would chain us down and steal our agency, making evil appear good and good appear evil. I've been wrapped in those chains and have no desire to be there again. I know that of which I speak. The world will tell you this is good, or that is good, or it doesn't matter what you do....but the reality is that it does matter. The choices you make today affect your tomorrow. My choices have affected my destiny, but at the same time there is always a way given to change that destiny if we but choose to follow and increase our faith.

That is the message I send this week. I just finished the book "The Peacegiver" and I highly recommend it. It teaches us so well that WE are the designers of our destiny. We have all "sinned and come short of the glory of God". (Romans 3:23) We cannot blame anyone else for our problems, our anger, our unhappiness, or our misery, because everything is our own choice. But what we can do is choose to love the way Christ did. We can choose to accept that he's already shown the way. We can't force anyone else to change, only ourselves. I know part of my biggest problem was not blaming myself for my own problems, but blaming others. How hypocritical! I am the master of my own destiny. The funny thing is that the world's "choice" actually binds more people down than anything else. Choosing to smoke, drink, commit crimes, and have sex before or outside of marriage, all lead to heartache and a curtailment of our agency. We hear this all the time, but do we internalize it. The world says, "eat drink and be merry for tomorrow we die". (2 Nephi 28:7) The Lord says, "Wickedness never was happiness".(Alma 41:10)

Ok, I'm off my soapbox. But, I love learning. I love sharing these things with my wonderful wife and best friend, because together we're growing in so many ways that we NEVER would have imagined a year ago. Together we can accomplish anything. I leave you with my blessing and wish that you will understand and hear my message and hopefully be able to gain a little insight into your own life. Looking back through my missionary journal and looking back at my life I see that I'm always trying to help and counsel my friends. I am here for you. I am here to listen when you have problems. I am here to help be that shoulder to lift you up when you're down. I don't give friendship lightly. I give a part of myself when I make that commitment, because to me a friendship is supposed to last a lifetime and then beyond. If you need anything, don't hesitate to ask Tiffany or myself. We're always here to help our friends and family.

Lastly, one comment on work! The main problem that I see with Afghanistan and the work that I'm trying to do here, is that, everyone is given something for almost nothing. The incentive to work is not there. There are some Afghans that work, but others seem to feel entitled to rank and power and money, without having to work for it. We give them airplanes, we give them food and weapons...and yet they are so used to GETTING things from the current invaders that the incentive to change really isn't there. Sad, but the saying really is true... “give a man a fish and you feed him for a day, teach him to fish and you feed him for a lifetime".(unknown) Too often I feel like we're just giving them fish!

You are all in my prayers and thoughts. After all, I have lots of time for both, I fly once a week and sit at a desk and work to unscrew the problems that leaders make for my schedule!!! Tomorrow will be another round of that! "I do believe in fairies, I do, I do!" (Disney's Peter Pan) Well, I for one do believe in fairies.

Chapter 25

RESPONSE TO A FRIEND'S QUESTION

First off, women are not silly because they cry...I feel silly when I cry, because I don't cry, not that I don't want to or to be able to, but just very, very, very rarely have I ever cried....but in my standard contradiction of life...I'm very in touch with my feminine side...I know our culture is messed up about a lot of things...it could very easily have taught us incorrectly....it teaches incorrectly about so many other things these days....

OK, now I'll answer your question about immortality and eternal life. Here's what I'll do, I'll expound on the doctrine, since I said in the first sentence that if you had questions, ask....but I'm not going to quote sources today, because first off I'm tired. I just got back from flying a night flight and so I'm not properly prepared to dig out the references. And secondly, I had already planned on expounding on this very doctrine in the long answer email I'm preparing, and I understand I don't have to answer it all at once, but I will expound tomorrow on some of the things you've asked and give you many bible references.

There is one other thing I want to say as we continue our discussions. I'll never be upset with you. I'll never contradict you (unless I do it without meaning to) and I'll always respect your beliefs. That being said, there is one thing that I believe that is important. That is, you can find out for yourself if these things I tell you are true. I know sometimes they seem 180 degrees out from what you've been taught. But, one of the tenet beliefs that we both have mentioned is that God can and will talk to us. He answers prayers and one of the many ways He answers is through a good calm, warm feeling inside. There is a promise, given in the Book of Mormon (Moroni 10:3-5) and other places in the Bible, that says that if we ask God, the Eternal Father, if a doctrine or something else, is true and we ask in the name of Christ, He'll let us know whether it's true or not by the power of the Holy Ghost. Personally, I've felt this, I've asked and I know that these things I tell you are true. In my messages over the next few days, I'll cover some of the references, and where the information comes from, but for now, let me expound on this question you asked.

The difference between Immortality and Eternal life...This is one of the points of doctrine that is not very well understood by the rest of the world, because many things have been lost over the years, but in continuing my discussion from above let me add some information. Earlier, I talked about how this life was a "time to prepare to meet God."(Alma 34:32) It's a time where we're being tested to see if we can obey the commandments and do all things our Father has asked us. We knew we would fail, from the pre-mortal existence; He knew we would fail, that we wouldn't be perfect, and that we would fail to be able to return to live with Him, unless we had a Savior. Christ came forth, plead for us in the Garden of Gethsemane, suffered for our sins, our pains and our sorrows, everything. Then, they lifted him up on the cross and He gave up His life. Three days later He was resurrected.

That moment, that experience, broke the bonds of death, allowing each and every person that's ever lived on this earth the opportunity to be resurrected. Everyone, good, bad, ugly ...everyone, will be raised from the dead and their body will be perfected. What happens to the soul between death and the resurrection? The spirits of the righteous go to Paradise and those that have not known Christ go to Spirit Prison to await judgment...However, it's not so cut and dry there because during the three days in between Christ's death and resurrection He went to Paradise, and organized the spirits there to be missionaries to those in Spirit Prison. They go and teach the Gospel to those that have never had the opportunity in this life to hear it. That way, at the Day of Judgment everyone will be able to be judged by the same rules. They'll have the opportunity to accept or reject the message of the gospel. But, that's not the point were making right now, we'll cover that in another discussion sometime....

Where was I? Oh yeah, everyone is in Spirit Prison or Paradise and then, at some point everyone will be resurrected and it will be time for the Day of Judgment. Then, based on men's hearts, their works, etc. they'll be judged. I guess you could say according to their faith and works. Based upon what is written in their hearts, they will receive one of three Degrees of Glory. Those that have accepted the Savior and completed all the necessary ordinances will be received into the Celestial Kingdom, which Paul the Apostle compared to the Glory of the Sun. (see 1 Corinthians 15:41) This is the Kingdom where God the Father and Jesus Christ will dwell, this is Eternal Life. Everyone will become immortal with a perfect body, but only those in the Celestial Kingdom will inherit Eternal Life, which by definition is living with God the Father.

The second Kingdom of Glory, which Paul compares to the light of the Moon, is the Terrestrial Kingdom; this is where the good people of the earth will be. It is a Kingdom of Glory, but, these are the people that weren't faithful to their testimony of the savior, or just couldn't accept the gospel, but were GOOD people on the earth. You've known people like this, that are good people, but just don't have room for religion, or God or whatever....

The third degree or Kingdom of Glory is the Telestial Kingdom, which Paul compared to the light of the Stars, This is where the wicked people of the earth will be, but is still a degree of glory, meaning it is better than here...but the wicked will be there.

There is one other place and that is Outer Darkness, where the devil and his angels will be sent, along with those few people who have committed the unpardonable sin of sinning against the Holy Ghost...

That in a nutshell, is the second half of the Plan of Salvation. Basically though, the other kingdoms are degrees of glory, they're also a type of hell, because those that go there won't be married, nor given in marriage, and they won't be with Heavenly Father.

In the Celestial Kingdom, Eternal life includes Eternal Increase...meaning that we believe that a man and woman may be sealed for time and all eternity and that their marriage covenant, when executed under proper priesthood authority, will continue forever, enabling those that are received into the celestial kingdom to have Spirit children.... That's part of the whole "becoming like God" thing. (See D&C 132)

I know you have trouble understanding the idea of us being able to become like God. Let me explain it simply. Think of God the Father as a great Music conductor, or teacher. We are all his pupils. He has this grand symphony (life) that He wants us to perform, but we need to learn how and we're tested, etc. We become better and better. Like any good teacher or conductor, what do you want for your students? You want them to become great, even so much that you want them, in a way, to become like you. God works the same way. He wants us, His spirit children to grow, to learn and to become like him as any father wants for his children. If you look at it like that, it's not such a difficult doctrine to understand and it's not contradictory to the Bible. Even if we become like God, for us there is only one God (God the Father) But, we'd have the opportunity to become like Him...It's hard to explain, without a belief in the basic doctrines of the Mormon Church, i.e. continuing revelation, modern day prophets etc.

First and foremost...is a belief that I know to be true, in continued revelation; in a knowledge that God sent further scriptures to help us understand. One of the hardest doctrines I have ever had to try to talk about, not Mormon doctrine, but the doctrine of other churches, is the doctrine that the Bible is it; that God won't send anything else. And yet we know that the Bible is incomplete. We know that it was compiled in the early centuries A.D. from books and writings from the Apostles scattered about and that a delegation decided what books could and couldn't be included. Prior to that time, the words of the prophets were kept on plates or manuscripts written by certain prophets. I understand that many churches point out the fact that in Revelations 22: 18-19 John stated that if anyone take away or add to the book, they would be cursed. I heard this a lot when I was a missionary, from many different ministers and preachers. The thing is, when John wrote that, the Bible wasn't put together as a book. The Bible was separate letters and books written at different times in different parts of the world. John was referring to his Book of Revelations.

Additionally, I hope I'm not offending...don't get upset....but let me ask a question... Why? Why would God, who appeared to prophets, from Adam on down until Christ, then appeared to his Apostles as He continued to give them revelation? Why would God cease to do miracles? Cease to speak to man? Cease to speak to prophets to tell them what he wanted concerning the world of THEIR day? Is God a changeable God? If He spoke to prophets and apostles for 4,000+ years, why would He stop? I have prayed about this and I know that God didn't cease to talk to man, man ceased to listen and to hear. Christ set up an actual church but, there was a falling away from the church Christ created. The Apostles were killed and with them the authority of the Priesthood, which is the power to act in the name of God.

I also know for a fact, because it's been born witness to my heart and soul, that in the early 1800's a young man, 14 years old, named Joseph Smith, read in the Bible in James 1:5, "If any of you lack wisdom, let him ask of God, that giveth to all men liberally, and upbraideth not; and it shall be given him." And verse 6, "but let him ask in faith, nothing wavering." He was confused because in his day there existed a great contention, or in his words "an unusual excitement on the subject of religion."

There were many churches teaching diverse things, and contending about different points of doctrine that he found confusing. He read the verse in James and decided to pray and ask God about it. He went to the woods near his home and began a prayer. He was overcome by a deep darkness, and could not move, then he mustered his strength and called upon the Lord and in his words he said, "But, exerting all my powers to call upon God to deliver me out of the power of this enemy which had seized upon me, and at the very moment when I was ready to sink into despair and abandon myself to destruction--not an imaginary ruin, but to the power of some actual being from the unseen world, who had such marvelous power as I had never before felt in any being--just at this moment of great alarm, I SAW a PILLAR of LIGHT exactly over my head, above the brightness of the sun, which descended gradually until it fell upon me. It no sooner appeared than I found myself delivered from the enemy which held me bound. When the light rested upon me I saw two personages, whose brightness and glory defy all description, standing above me in the air. One of them spake unto me, calling me by name and said, pointing to the other --*This is My Beloved Son. Hear Him!*"

Joseph Smith saw God the Father and Jesus Christ, separate beings with separate bodies. They spoke with him and called him to be a Prophet to RESTORE the things that had been lost over the last two thousand years. Many plain and precious truths had been lost. While there are many references to them in the bible, the meat is missing in many respects. He went through much persecution, much opposition, eventually he was directed by an Angel that appeared to him and directed him how to find a set of Golden Plates which with the power of God, granted to him by an ancient prophet, he was able to translate as the Book of Mormon, which is another powerful testimony of Jesus Christ, but written by his prophets who were guided from the Holy Land to the Americas 600 years before Christ. Additionally, it contains the visit of Christ to America following his ascension into Heaven. In the Bible it's written that Christ said, "Other sheep I have which are not of this fold, them too must I visit and they will hear my voice and it'll be one fold and one shepherd..." John 10:16

These are the main differences between the Church of Jesus Christ of Latter-day Saints and other faiths. We believe that we have been given revelation in our day, that prophets have been called by God the Father and Jesus Christ; that through this revelation The Plan of Salvation was revealed. This plan is found in the Bible, but it is not fleshed out, because many plain and precious truths were lost. I've prayed and know that these things, though maybe hard for you to understand, or accept, are true, because I've felt the Spirit testify to me that they are, verbally as well as with a burning in my chest that let me know, not just believe. I know these things are true....

I hope you have more questions...I know, you ask a simple question...get a longwinded answer, but I love sharing and I've always enjoyed talking with you about this stuff. Seriously though, if something sounds so outlandish or crazy or 180 out from what you've always been taught...take it to the Lord. If you want a Book of Mormon, I'll happily send you one with my testimony inside. I'm not trying to convert you...just explain so you understand where these things come from. I know who I am, where I came from and why I'm here and I know where I'm hoping to go after I die. There's a lot more information out there that I would love to share with you all based on scripture and revelation.

One of the points most people take offense to is Joseph Smith and the Book of Mormon, but it's really pretty simple. If one can accept that God spoke with prophets anciently, then we can make the logical jump to Him speaking to prophets today. If we can accept that He would appear to a prophet today, then, we can accept that He could appear to Joseph Smith and that the Book of Mormon could have come through a prophet and therefore can be accepted as scripture. It's not adding or taking away from the book of Revelations, or the Bible, it is another testament, a scripture unto itself. If you can make these assumptions, the key is to ask God if I'm smoking crack, or if I'm telling the truth. I, or anyone actually, can tell you many things. I can say something, your pastor can say something, another leader or teacher can say something...but the truth, that only comes from God. One last assumption--if Joseph Smith is a Prophet and the Book of Mormon is true, then, the

Church of Jesus Christ of Latter-day Saints is the restored kingdom of God on the Earth.

"Ask and ye shall receive, seek and ye shall find, knock and it shall be opened unto you"...that's what this is all about...I enjoy sharing and am enjoying our discussion...and Heavenly Father, can let you know for yourself if these doctrines that I'm discussing are true! That's my challenge to you...

Ok...I'm done for now...it's almost one o'clock in the morning. I'm sure I'm stirring up a hornets' nest of questions or defenses with this chapter, because many other churches have a misunderstanding of the Mormon Church (The Church of Jesus Christ of Latter Day Saints) and therefore many of the doctrines are attacked.

Chapter 26

EVERYONE NEEDS A TRUNK MONKEY

Don't mind the title, every story needs a good catch phrase. I remember when I was in AP English class and we were studying King Lear by Shakespeare and we had this project to write a two page synopsis of some metaphysical psychobabble something or other about King Lear and his madness. I had forgotten when I wrote that we were supposed to have a title for our project. So, quickly, before handing it in, I wrote a title that appropriately was perfectly suited to my warped sense of humor...and also had absolutely nothing to do with King Lear...I didn't realize as the teacher collected the stories she was going to read the titles out loud, just to see what sort of psychobabble we were able to come up with. She began, "King Lear and His Madness, King Lear and His Heart of Stone, King Lear: An Extrapolation of Psychosis, King Lear and Freud's Theory About Mothers....." and on and on...then she got to my masterpiece...."Joe is dead!" For some reason she didn't find the humor in it that I did.

I busted a gut, but just got the evil eye....Aww, she loved to hate us. See, there were four of us in her class from band, and we ALWAYS got out of class and she had to excuse us, so she hated us, but she loved us. We were unique and didn't take life too seriously. Besides, if you take life too seriously you'll never get out alive. Ok, bad pun. But, anyways, she loved to hate us and loved us because we wrote well, we had unique points of view and we were fun (I'm ad libbing here but I thought we were fun) She did have to separate us all since we talked too much. Therefore, we practiced sign language so we could still talk!

Why do I talk about my high school English class? I don't know except that it reminds me of things that are important which I'll talk about later...such as agency, freedom, abilities and all the other things I continue learning on a daily basis. But first, as always, craziness speaks and indifference departs, the cow jumps over the moon and the fiddler blows his horn, or was it the cat ate the fiddler...oh I forget, but what I mean to say is that first, flying fun for the week.

I actually didn't fly with any Afghans this week, but I flew twice. In a war zone one of the many ways that troops get resupplied is via a means we term air drop. This is a literal description as well as a method. Literally it means that we drop stuff from the air. And as a method it's fairly obvious that we throw crap out the back of the airplane with parachutes on it and hope it doesn't explode when it hits the ground. This week I got to participate, and since I'm one of only a couple airdrop qualified instructors here, I'm one of the first to help continue validating the procedures developed for the C-27 to airdrop supplies. Last Saturday, which just happened to be September 11th, we flew a memorial flight around to different points where the Special Forces were dropped off to begin the assault on Mazar i Sharif back in 2001. We overflew these sights at about 300 or so feet through the mountains.

Then we did the most important thing of the day.....we stopped for lunch. Flying low level on a semi-empty stomach can be a little difficult and we had a couple people a bit, shall we say, nauseous, what with all the bumping and bouncing around in the mountain thermals. We stopped for lunch, but there was a helicopter blocking our parking space and we had to wait for him to move. Then, our fuel took forever to arrive at the plane. Finally, we got a bus and headed over to the German side of the base to go get some schnitzel. That's all we wanted, and we arrived one minute after the kitchen closed and they refused to open back up! We had to settle for chow hall food, which actually tasted good but it wasn't schnitzel. We were sad, but we flew back to base with full bellies.

The next day I was supposed to have two Afghan students, but, they decided to take an extra day as part of one of their three day holidays. It soon turned into five. When they didn't show up, another instructor and I took the plane and went and practiced for a couple hours. It didn't happen often, but it was always worth it. We stopped and got schnitzel for dinner!!!!!! It was sooo good!!! We flew back at night. I enjoy night flying! It's calmer and not as busy. I tried out NVGs in the airplane and found out how bad the airplane lighting is to fly on Night Vision Goggles (NVGs)--I had to turn off all my lights, but I enjoyed it and could see a lot, especially stars.

A few days later I got to fly again, I know, crazy isn't it. I flew an actual airdrop mission to resupply a forward base. It was kind of funny. The silly Afghan Army guys parked their Humvees on the drop zone and we dropped, almost on top of them. Luckily we didn't hit anything, but equipment can be destroyed so easily. At least one bundle of water exploded on landing when it's chute failed to open.

This brings me to my study and learning topic of the week--agency and communication. I've talked a lot about agency. Agency is one of the primary reasons we came to earth, to see if we would do all that the Lord commanded us. I read a great description of agency this week. The story asked, if we saw a man that was tied up, bound and gagged so that he couldn't move, couldn't talk, couldn't blink, and couldn't see, would he have his agency? Most times we define agency as being the ability to choose. However, this example brings up a good point. Would that man have his agency? What do you think? The answer is a little surprising, or at least it seemed so the first time I read it. The man tied up so he couldn't move would have just as much agency as you or I. The reason is the nature of agency. Agency is choosing who we will follow, the Savior and His teachings or the devil and his. The tied-up man has as much agency to choose to follow the Savior as we do.

One other aspect of agency that I know I've touched on before, but I feel needs to be brought up again and again is the fact that we are free to choose, as many people often do, to give up our agency. The world continues to teach that drugs, tobacco, premarital sex, alcohol, etc. are choices that are our rights. It teaches that we have freedom only if we choose them, along with any other guilty pleasure available. The sad thing is that these things bind the person who chooses them down and restricts their ability to make choices until they become a slave to the very thing they chose and no longer have a "choice" in the matter. It's sad but true. Satan holds the chains of the earth in his hand, the cords that he wraps men up in one slender line at a time, and laughs.

Debt is another one of these chains and we as a society are bound. Look at what we're doing to enslave not only ourselves but our children in debt. The Savior said a man cannot serve two masters. When we are bound by debt (and I fall into this category though I am working steadily to get out) we are slaves. We lose the agency we thought we had; we work to pay interest and others instead of ourselves....So sad, but credit cards come cheap these days...until the interest bites.

You could say I get on a high horse sometimes and I probably do. I worry about everyone, I worry about the way I've responded to things in the past and don't want to go down that same road ever again. I study and attempt to learn and grow so that I can stand before the Savior and express my gratitude for what He did.

How many songs are there on the radio? How many lyrics do you know? How many of those songs are good? Good question! What we listen to communicates to others who and what we are. Do you believe that? I think it's interesting because music has a powerful ability to either bring the Spirit of the Lord, or cause it to depart. I've been very interested in music throughout my life. I got involved in band in 8th grade because I hated my 7th grade Spanish class and music clicked with me. I had fun, it brought life, and it brought spirit and kept me centered. I learned piano and a little guitar...I don't brag, I'm not good. I just tinker with it and it's brought me much joy.

Right now, the joy I get especially comes from being able to play, even though I mess up, each Sunday, the little keyboard in our meetings. It's my little contribution to our meeting and I'm thankful that I can do so. I also have thoroughly enjoyed writing music. It's a unique undertaking and I finished two songs this week and actually was able to put them on my IPod. They're different and spiritually minded because I find so many songs that I can't stand, mostly songs with curse words and inappropriate messages. But, I love music. It brings the Spirit and helps me to focus, when the world around me is filled with people devoid of light. Life isn't easy, but communicating with the Spirit sure makes it go a lot better.

The last thing I need to write about is Happiness. I'm generally a happy person. I choose to be happy. I choose to have fun and laugh at life. I choose to take joy in life. I listened to a 2005 General Conference session this week and one of the talks struck a chord in me. Elder Hoyos said, "We need to recognize that 'wanting to' is the key to living the Gospel. And that living the Gospel is the key to happiness." Most times we find happiness in the midst of the trial of our faith. Happiness comes as a result of righteous living. Joseph Smith stated, "Happiness is the object and design of our existence; and will be the end thereof; if we pursue the path that leads to it; and this path is virtue, righteousness, faithfulness, holiness, and keeping all the commandments of God." (Teachings of the Prophet Joseph Smith, pgs. 255-256) People tend to ask me why I'm so bloody happy all the time. The truth is that I'm happy because I know that I'm on the right path. I'm happy because I choose to laugh at most troubles in life and to try to learn from my trials and become better. I'm happy because life's too short to not take joy in it.

I've quoted the movie "The Last Samurai" before, but it fits here. "Life in every breath" meaning we can see the end, we can see the joy in each second of life, because we only have this one mortal life; though we had a pre-mortal life in the Spirit World and we'll have a time in the Spirit World after we die. Then, cometh the judgment where we'll be judged after our resurrection, in our immortal body and we will attain that kingdom of glory to which we rightfully earn. I don't know if I'm explaining this right but I'm trying to say that I know that we can be happy in this life and in the life to come and as has been said before, happiness comes from living the commandments.

Life is an adventure. Life is fun and crazy. Life is a pain in the butt at times, but it's a good one that we can learn from. Life gives us trials. Life is a beautiful mess. I love it. I love life. I love my family. One thing being apart in a war zone does is helps you focus on what really matters. My wife is my best friend and I have fun spoiling her at times, and at others I'm the bane of her existence, as all husbands are to their wives at times. She stands by me and supports me and I love her for that. Together we can get through anything. She doesn't enjoy her current role of being a single mom for a year and a half. It's not fun, it's difficult and stressful, but she's a good wife and mother and I love her for it.

I know that these things I am learning and expounding on are true. I feel it as the Spirit whispers to me. I know and my witness of its truth. The best part about what I learn and teach is that the same Spirit that tells me these teachings are true can tell you, if you ask. James 1:5....That's the key to knowing.

HIT IT - By ME

Try - you've gotta chance

So take it

You may learn to dance

As your life

Unfolds its mystery

You've got to take it, you'll always make it

So Try

Do - just do what is right

Don't look back

Don't fall for the world's tactics

Just go

Down the straight and narrow road

And run

Run from the wicked, so you may

Be where he can accompany you

Every day and every time you're faced with challenges

In your life

You act and make your choices

Every day

And you know that you are

Where you should be

So try - you've got to take your chances

When you're given

Each and every day a new stance

Built on gospel plans

You can know what you must do

Just Ask

He'll answer always

He's there

And he'll listen to you

If you just ask

Every day and every time when you face a challenge

Hit your knees

He'll help you act and make your choices

And each and every day you can know just what to do

To live

So, Try, Do, Run, and hit your knees

He'll watch over you....

Chapter 27

TRUNK MONKEYS PART TWO

Emotions overload. Feelings of peace. Tears flow down. Bring on the Rain!

I just feel that there's a second piece to everyone needing a trunk monkey. And so I'm writing again. I'm going to get a little sentimental. :) Looking back, I see through the years all the insanity of my life. There've been highs and lows. There's been right and wrong. There's been joy and sorrow. I think about my best friend of the male persuasion (Since my wife is my bestest friend I must differentiate), Rusty, it's hard to realize we've been friends for over twenty years. We've laughed and cried and made everyone around us, when we were growing up, think we were insane, because we were. We laughed at life and life laughed back. We were like Amos and Andy, Abbott and Costello, the three amigos, (without the third, though there were several that fell into that category over the years) but through it all we've been friends.

Marriage, complete differences in types of careers, distance apart, and time in between conversations have never diminished that friendship. I've said before I take friendship seriously. There are those that receive this that were a part of our tripod, our Musketeerhood, our insanity. We have good memories of those times. There are very few people I've maintained contact with over the years, and the ones I do it's because of what your friendship means to me. My bestest friend, as I said, is my wife, Tiffany. She puts up with a lot being married to me and in the past year we've truly gotten to see each other in a new light. We've grown closer and stronger and better as we've sought to put the Gospel first in our lives. I make no apologies that all these chapters deal with my spiritual lessons learned and often times I'm giving counsel.

I find it funny to give counsel. Reading through my journals and looking back on my life, I've been a counselor. I've counseled friends and family in troubles and stress and problems and I've always enjoyed it and tried not to judge. After all, with all the mistakes I've made in my life, I'm no one to judge anyone. I'm truly thankful for the truth that repentance is not only possible, but expected. It was a hard lesson to learn and I'm glad that It got through and that I'm able to progress each and every day to become a spiritual giant. That's why I say it's funny to give counsel, because for a long time I had a hard time taking counsel, even though I was always good at giving it. My dad can attest to that, at least in the years I've been married. I suffered from pride. I thought I could do things and was above things and that I was exempt from counsel...I wasn't and I'm not. It took some humbling experiences to let me realize this.

I am not anywhere near perfect. I make mistakes and will continue to do so. Life, each day, is an opportunity for me to grow and change and become better, now that I'm of the proper mindset to do so. I no longer can reject counsel when I realize how dependent I am on the Lord for everything in my life. He protects me while I'm at war, He watches over my family while I'm away, He strengthens me when I'm down, which happens more than many would think, because I USUALLY am laughing at life as previously expressed. But there are times when I struggle, and those times I need the love and support of the Lord and also of my beautiful wife and help meet.

Where was I? Oh yes, what I'm saying is that, this week, I've really learned about balance; Balance and focus and separating the wheat from the chaff. What is really important in life? Money? No, though it helps us live. Our job? Nope, though it does come with commitments that must be honored. Family? Absolutely! And there are times I categorize friends under that category as well. But it's our familial relations that matter most. One of our modern day Apostles, Elder M. Russell Ballard stated, "We warn that individuals...who fail to fulfill family responsibilities will one day stand accountable before God. Further, we warn that the disintegration of the family will bring upon individuals, communities and nations the calamities foretold by ancient and modern prophets." (Let Our Voices Be Heard - Ensign, Nov 2003)

In The Proclamation to the World on Families by the LDS (Mormon) Church it states, "Family is our first and primary priority. Families are eternal. Families are the basic unit of the Church and kingdom of God. The plan of exaltation and happiness is centered in the salvation of the family and its individual members. What are we doing to magnify our eternal roles and serve each other within our family unit--fathers and mothers, husbands and wives, brothers and sisters, and sons and daughters?" This hits home, especially when I'm so far away. Oh, how I miss my family. I miss my wife and kids. I miss hanging out in the evening and sharing a laugh or a joke or even breaking up a fight. When you have four kids there's always fighting...especially when you had four within four and a half years. Life is and was crazy. But I love it; the crazier the better. I enjoy the insanity, the chaos and the change...life is change and growth and I like it.

It's interesting the way life is viewed by those around me. There are those that I work with that are in a continual state of anger. There are those that are always stressed out. There are many whose mouths are excessively foul. There is very little of humility around and there are many people that just seem lost. Contrast that with talking to my wife and having her tell me about her inspiration and the schedule she's making too, improving her life through study and prayer as well. One of my cohorts made a comment that I liked and find it to be true. He said, "Everyone has a God sized hole in their heart and they'll try to fill it with things that can't fill it the same way." They fill it with football, or work, or teams, or porn, or drugs or whatever....It's sad, but it doesn't work. True happiness comes, as I said in part one of this blog email, through living the gospel. Elder Hales said in his book *The Return*, "In life, how we respond to wise counsel--even if we may not understand the importance of the counsel at the time--can prepare us for life's tests and save more than just our ankles."

Going back to reminiscing...I was insane in high school. I admit it. I know it and I relish it. I'm still insane, but I keep it toned down a little, mostly because I've matured....a little. I still feel like a kid. I know Tip would say the Eternal Peter Pan. And to me that's a good thing. In my opinion you have to be able to be childlike at times to really understand things and realize that this life really is a fun life and we stress out about things way too much for silly reasons. Some humorous and fun memories that I don't mind sharing....jumping my Volkswagen bug coming out of a dirt field, toilet papering a friend's house in the middle of the day because she was late for Rusty's date...Her siblings shredded it all in my car and we found shredded bits of toilet paper for years afterwards in the car; learning to fly when I was fifteen and having to have my mom take me to the airport; reminiscing with Rusty while sitting at the park planning our lives, and amazingly our lives have not followed the paths we thought they would; Hanging out with friends from PLT (Peer Leadership Team) and performing at elementary schools...giving WAY over the top performances, all good memories and many, many others.

What are the crazy facets that link all this together? LIFE. Most of my memories stem from band and music and mission and college and lots of fun memories with my wife. She thought I was strange...admittedly I was and still am! I love being different. I love being unique and I don't worry about what others think about me. I relish it. On my second date with Tiffany, I flew up to Idaho to visit her. I had to do a long cross-country flight while I worked on my pilot's license, so I flew up there. I was already smitten, and we walked around campus for a couple hours....to this day she still holds the fact that I found twenty dollars on the ground, and used it for gas and didn't give it to her, against me...but then, she took me out to the airport and I got the airplane ready, hopped off the plane's wing kissed her, jumped back in and flew off into the sunset!!!! Three weeks later we were engaged....She's my best friend and stood by me through thick and thin.

Now why are people so afraid to express feelings, other than rage or anger? Why are people afraid to talk about religion and spirituality? Why does the U.S. get further and further away from the principles that founded it? FEAR. We're afraid of doing what's right? The Afghans are afraid that we'll leave...yet they don't really want us here. The Iraqis are afraid that their country is going to spin out of control! Many religious leaders in this area teach fear instead of peace! One of the many ways that we stumble and fall is due to fear. Too often good men fear men more than God. People don't share their feelings, don't talk about important subjects; parents don't teach their kids, or talk about sex, or other important topics, so they learn crap in schools that is just WRONG!!! We fear, we can't talk, we stumble, we worry, we aren't open....I'm so thankful that Tiffany and I have been able to break years-long problems of not being able to talk about things. Now, it is so freeing and nice to not FEAR what we say and to talk about everything. It is sooooo cool and nice. Am I bragging about how Tiffany's and my relationship has improved? Absolutely! I love it and I don't mind sharing with you all how our spiritual growth has affected our marriage in so many positive ways and I love it.

With regards to the man's fear, Elder John A. Widtsoe said, "As leaders in Israel, we must seek to dispel fear from among our people. A timid, fearing people cannot do their work well. The Latter-day Saints have a divinely assigned world-mission so great that they cannot afford to dissipate their strength in fear. The Lord has repeatedly warned His people against fear. Many a blessing is withheld because of our fears. He has expressly declared that men cannot stop His work on earth, therefore, they who are engaged in the Lord's latter-day cause and who fear, really trust man more than God, and thereby are robbed of their power to serve." (LDS General Conference report, April 1942) So true! We need not take counsel of our fears. The Spirit and fear cannot comingle. Am I afraid of being in a war zone? Nope...I'm secure in my faith that the Lord will protect me and I don't fear.

Can one person make a difference? I hope so. I hope that as I write about my life, my adventures, my family, my growth, that my life can make a difference to you. I hope that I can set a good example. I know I haven't always been the best example, but I'm hoping that my personal growth is helping you to have a better day, a better outlook, a better life. I want to be a good example. I want to have the Holy Ghost with me always. I love feeling the spirit talk to me. That's why I'm writing this part two. I was working out and felt that I hadn't covered everything that I needed to this week. I could pretty much hear the Spirit tell me to write again. I'm writing whatever I feel as it comes through my head. Elder Bednar, in May 2010 stated, "Agency is the power and capacity of independent action. It is the ultimate gift through the Atonement. With agency, everything is not a choice or option." It's deciding who to follow! When we decide who to follow, we make a decision to abide by the laws that govern our actions. I hope that what I write will touch one of you that read this and make you go Hmmmmmm!

I love sharing, my stories, my studies, my beliefs. I don't fear that I will offend any of you. I share and know that my true friends understand where I'm coming from even if you don't know what I'm talking about or understand what I'm teaching. I always love to teach. YES!!! I say I like, I love, I want etc.....a lot...and that's ok.

The world is only getting worse. There are wars, rumors of wars. There are earthquakes...in fact it was funny, I was on the phone this week with Tiffany when an earthquake hit. It was a small one and I sat and joked with Tip about the fact that my bookshelf was rocking and my chair was rocking a little. I joked that someone would be running around saying "get in a doorway, get in a doorway!" I guess with growing up in California it didn't bother me at all...it was a nice, small, little earthquake.

What's forgiveness? It's important. He, who doesn't forgive, denies the Atonement and basically says that he doesn't accept

Christ's paying for ours and other's sins. It's worse for the person who refuses to forgive than it is for the sinner.

I'm brain dumping all my feelings and information into this email that I feel an urge to share.

What is the Bible? In olden times prophets received revelation and it was collected together, eventually becoming what we now know as the Bible. But, where in the Bible does it say that God ceased to give revelation....NOWHERE...it doesn't say anywhere in the Bible that revelation has ceased. In fact it has not ceased and the Lord still reveals things to prophets and apostles. There was a long period without revelation, because man wasn't listening. The Lord continues to reveal His will to man...but very few people listen. (If you want to know more, just ask!) God loves us just as much now as He did back then.

I wrote this week in my study journal, "Why do I love the Jayson Wolfe series (a five book series by Anita Stansfield)? I don't think I've read anything that's touched me like this and this is the second time I've read them. Second chances are so true. I'm thankful for the Atonement. Now, in this series I see myself. True, I don't have the skill in music, but I have the passion and love that I see in Jayson. I write words, he writes music. I also write lyrics, but the love, the Gospel, has made me cry each time I read it even though I know the story now. It's like reading about a good friend or seeing your life in a different way. I want to be like Jayson and experience growth and passion and joy and music and love. I want it, I need it, and thankfully, I recognize that I get it with the Gospel."

Lastly, this week I learned from Pres. Gordon B. Hinckley that, "Ours is the great and solemn duty to reach out and help them (those that are lost or struggling or poor), to lift them, to feed them if they are hungry, to nurture their spirits if they thirst for truth and righteousness."

Thank you for listening. Thank you for hearing me out. After all it all boils down to choice...we choose to be happy. We choose to do what is right or wrong. We choose to be grumpy or not. We choose to like washing dishes or not. We choose to be happy when 7,000 miles from home and it's already been a year since I lived with them. Life is choices ... choose wisely!

Chapter 28

FLIGHT, NATURE, AND THOUGHTS

I sit here wrapped in my pirate flag as the air conditioning blows and I think on what is important, and what is interesting. (Yes, I did say pirate flag…I always deploy with one…Why? Because I want to!) Well, officially I will no longer be a Captain in the Air Force as of next week….I'll be a Major. I look forward to pinning on and moving up in rank and responsibility. I have a lot to talk about this week if you can believe it, since I never talk a lot, I have stories to tell and lessons learned. This week is one of those crazy weeks with lots going on and I must add that I was blessed to have an insane flight this week…..sit down, buckle up, strap on the booster pack and realize this will be a bumpy ride. The hardest part of the week was the fact that the internet has been really bad, making it difficult to talk to Tiffany and I really miss our hour's long conversations, though when I've seen her she's looking very good and gorgeous.

Oh, how the plans we make change on a daily basis! I move about throughout the week from scheduling, teaching, flying, watching conference talks, studying, having a Twilight marathon, spending an hour chatting with Rusty and Tiffany via email – reminiscing and acting goofy, working out and eating….what a week. Oh, how work is crazy and drives me to insanity! I like the insane part, but not so much the schedule change part, though the changes that comes across my desk do cause the days to pass quickly and helps me feel like I'm accomplishing something. I relish the times I can sit and email Tiffany when I don't have much going on. At times it's hard to understand who's advising whom here. In many ways U.S. personnel seem to fall into an Afghan method of accomplishing change to the flying schedule. This method is not exactly useful, from an advisor perspective. When the Afghan Ministry of Defense (MOD) decides to make a change, they call our group commander. He calls us, for some reason this usually occurs when I'm not around, and directs whoever answers to make the change for the next day's schedule. The problem is that this happens after all our Afghan counterparts have gone home. We're not in the habit of acting like Air America. We are trying to teach the Afghans how to plan and execute missions. So, when they're not around to learn…it's kind of a pointless task. Therefore, we jump through hoops and make things happen, but in essence we are teaching them how to eat fish we give rather than teaching them to fish.

That was point one for the week. It happened while I was out flying and it spun some people up because it was major change with less than 18 hours until mission accomplishment. Everyone had left for the day. The instructor for the flight just happened to not have left work yet and was upset because it was a mission that the Group Commander knew about for over 5 days, but kept close hold…meaning he didn't tell us and we could have been a lot better prepared. We've tried to teach the Afghans that we won't make changes less than 24 hours out unless it's for an emergency. Amazingly, at times our leaders are the ones that succumb to the pressure to make changes, to "make it happen", or "hack the mission" as we like to call it. I'm not against mission hacking. In fact, I've always been a mission hacker. I've pushed the envelope within limits to get things done. Sometimes stuff happens, and I'm sure will keep happening as we progress through this program.

Life is about making the appropriate choices, flowing with the punches and doing what we need to. After all, we do the best we can with the information we're given. Sometimes we choose correctly, sometimes we don't. One of my favorite sayings is "play the cards you're dealt". We're not the dealer of the cards, but we choose how we play them in our life.

Point two for the week developed through my flight, which I was on the day when chaos erupted in my office. I had the opportunity to fly and instruct one of the students that has major difficulties. It started off badly and got worse throughout the flight. This student is on the verge of being removed from the program. He is one of the nicest guys, but he has issues. Even though this was somewhere in the neighborhood of his twentieth flight, and he has around forty hours in the airplane, in many ways it was worse than his very first flight. I should know....I flew his first flight with him. The problems started out minor. It seemed during his pre-flight that he didn't know anything that we normally do to check radios, instruments, and navigation systems...all the things that keep us safe and straight when flying at night or in clouds. He attempted to test his bailout switch (which we test every time) by attempting to use the emergency fire bottle switch. (They're about a foot apart in location and clearly labeled.) They were minor discrepancies, but enough to have me on guard as we began the flight. As we taxied out, we check the brakes. There are three steps to this process. I check my side, have the copilot select emergency brakes, then I check those, then back to normal and he checks to make sure that all of our systems are working. As a courtesy to crew members when taxiing, whenever I need to use the brakes, I state "Brakes" over the interphone system. This prevents loadmasters or others from falling or getting hurt because they expect a possible slowing down of aircraft momentum which could throw them off balance, if they're standing in the back. Well, as we taxied.....I called out "Brakes" and I see the copilot jam on his brake pedals and the plane jerked to a stop. This happened twice even after I told him that I had the aircraft and that HE was not allowed to touch the controls unless I told him...so, the next time I said "Brakes", he did it again. My loadmaster was not pleased.

We finally made it to the runway and I briefed the takeoff. Since we were making a short hop to Bagram, I wanted to just fly it and work it since he'd get a lot of flying later on that day. The pilot not flying has certain duties on takeoff, on climb out, and prior to landing. He did none of them. In fact, he did nothing. I had to make my own liftoff call, get my own gear and flaps up, fly the airplane and talk on the radio while, apparently, I had a passenger in the right seat. He sat with his hands in his lap, oblivious to what was going on around him. This didn't bode well, since he'd already failed his previous sortie. Landing at Bagram was pretty much the same, I contacted approach control, who sent me straight to tower for the straight in landing…the airfields are very close…and I requested the copilot run our checklists. Nothing! It was an exercise in chaos as the loadmaster and I did the job of three people, and had to repeat items over and over until the copilot would respond. Ay yay yay…I was happy to put the plane on the ground and tell my copilot exactly what I thought about how helpful he wasn't being. He got the hint. (Not much of a hint when you tell them that if they don't get it together they won't get to touch the controls, period!)

We departed Bagram and flew to our training base. There our pattern practice actually went fairly well. He was off altitude, off airspeed, but these didn't concern me too much. What concerned me was that he was constantly behind the airplane. This means that he was letting the airplane fly him, not anticipating what needed to be done. I sent him around, not letting him land, three times for forgetting to request the Before Landing Checklist. (It's a safety requirement for us to run it to prevent minor things like gear up landings!) And that is when I decided to hook him. UNSAT, hook, call it what you will - the wording doesn't matter…it means he fails the flight lesson. I made the decision as a matter of safety because on our go-around with full flaps down he allowed the nose to climb to twenty degrees above the horizon. And, without requesting to move the flaps to a lower setting so we could accelerate…he allowed our speed to drop to dangerous levels. When we reached my threshold for slow speed, I forced the nose down and moved the flaps on him, accelerating. Then, I explained what he did wrong, quite loudly I might add. When he did it a second time in a row, that's when he failed his ride. I'm just glad that I have controls when teaching in order to take over, or make adjustments, because some of the things these students do just don't make sense and can be hazardous to my health, if they were the only people in control. But, that's my job as instructor to let them make mistakes. However, I can't allow the mistakes to get to a point of no return. I have a pretty rigid safety threshold that doesn't get crossed. Many an aircraft mishap can be attributed to mistakes that weren't corrected.

On that note, I must add that the flying IS fun. The training is a challenge, and I'm proud to announce that the student passed his next lesson. I sat him down after our flight and explained in detail how dangerous the things he did were and that he was on thin ice. He focused, apparently, on his next flight. Like I said, he's a good guy, just gets out of it sometimes. And isn't that how we all get. We all tend to be out of it, or out of sorts, at times throughout our lives. We strive and climb and want and do, but there are times when we just don't know what we're doing or why. Have you ever asked yourself, "Who am I? Why am I here? Where am I going?" Everybody has at one point. We are all children, even as adults. We all wonder, at times fear, and at times lose our focus. I know, I've been there, done that and got the t-shirt. Now that my focus is strengthened on who I am, where I'm going and what I need to do. I feel good.

This week I began studying topics. I decided that each week I'm going to take a topic and research it to enhance my own understanding of the Gospel topic I want to research. I find that this fits me perfectly, especially this week. I've been working out, I've been sore, I've been tired, I've been stressed, I've been happy, I've been hungry, I've been full….in all, it's been a busy full week and I've really enjoyed it.

I feel the Spirit stir within me as I write. There are things I love and things I've learned. Many of the things I'll share, I've known for years, but it's so nice to be able to reinforce my personal beliefs and strengthen my testimony. The focus of my study this week has been the nature of God. There is much confusion among different sects, churches, religions, etc. throughout the world regarding God the Father. Many of these beliefs stem from the Nicene Creed published in the 4th century A.D. which tried to tie a bunch of differing views together. I won't disparage any particular view. I am thankful that I know for myself, through personal revelation, about the nature of my Heavenly Father. This is what I know. God the Father is a separate, individual being from the other members of the Godhead. He has a body of flesh and bone and is the literal father of our spirits. We are his children. He is the ultimate creator of the Universe and it is by His laws that all things are accomplished. He is a God of love and law.

His firstborn son, Jesus Christ, is the second member of the Godhead…again a separate, individual with a glorified immortal body just like His Father's. He is Jehovah, the God of the Old Testament, He answers to His Father, our Heavenly Father and the one and only God. Jesus was chosen as our Savior, to bring us back to His father to be judged. Through Christ, God the Father created this world and made man in their image. Just as a son may look like the father…so, too, it is with Christ.

The third member of the Godhead is the Holy Ghost, who as His name implies, is a personage of spirit. That way He is able to dwell in us and influence our spirits. It is through His influence that Heavenly Father and Jesus influence us here on this earth. He is the comforter, the revelator, the one that brings us the love of the Father.

Now, why do I go over this topic? I go over the nature of the Godhead, because there are many things that confuse people, and I just want you to think about this. The Bible is often misinterpreted when it says that God and Jesus are one. I know this to mean they are one in purpose. After all, I can say that my wife and I are one, especially since we are now of one mind and one heart, but we're two separate people. So too with the Godhead! It is three separate individuals, though God the Father is the One True God. This is why Christ always prayed to the Father. He wasn't praying to himself. He was praying to His Father. I want you to realize this because for me it is such a freeing knowledge. We are created in the image of God, the perfect man. We are His spirit children and He wants us to learn and grow and become like Him. That's a doctrine that many people have a hard time with, but I know it's a true doctrine. Why? I know it because it's been born witness to me and because it makes sense. It's not presumptuous of us to think that we can become like God and does not contradict the Bible. As we progress and become like him…he will still be God Almighty, God our Father. We will always be His children. We're children of a Heavenly Father and He wants us to grow and progress. That's the whole point of the Plan of Happiness, the Plan of Salvation. We're here to be tested and to grow. I look at all the people here in Afghanistan and I realize they're all children of God too. The Taliban are children of God, the Nazi's were children of God, Stalin, Lenin and all the rest of the despots throughout the centuries were children of God.

Why then does He let things happen? People ask this often. I've learned and studied a lot about this. This question came up a lot on my mission. I knew a couple families that refused to attend any church because they couldn't believe that God would let calamities, catastrophes, evil doings such as the wars going on in Sudan and the murder of innocents in Russia, the killing of the Jews during World War 2, and other things, happen. At that time, I didn't know how to rightly answer their questions. This week I studied some of the answers to those very questions. The truth is that Heavenly Father is a God of Love and Law. What does this mean? It means that He loves each and every one of us. But that doesn't mean He can or will put aside eternal laws just because He loves us. I've talked about agency in just about every single one of these messages, and that's because He gave man the ability to choose; sometimes our choices affect other people. For years the people of New Orleans were warned about the levies, but chose not to fix them. Then, a hurricane hit dead on and they suffered. Was this God's wrath? No! It was the natural consequence of decisions made by a few people that affected thousands of people. This is just one example. God allows some things to happen because He can't and won't break eternal law.

If God put aside laws to prevent all suffering, to prevent the consequences of choices, He would cease to be God. "If ye shall say there is no law, ye shall also say there is no sin. If ye say there is no sin, ye shall also say there is no righteousness. And if there be no righteousness there be no happiness. And if there be no righteousness nor happiness there be no punishment nor misery. And if these things are not there is no God. And if there is no God we are not, neither the earth; for there could have been no creation of things, neither to act nor to be acted upon." (2 Nephi 2:13) I'm thankful that there is a God, that there is opposition. There is opposition to the plan. Yin and Yang is not just a Chinese riddle. There is always light and dark, good and evil, for we must look to the good to oppose the evil. If there wasn't right and wrong, what would we have? We'd have anarchy and life would not have meaning.

Yet life has meaning. Life is good. I love this life I have. I love the fact that I can look at my wife and know that she loves me and that we are one. I love the fact that we can raise our children to look to our Heavenly Father for direction. He gives us revelation to help us direct our lives. He knows the end from the beginning. He wants us to progress. We have prophets and apostles today at the head of the Church of Jesus Christ of Latter Day Saints that receive revelation for our day, just as did the prophets and apostles of previous dispensations of time. The church was restored as was required. Paul wrote that there must be "a falling away first" (2 Thes. 2:3) – an apostasy from the true teachings of Christ-- before the Lord comes again. And before that day there had to be a "restitution of all things" (Acts 3:21) and Paul continued to say to the Ephesians that in the "Dispensation of the fullness of times" the Lord would "gather together in one all things in Christ". (Ephes 1:10) This is a topic for another day, and I will cover the Restoration another week. For now suffice it to say that I know these things to be true.

I'm not perfect. I've made mistakes and I'm sure I'll make more. I spoke a lot about God the Father, not touching on the fact that Jesus came to atone for our sins. Does this fact eliminate our need to follow his commandments? No. Too often people think that accepting Christ as their Savior excuses their sins. Yet all of Christ's teachings showed that we are required to believe on Him, accept Him, and OBEY the commandments; obey His teachings. "There is a law irrevocably decreed in heaven before the foundations of the world upon which all blessings are predicated—And when we obtain any blessing from God, it is by obedience to that law upon which it is predicated."(D&C 130:20-21) This is profound. We are blessed through obedience; we are saved through obedience and faith. I'm glad I can share my studies and learning. I'm changing my life. I'm trying to "become" and not just learn as Elder Bednar, member of the Quorum of Twelve Apostles today, said in a general conference address in 2005. We must learn and change and grow and become Saints through adhering to the gospel of Jesus and participating in the saving ordinances predicated from the foundation of the world and we must endure to the end, which is where Satan really tries to get us. He wants us to fall. He pushes us to fall. He glories in our faults. He glories in our anger, or in our false beliefs. He urges us to be closed-minded and not seek truth. I was closed-minded and hard-hearted for too long. No longer! I refuse to let him have one more minute of my life. Thanks again for listening.

I do not want to detract from anyone's beliefs. I just submit mine because I feel the desire to share my knowledge grow in me as I study every week. I love to share. And I feel the need to share my testimony with you all. Again, I promise the same promise that James gives in the Bible and that Moroni gives in the Book of Mormon. It is that, if we ask, we can be given knowledge of the truth through the Holy Ghost. I've given much space to my feelings, beliefs and knowledge. As always thank you for listening. I don't expect you to believe everything I write. I am just a man and extremely fallible. But, I know that you can know for yourself the truth of what is right or not, if you ask in faith. If you desire it, you can know if these things are true.

I am calm and at peace with my life right now. I miss my wife and family. I wish I were home, but with regards to where I am spiritually, I'm at peace knowing that my Heavenly Father is proud of me and where I've come to, from where I was.

Kabul Airport; Loading a plane (below)

Chapter 29

LETTER TO LYNN

Again as usual, I am taking the time to seek the Lord's guidance as I respond to your questions. I'll agree with you that the Lord's grace saves us before we try our best, in that all mankind is saved from the fall. In my last post I mentioned that Stalin, Lenin and all the other despots are children of God and it's true. Thanks to Christ, they too are saved from the Fall of Adam which brought death into the world. All men are saved from death, and I agree that as we draw closer to the Lord our desire to do our best increases! And then as we go through enduring to the end, we'll be saved from spiritual death ... which is separate and distinct. That's topic for another time.

You asked a couple key questions.

In a previous email you asked, “What is a prophet and apostle and how are they called?”

In ancient days a prophet was called of God to speak repentance unto the people, to call them back to the fold and to clear up the disputes that arose regarding doctrine. Additionally, the prophets were ordained to their work. They were given authority to act in God's name. This actual power and authority is called the

Priesthood and the Prophets hold the Keys to the Priesthood. For example, they can ordain others to office, give portions of that priesthood to others, perform certain ordinances which are covenants made with God and sealed on earth through the power of the priesthood. The same is true in modern days. This will take a little longer explanation and I hope you enjoy long stories....

I want to preface this though with the comment that I understand the "culture of belief" comment you made. I understand that for either to change their culture of belief could require major changes. I also want you to know that I am not a “closed-minded, Bible bashing, only I’m right, member of my church”. Those things I know to be true about this Gospel, I know, because the Lord answered it to my mind and my heart after I studied and prayed. I keep my eyes open at all times, because I do not want to be deceived ever! I agree that there may be times when we agree to disagree and I'm fine with that. You're my friend and you're asking questions and I respect that. I truly do. I don't want to shove anything down your throat. I humbly thank my Heavenly Father that we have this opportunity to share and discuss our beliefs. Speaking of the Book of Mormon, it is the biggest sticking point most people have with the Church of Jesus Christ of Latter Day Saints.

The Book of Mormon is "Another Testament of Jesus Christ" and it clarifies many of the plain and precious truths that are hard to understand in the Bible. It was written by a branch of the House of Israel that were taken out of the Land of Jerusalem 600 years before Christ's birth. It tells how they were led by the Lord to the America's and tells of how they ended up dividing into two groups of people. The Lamanites were a fallen people that didn't believe the "traditions of their fathers" regarding the coming of a Messiah, even Jesus the Christ. The Nephites were a people that believed in the prophets of the Old Testament, followed the Law of Moses, and had prophets to teach and baptize among them. The Book of Mormon is the record of their history and the teachings of the prophets in America. It records how after the death and resurrection of Jesus Christ in Jerusalem, He appeared to people here on the American continent. (The Other sheep, not of this fold) For another 400 years following this the Nephites continued on, yet they eventually fell away from their beliefs, became hardened and were annihilated by the Lamanites--who are the ancestors of the American Indians, the Aztec, and Maya. The last prophet of the Book of Mormon, Moroni, hid the plates, since it was written on gold plates, for a future purpose, to come forth at the Dispensation of the Fullness of Times, as prophesied in the Bible. That same Moroni appeared to Joseph Smith and showed him where the plates were buried, and taught him how to use the Urim and Thumim (seer stones), with which, through the Lord's help, he was able to translate the plates into the work we now have as the Book of Mormon.

How are modern prophets called to be a prophet? We first need to ask where they were for almost two thousand years, why there weren't any prophets. After Christ's resurrection, the Apostles (an apostle is a follower and a special witness-in this case a special witness of Christ) went to the world to preach the gospel. All the apostles save John were eventually killed, and they were unable to get together to ordain new apostles, through the laying on of hands. Jesus had laid his hands on their heads to give them the priesthood. There was much confusion, dissension, disorder and false teaching creeping into the church at that time. For the Bible references, look up the following scriptures:

Matt 24:9-11, Mark 12:1-9, Acts 3: 19-21, Acts 20: 28-30, Galatians 1: 6-9, 2 Thessalonians 2: 1-12, 1 Timothy 4: 1-3, 2 Timothy 4: 3-4, 2 Peter 2:1-2, Amos 8: 11-12, Isaiah 24:5, Isaiah 60:2, 1 Corinthians 11:18, 2 Timothy 1:15, 2: 18, 3:5, James 4:1, 1 John 2:18...

I draw specific attention to 2 Thessalonians 2:3 when we are told that Christ won't come again "except there comes a falling away first". We can look at history and see what happened. We see the councils of Nice, the changes in church doctrine, the Dark ages...followed by reformers. The reformers didn't call themselves prophets and weren't prophets, they tried to reform the church back to what, according to their understanding, was missing. The problem was that there was a missing ingredient. It was like a mirror that has been cracked. If you've ever cracked a mirror and tried to piece it back together, you know it doesn't look quite right. While there were many good portions and many truths...but I was missing bits and pieces, and required a restoration (in the case of a mirror, a re-firing) in order to be put to right.

When Joseph Smith went to the grove of trees and prayed about which church to join, God the Father and Jesus Christ appeared unto him in person, two separate beings, and the Father spoke to Joseph, telling him to listen to Christ. Joseph asked his question and was told to join none of the churches of that time because they were missing key pieces of the gospel with many plain and precious truths having been lost. Then Joseph was told that the Lord had a work for him to do. After Moroni brought Joseph to the plates to translate the Book of Mormon, Joseph and another, Oliver Cowdery, went to pray about certain principles they learned about as they translated. John the Baptist appeared unto them and administered unto Joseph and Oliver, laying his resurrected hands on their heads and gave them the Aaronic Priesthood, which was the authority to baptize, among other things.

Later, Peter, James and John, the same Apostles from the Savior's time, came as resurrected beings and laid their hands on Joseph and Oliver's heads and gave them the keys to the Melkezedik priesthood, and ordained Joseph as Prophet, Seer and Revelator. Oliver was in turn ordained an Apostle and from that time forth, the Priesthood has been ordained upon worthy men so that it is not removed from the earth again. As the Gospel was preached and the Church grew, twelve Apostles were ordained and each was given the keys to the priesthood. They were set apart by those who had received it, as Prophets, Seers and Revelators. Each Apostle holds those keys, and from that time forth, as one Apostle dies, the others gather and take the matter before the Lord as to who to call to be an Apostle. A Prophet and Apostle hold the keys to revelation for the church and the world. We're each entitled to personal revelation for ourselves and our families and sometimes even our friends in answer to their prayers, but only the prophet, as in ancient days, and the Apostles, as in Christ's time, can receive revelation for the World or the Church.

OK, is your head about to explode? That's a lot to take in. I speak casually of resurrected beings coming in our day to speak to men, of them giving authority to men in our day, of a restoration...but that's what we claim. That's what I know to be true. I don't want you to take my word for it. Like you said, we each come from different cultures of belief....and that's the beauty of it. I don't expect you to believe me. You couldn't have put it better in your last line...we both could bring out scriptural commentaries and there are many out there, some that would claim that I am full of it...but the truth can only really come from our Father in Heaven. We claim as it said in the Bible that there was a falling away, an apostasy. The Church had to be restored to be able to bring, in the latter days a "restitution of all things" that had been missing. OK, there's my diatribe...One last thing.

Regarding that portion you were asking about, “who is Elder Bednar?”: Elder Bednar, is one of the Living Twelve Apostles that are special witnesses of Christ and have been set apart as prophets, seers, and revelators. He came and spoke to several congregations. We call a group of congregations Stakes. He spoke at a Stake Conference where Tiffany is attending right now. I know that there are Apostles and Prophets on the earth today. I have met several of them and the Spirit has born witness to me that they ARE true apostles of the lamb.

The Plan of Happiness I mentioned is another name for the Plan of Salvation that I've mentioned in several emails now. In Moses 1:39 (the Pearl of Great Price) the Lord says, "For behold, this is my work and my glory--to bring to pass the immortality and eternal life of man." Another scripture, 2 Nephi 2:25, says, "Adam fell that men might be, and men are that they might have joy." The Plan of Salvation is a plan of happiness, because we can only TRULY be happy to make it back to live with our Heavenly Father in the Celestial Kingdom.

I understand a quandary and a conundrum of looking at something like this totally out of your "culture of belief". My brother-in-law was raised Southern Baptist and he spent the last ten years basically condemning his wife, who is Mormon....until he read the Book of Mormon and two weeks ago he was baptized a member of the Church of Jesus Christ of Latter Day Saints. Am I going to lie and say I wouldn't be overjoyed if our discussions turned into something similar with you? No, I would love it, but I will also honestly say, that I will not shove anything down your throat, nor will I discredit any of your beliefs should we choose to believe differently. I will be a faithful friend and honor your beliefs, because they're yours! So no fears....bring on the questions and we'll continue our chat. Like I said I've always got my eyes open.

Thanks for being who you are. I know some of what I say sounds outlandish or crazy at first, that's why the Lord promises us He'll let us know if something is true or not. There's a promise in the Book of Mormon, in Moroni 10:3-5, that says, "Behold, I would exhort you that when ye shall read these things, if it be wisdom in God that ye should read them, that ye would remember how merciful the Lord hath been unto the children of men, from the creation of Adam even down until the time that ye shall receive these things, and ponder it in your heart;

And when ye shall receive these things, I would exhort you that ye would ask God, the Eternal Father, in the name of Christ, if these things are not true; and if ye shall ask with a sincere heart, with real intent, having faith in Christ, he will manifest the truth of it unto you, by the power of the Holy Ghost. And by the power of the Holy Ghost ye may know the truth of all things."

That's the promise. I took it and I've been told time and again of its truth. And if the Book of Mormon is true...then Joseph Smith was called as a prophet...and so on and so on....we learn line upon line, precept on precept. The Lord is mindful of US. He loves you, he loves me, he even loves the idiot Taliban...I've heard the voice of the Lord's spirit speaking to me in my mind and heart...a lot lately as I strive to do what is right and grow in His eyes...

Chapter 30

THIS TOO SHALL PASS

"This too shall pass!" These words of wisdom from my mother have been found throughout my life to be at once perfect, mundane, eye-rolling, frustrating, enraging, thoughtful, hopeful, treasured and blessed. These words are words I hear over and over now whenever I feel a sense of frustration, or feel like nothing is going right. "This too shall pass!" What inspiration! It's funny because for such a simple phrase it packs so much information into it. It embodies knowledge of the infinite, empathy for the moment, hope for the future, and encouragement for the present.

This has been a very busy week and as I get closer to going home for a couple weeks of rest and relaxation to see the family, the feeling of time flying by grows stronger. I've been fairly occupied this week with many changes to my otherwise perfect schedule. I pretend it's perfect when I write it, and then it changes 8-10 times by the end of the week, but then I've at least got another week's perfect schedule made so I am perfectly happy with everything...except when I'm not! This week encompassed several aspects of life in Afghanistan with which I had to deal with. First, airplanes break. It's a natural part of the job, but can be stressful at times. When airplanes break it means I have to shift people and missions around and juggle five balls with one arm tied behind my back. We had our fair share of broken airplanes this week. There were engines that wouldn't start, pressurization that wouldn't work and, in fact, blew out the pressurization tubing, tires that exploded, smoke in the cockpit, and hydraulic pumps that blew circuit breakers! Maintenance recovery teams had to be launched to fix the plane that blew a tire. And throughout all this, I had to figure out who was going on what airplane, what student training was getting accomplished and what could be pushed back a few days. All in all, not a bad week's work! I love the challenge of it. I love the complexity of taking a certain amount of hours of flying each month, breaking it down into each week's plan, settling on who and what is going to fly where and how and then....have it all torn apart by Murphy and his bag of tricks! Life is crazy! I love it. It's crazier here in Afghanistan where parts are hard to come by, maintenance is doing their best with an old airplane, and everyone thinks they have the best idea ever for what we need to do.

I spent a fair amount of time doing counseling sessions with my leaders this week. Not me being counseled, but counseling with them! There are just certain things that are good policy and certain things that aren't and sometimes leaders need someone to not be a "yes, man" and tell them what makes plain old common sense. Tiffany always says that I've been a counselor by nature and I agree with that. It's one of my favorite things to do, to just listen and provide counsel.

This week it was hard to get a hold of Tiffany because she's been working for her sister. The fact that she can help, and has been helped in return, and was compensated for her efforts, is such a blessing. She's a wonderful wife and I'm so blessed to be married to her. She is helpful and considerate of others and when she gets working...she's a dynamo. She takes the bull by the horns and amen to that bull! :)

Of course I flew this week. I actually got to fly twice. Both interesting and both very different flights! The first flight was with a student. This is the same student that I hooked last week. He had flown poorly the previous week, with which I regaled you earlier!

However, he passed his follow-up sortie and it was my turn to fly with him again. He flew well. Not great, but satisfactory. We departed and I could tell he was making an effort to do better. He struggles, because he wants to do well, but spaces out at times. His flight went well as we flew up to Mazar e Sharif and entered the pattern. We did several patterns and everything was flowing smoothly. He flew some nice patterns around the airport and his landings were not bad. I turned up the heat and re-introduced single engine work to him. Ha-ha! This is where things got interesting. Still not a bad sortie, still doing well, but interesting because he OVER EXAGGERATED everything on single engine work. In an airplane with two engines, mounted far apart, one on each wing, if you lose one engine, i.e. it stops or has problems, it can still fly. But, the tendency is for the airplane to want to fly sideways. We call it crabbing into the good engine. To prevent this we have some simple techniques which work very well and keep you flying straight and level. First, you raise the wing with the dead engine a few degrees above the horizon. Then, you step on the rudder pedal on the side of the good engine. These two things, when coordinated with increasing power on the good engine, will allow you to fly straight, and level, allowing you to accelerate and fly somewhat normally until you can land. That's the technique...it's easier to say than do.

After all there are a myriad of things affecting the airplane when you're doing this. First, there's temperature, which makes the plane not perform as well if it's hot. Then, there's turbulence and the altitude of the airport that can have significant effect. The third major factor is the weight of the airplane. There are times when you take off and you barely have the ability to climb if an engine fails, especially in this mountainous terrain. Not a pretty contemplation, but we make it work.

Now, with all of this going on, our students have to learn to control the airplane, especially because around here it can be hot, high altitude, turbulent, thanks to the mountains, and the planes are usually pretty heavy when we're taking passengers or cargo. Personally, I believe smacking into a mountain to be a bad thing. It really would put a damper on my leave to go see my beautiful wife and kids. Therefore, I take it personally to teach these guys NOT to crash into mountains, as I've explained. Lucky for us on this flight we were able to practice on the side of the airport that DOESN'T have mountains. We had time and space to put the plane and my student through their paces. I failed his engine, simulating a fire, and this is where he over-exaggerated his controls. I had to struggle not to laugh, because when you fail an engine you need some rudder pressure on the good engine. There's this little ball on the instrument panel that sits between two lines when you're flying straight, if you're crabbed, it's off to the side. Well, my student stepped on the correct rudder, then the other, and then back, basically we were yo-yoing back and forth across the sky for a minute. My loadmaster, who was trying to sleep in the back, was not appreciative of the tail kicking back and forth, back and forth, up and down, almost like a broken merry-go-round! It reminded me of my favorite Croatian word "ljuljati se"...which means to make one-self dizzy!

I finally had to laugh as I showed him how to put light, solid, constant pressure to keep the ball centered, not blindly chasing it as you over kick the rudder. The rudder is a huge barn door on the tail of the airplane that will kick the nose right and left. The rudder will move the tail back and forth erratically and can easily make people sick in the back. Be patient, I am coming to my point...unless I don't! In reality, control is accomplished by applying certain select principles in an organized way with determination and constancy!

Anyways, to make a long story longer....he did well, except for the ljuljanje (going on in a dizzying manner) of the airplane, which thrilled my loadmaster!!!! Ha-ha. That flight was fun and challenging. My second flight of the week was a VIP aircraft upgrade. We have one airplane that is a lot heavier than the others because it has a VIP module built into it and needless to say, it flies like the other airplanes, but we still have to get checked out in it. So, a few of us flew down to Kandahar, ate a nice lunch, and flew back. The ride down to Kandahar was nice; I sat for half of it in the back in the VIP seats with my IPod playing in my ears and listened to some nice calm music. On the way back, I flew! It was a nice calm ride, the kind you don't get that often, but I'm looking forward to more VIP flying when I move with the family to Germany to fly the C-21. For those of you that don't know, I found out my assignment. I'm going to fly the C-21 when I move to Germany, which is a Lear Jet and should be an absolute blast to fly!

Now, with this information we can talk about the things I'm learning. As you can see there have been a lot of experiences that I've gone through this week, the highs of finding out locations and getting promoted and the lows of.....being in Afghanistan! Last week I talked about the nature of God, and the Trinity. That typifies much of my studying for this week as well. But there are some things that have really stood out to me. Today, being church day for us here, stands out because it was a day of testimony. I've born my testimony a number of times in these chapters and today won't be an exception, but I want to start this with an acknowledgement. I want to acknowledge that I know I'm a son of God. I know you are a son or daughter of God. We're all brothers and sisters, created by our Heavenly Father and endowed with infinite potential as the offspring of God. However, our own shortcomings, our own attitudes, our own lack of self-worth or self-esteem limit what we can do and how much we can grow. There's truth to the saying, "As a man thinketh, so is he!" We have been created to act, not to be acted upon, hence the agency that I've talked many times about, but we give up bits here and bits there, not realizing that our very thoughts about ourselves challenge the ability of our Heavenly Father to answer us in our times of need.

What is self-esteem? What is worth? What is value? Do you know who you are? Do you know that you are a child of God? I'm not asking for you to tell me, I'm asking because I learned this a long time ago, but it wasn't until recently that the answer to the questions hit home. Self-esteem, it's the essence of who you THINK you are. If we think we're crap, we live in a manner that denotes it. If we think we're the king of the world, we likewise live in a manner that denotes it. Where do we draw the line? What is correct? People talk about low self-esteem or high self-esteem, but I think there's really only one thing, esteem...either you have it, or you don't. You can always tell when someone doesn't deem themselves of worth. They don't look people in the eye, they don't consider their views as valuable, they don't treat themselves with respect, and they get into things that harm their bodies and for what....nothing. Nothing good comes of it.

Yet, as we realize that we are children of God, that God the Father is literally the father of our spirits...our esteem changes. We tend to look at ourselves and others in a new light. After all, every person on earth, be they a saint or a sinner, is a child of God. He loves each and every one of us and wants the best for us. We sin and fall away from the presence of God, yet He is always willing to forgive, if we sincerely repent. Looking at esteem again we see, and we all know people, who have completely changed their lives as they recognize that they are children of God and that their life has worth and meaning to it. Are we one of those? Do we look at our lives the same way every day or do we discount that miracle that is ours. Our life is a miracle and we can be thankful every day for what we have, even when we have almost nothing! When we realize that our life has meaning, that we are children of God, we act. We make different choices. We learn of the greatest of all gifts, the gift of charity. But, charity is not a passive gift. Charity, as the pure love of Christ, requires action, it is putting into practice the teachings of love that strengthen our spirit and helps our neighbors and ourselves.

In many ways I am writing a hodge podge of thoughts and feelings because I was struck by a key that intertwines through all these scenarios and incidents, from my flying, to the self-esteem issue, to charity...basically through everything. The link that runs through all these things is the fact that there must be opposition in all things. There are also blessings in all things. Every moment of opposition provides stark contrast and, ultimately, often ends up in great blessings. A Book of Mormon prophet said of opposition, "For it must needs be, that there is an opposition in all things. If not so....righteousness could not be brought to pass, neither wickedness, neither holiness nor misery, neither good nor bad....Wherefore, if must needs have been created for a thing of naught; wherefore there would have been no purpose in the end of its creation......I speak unto you these things for your profit and learning; for there is a God, and he hath created all things, both the heavens and the earth, and all things that in them are, both things to act and things to be acted upon. ..... Wherefore, the Lord God gave unto man that he should act for himself. Wherefore, man could not act for himself save it should be that he was enticed by the one or the other." (2 Nephi 2: 11, 12, 14, 16) Opposition is necessary in life for us to grow. We learn to make choices, being enticed by good or bad, learning right or wrong, seeing the commandments of God and what he requires of us, and then making choices... We are agents unto ourselves to be enticed by good or bad. That is what agency entails, making choices.

However, we are not left with opposition constantly in our face with no hope. The Lord tells us to make choices, and then He states emphatically that if we do His will, He will bless us. Too often we forget that and make wrong choices for instant gratification, which leads us to momentary happiness and eternal misery. I've made many wrong choices in life and know what I'm talking about. Yet, when we give in to the enticings of the Spirit, the Lord doth immediately bless us, whether we realize it or not. In a revelation to the prophet Joseph Smith the Lord declared, "There is a law, irrevocably decreed in heaven before the foundations of this world, upon which all blessings are predicated--And when we obtain any blessing from God, it is by obedience to that law upon which it is predicated." (D&C 130:20-21)

Now, I know for a fact this is true. I've seen it time and again. A classic example in my life is the law of Tithing. It's one of the only commandments where the Lord actually says, "Test me"!!! In Malachi 3:10 we read, "...and prove me now herewith, saith the Lord of hosts, if I will not open you the windows of heaven, and pour you out a blessing, that there shall not be room enough to receive it." Talking about tithing, the Lord says to test Him. In my own life there have been many instances where, literally, the windows of heaven have been opened. Recently, for example, when our budget was tight, due to working hard to pay off debt that we incurred when we weren't following good financial practices, the Lord opened a way for Tiffany to work and make some money to be able to get the tires fixed on her car. This was when, by my budget, I wasn't going to be able to get it done for another 2 months (bloody expensive special rotten tires!!!!) But, since we've been paying our tithing, the money came available when we needed it! This has happened many times, and this is just one example, but I've been more open to seeing blessings the last few months since Tiffany and I began our spiritual journey together.

While there has been a lot of opposition, there have been a lot of blessings too, especially as we've worked towards being more Christ-like and living a gospel centered life. Some oppositions have been financial, emotional, personal, familial, and I'm not going to go into specifics because sometimes opposition is just personal, for us it has been too, but it's provided us with much growth spiritually these last six months I've been in Afghanistan. But I do want to list some of the blessings that have occurred while I've been here.

1. Our marriage has been strengthened.
2. Our finances are being straightened out.
3. Our testimonies have grown along with our reliance on God.
4. We're getting the assignment we've wanted for a long time.
5. We're becoming closer to our friends and family.
6. We're able to talk to the kids about anything and they ask gospel questions all the time.
7. I don't feel uncomfortable sharing my testimony or beliefs with family and friends, even though some of you are not members of the Church of Jesus Christ of Latter Day Saints.
8. My personal relationship with Christ is growing daily.
9. My personal relationship with my Father in Heaven is growing daily.
10. My desires to do wrong have diminished in direct proportion to my desires to do right increasing.
11. I receive personal revelation again, on a recurring basis.
12. I feel peace, even though I'm in a war zone, I have no fear, because of my Faith that all will be well.
13. My love for all people increases every day.
14. I'm playing guitar and writing music and writing all these things...focusing on the good.

and

15. I'm happy....I've always been a happy person, but I am truly happy and comfortable with where I am. I know that I am a son of

God, that He loves me, that He forgives me of my sins, and that He gives me peace and that peace gives me happiness.

That's just a small list of the many, many blessings that I receive at the hands of the Lord every day. I'm blessed with peace and safety and I feel Him guiding me as I make my choices and teach my students. Being in a war zone is an interesting experience and I'm thankful that I have this experience to learn and grow and share this growth and learning with you. Without opposition we can't see the blessings, but the Lord gives us blessings as we do his will. I share my knowledge and testimony that his work is progressing on the earth. He restored his gospel, through prophets called in our day to bring to light the missing truths that were lost for so long. I am thrilled that I get to try to listen to the Prophet and Apostles speak tomorrow at the General Conference of the Church, even though I'll have to be up all night long to do so. "The Spirit whispers this to me and tells me it is true, He tells me it is true!" (Children's Song Book)

Thank you as always for listening to me. We are children attempting to become like a parent through the help of an older brother. I hope you enjoy today's rant; I enjoy writing it and sharing my learning with you because as I write and teach you, I actually learn more, so it's really just a selfish kind of writing because I want to learn more!!! :) As always, you are my family and friends and I love you. I love the Gospel and I love sharing it with you.

WELCOME
HOME
FLYBOY
!

Chapter 31

THIS TOO SHALL PASS TWO

This too shall pass; a phrase as old as time itself and just as appropriate. We live in a world that is becoming more like Sodom and Gomorrah every day. We see envying and strife, selfishness and misery, all because people have bought into the lie that they must "get" as much as they can out of this life, at the expense of everyone else. When did this lie perpetrate? So long ago that we can't even pinpoint a date. Yet, we can read about the first lie, the serpent telling Eve to partake of the fruit to become as the Gods, knowing good from evil, but that they wouldn't die…From then on the lie has grown and propagated throughout the world. Jealousy, revenge, strife, maltreatment of others, and prideful woolgathering are the rage. We see one of the number one tools of man – rationalization, to protect oneself from guilt.

I am so thankful for Prophets, Apostles and teachers that can show us the way to live to deal with the world without being part of the world. We must live and survive in a world that is increasingly vulgar, uncouth, and prideful, yet we don't have to succumb to following the way of the world. Today is the 180th Semiannual General Conference of the Church of Jesus Christ of Latter Day Saints. Unsurprisingly enough, many things are poignant to what we're doing today in our life. The privilege we have each day to study and learn the fundamental aspects of the Gospel of Jesus Christ inspire us as we grow every day! I love taking notes as living Apostles and Prophets speak to us, in our day, letting us know what is important in our day. I attest that there are living prophets and apostles on the earth today that receive revelation for the church and the world from our Heavenly Father.

One of the overriding themes of the first session was our need to develop a personal relationship with our Heavenly Father. We are asked to consecrate our life to the Lord. We are not forced to do anything! In fact, we have our agency to choose what we do. One of the saddest stories that I heard was that of a member of the church who was asked if he thought he had a personal relationship with the Lord and he said "NO". When asked why, he responded that if he did, the Lord would require commitment from him. How sad! One of the great blessings in life is to develop a commitment to do what is right. As I wrote yesterday, there is much opposition and it's a required part of life, but the Lord promises us abundant blessings as we learn and grow and obey his commands.

I feel the need to share information about prophets. I know there's a prophet, and I might have mentioned this once before, but humor me. Common sense tells us that a living prophet would be more important than a dead one. In fact, we are counseled that living prophets ARE more important than dead ones because they receive revelation for our day, for our time, for the situations that are occurring in our lives and in the world of our day. The Lord will not let a prophet lead His church astray. "Prophets are not required to be academics. In fact Joseph Smith wasn't an academic, he was a farm hand." Some key things that we need to know about prophets are: "1. Prophets don't have to say, 'Thus saith the lord' for his words to be scripture. 2. A prophet tells us what we NEED to know, not what we WANT to know. 3. A prophet is not limited by man's reasoning. 4. Prophets are able to receive any revelation for any situation. 5. A prophet may give advice in civic matters. 6. The proud and the rich have a harder time following the words of the prophet." A prophet was required to bring about the restoration of the Church of Jesus Christ upon the earth, and a prophet is still alive on the earth today.

The words of the prophets lead us and guide us to make correct decisions. After all, this life is a time to prepare. It is a time to make choices. We are in the twilight of the world before the second coming of our Lord and Savior Jesus Christ. So far, the focus of the conference has been on agency and choice, faith and character, and the need to follow the counsel of the living prophet. The Plan of Salvation, also known as the Plan of Happiness, teaches us of our pre-mortal choices to follow Christ and come to earth to be tested. We must learn to exercise faith unto repentance, faith in our Savior, faith in the Gospel of Jesus which teaches us all things what we should do. There were so many good talks this conference and I was excited to see that my blogs and personal study have been following the guidance of the General Authorities of the Church so far as detailed in this conference. It seems that Satan concentrates on alienating people from a personal relationship with God, telling them that anything goes as long as they love the Savior. That doesn't work though when "anything goes" is an attitude that contradicts the very teachings of the Savior.

Too often we stay busy, just to stay busy and thereby are so occupied that we are unable to listen to the Spirit. How does the Spirit speak to us? Each person is different, because the Lord understands us each as individuals and knows how we respond best to the Holy Ghost. However, there are certain ways that He responds to all of us. The Holy Ghost speaks to our mind and heart with peace and in a still small voice. Often, prayers are answered through another person. But, personal witness and revelation is a quiet personal matter between the Lord and the individual. What does this mean when we occupy our days so much that we don't even have time to think, let alone ponder on the things of eternity? It means that we're too busy. The Lord will continue to try to speak to us, but so often the problem is not with the Lord but with ourselves. Elder Uchtdorf, member of the First Presidency of the Lord's church, stated that there are four relationships that really matter and that we need to focus and spend our time on. The four are: our relationship with God, our relationship with our family, our relationship with our fellow man, and our relationship with ourselves.

So often we are told about agency. This is because our agency was the central theme of the war in heaven, the Plan of Salvation, and the way in which we will grow and become like our Heavenly Father. I love this. I love the discussions of agency, because it is a doctrine I understand well. The fact of the matter is that we choose each and every day exactly who and what we want to become. We are enticed by good or evil at all times and as our character grows by our faith we are able to develop into strong, obedient, stalwart followers and Disciples of Christ.

As always, thanks for listening. I'd write a lot more, but it's almost three in the morning and I've been up for going on 24 hours so my brain is clouded and tired. I bear my witness that these principles I write are true and they echo in my mind and heart. I know of their surety and truth. I'm blessed every day in so many ways and love just sharing these with you. Thanks my friends.

Ahh, the joys of staying up late....reminds me of a personal story which I must share, If you've read this far...you'll enjoy this.

When I was 17, we had a youth conference in UT and we were spending the night camping out, I had to work so I arrived late and my plan was to just sleep in the minivan. My friend, Adam, was feeling sick so he and I went to a gas station and got him some generic cold medicine...which he had a reaction to...it made him seem stoned out of his gourd and he laughed himself to sleep in the minivan...by himself, laughing for three hours straight until he basically passed out. This wasn't the end of the story though. I stayed up all night, talking and hanging out around the campfire. We enjoyed the peaceful calm of the late night, the flickering flames of the fire, and our company. The next day we were hiking Mount Timpanogas, at the top of which is a glacier, which you traverse, back and forth, until you get to the top....Well, with NO sleep, and downing mountain dew like it was water to stay awake we hiked for 5 hours up this mountain. Suddenly, I looked at my watch and realized I had to be at work in two hours....do the math...5 hours up, plus one hour drive...and only two hours to do it....I figured I was going to be late. Well, Rusty, my best friend, had to get home too. We did the smartest thing we could to cut down on time....We flopped on our backs and slid down the glacier until we reached the end and hit dirt. We cut over two hours off our hiking trip and it was a BLAST! Then, we cut through the woods hiking straight down the mountain, not on the trail. We figured we'd hit it since it traversed back and forth. Well, it was not quite that way and we ended up travelling lost in the woods for quite a ways, but we found the trail and literally ran down it. We reached my car right when I had to be at work....yes, 5 hours up, 2 hours down...we were awesome, and tired and hyper-as-all-get-out with all that caffeine in my system. I dropped him off and made it to work only two hours late. OOPs! That night I had to down soda every 15 minutes just to try to stay awake, I was a busboy at a Mexican restaurant!...Finally, I got home and made it to bed....after being awake for 41 hours. I was a little tired. I actually enjoy nights when I'm deployed because the nasty, vulgar, and frustrating people are all asleep and I can relax and enjoy the Spirit.

Wow, what a day! What a week, really! It's been busy. I'm officially enjoying taking a rest day. I needed it. Every week, we work, we make changes, we attempt things, and a majority of the stuff we do is mental. It's dealing with attitudes, expectations, and attempting to make everyone happy, which isn't easy to do. I am not complaining, just stating facts. This has been an interesting week. I flew two days in a row and will shortly tell about those flights, because it’s fun and I always learn things and find things to share when I fly. The biggest thing this going on was the fact that we're attempting to send a crew to Italy to pick up another airplane and the Afghan Embassy LOST one of their passports. Yeah, that makes it real easy to go get an airplane! Actually it doesn't, but who's counting. They were supposed to leave yesterday, but now might leave tomorrow. I'm going to go pick one up hopefully in December, but as always, we shall see. I try not to count my chickens till they've hatched.

This week I flew a training sortie and an operational mission--very different experiences and for different reasons. First the operational mission, even though I actually flew that second, I have more anecdotes to share from the training sortie. For the mission, we flew into Tarin Kowt, a tiny dirt runway not too far from Kandahar. We carried a full load of passengers, dumped them off and picked up another load to return to Kabul, plus one Afghan HR. HR stands for Human Remains, meaning a dead person. We departed. I worked the radios on the flight in, but I got to fly the return leg, since we alternate who gets to fly. On takeoff, I kept the airplane low, between thirty and a hundred feet and brought up my gear and flaps. I stayed low, flying over the valley at 300 feet, scaring goats and sheep. :) Turning to our departure corridor, I stayed low until I was about ten miles out from the field and then, making sure everyone was strapped in, hauled the nose to the sky rocketing up in a nose high attitude, until our airspeed slowed to our climb speed and I let the nose track down to hold our climb speed. We gained altitude instantly and the maneuver was very fun to do. Then, everything settled down and we returned to Kabul, a nice relaxing flight. It was a nice day and we got a lot accomplished, but operational missions tend to be like that, predictable, and nice and relaxing....assuming you have a good copilot. The one thing to note is that along that flight path the communication is unpredictable and you fly most of the flight without talking to the controllers. That's sad but true. When you finally get hold of them, then they guide you around traffic and other obstacles such as mountains, if you're in the weather, to return safely home. Kind of like the Spirit--at times it's hard to hear it, there may be static as we hear every time we're near base, but listening correctly will help see you safely home. (More on this later)

My second flight, the training flight, was a lot of fun. It was with the same student that I hooked a few flights before, but we also had a qualified copilot along to get a local proficiency sortie. I'll actually end up talking about him more than the first student, because of his attitude. My student actually did a good job and progressed nicely. He flew well, was well prepared, had studied, and is progressing adequately since his near miss for getting kicked out of the program. Aside from some minor problems when doing single engine work, i.e. raising the wrong wing, and descending too low when told to go around, he did just fine. The descending too low on a go-around is another case in point for communication. Sometimes we're told, as he was, directions about what specifically to do. In this case we were told to make a low approach to the airfield because there were men and equipment on the runway. We were told to fly no lower than 500 feet. This is pretty standard, it happens all the time. Well, he understood the low approach, in fact he even commented that we were making a low approach...but then he continued his descent, 500, 400, 300...finally, I grabbed the controls added power and pulled us back up to 500 feet. He immediately asked, "What?" I asked him if he had heard the controller tell us to "fly a low approach not below 500 feet". He said he had, but hadn't understood the 500 feet part, and instead of asking for clarification, he was just going to fly a low approach....at probably 50-100 feet, above the heads of the fire trucks on the runway...not good, and not legal! We discussed that problem, and talked about the need for communication. As a crew airplane, in this case with four crew members, we MUST talk to each other about what we're doing. Especially when two of those crewmembers don't have controls, they are depending on us to safely get them around and back on the ground. Communication is essential! It is required and too many problems and even crashes have occurred due to people NOT communicating their intentions, or not understanding the controllers and MISINTERPRETING what they're told to do.

I had a personal example of this when I was a student pilot, well before ever joining the Air Force. I was flying a little Piper Warrior, four-seater, and flew into McCarran International in Las Vegas, Nevada, for one of my two required cross-country flights to get my pilots license. At this point I had only about 30 to 35 hours of flying experience, ever, and I was flying into an international airport. The controllers had to talk me in to find it. I remember vividly them asking if I had the airport in sight. I said, "No". They then asked if I had the Boeing 737 in sight ahead of me. I did, it was flying a lot faster than me, but they told me to follow it into the airport, but keep my speed up because I had another 737 flying behind me....Needless to say, it was a roller coaster, stressful, and a lot of fun, this little tiny airplane sandwiched between big airliners. But, I landed safely, got some gas and took off back to Salt Lake City, Utah. On departure, I heard my call sign and some instructions, although I didn't understand them. I just answered with my call sign, thinking I was doing well. I continued on my heading and after a few minutes, the controller came back on the radio and

YELLED at me. He asked if I had the traffic in site, which was right in front of me and passed over my head 500 feet above me. From a controller standpoint, this is a near miss, and even though legally it wasn't bad, I got an earful. What I'd been told, and I acknowledged was to change headings so that I would be steered clear of the traffic and not pass so close, but in my not querying, just flying along all happy go-lucky, I could've caused an incident. That is why listening to the controllers is so important. It's also why communication with crew members is so important. It's essential that everyone knows what we're doing to back each other up.

Now, to take a spiritual turn with this! This is how the Spirit talks to us too. Sometimes we hear clearly. Other times, there are static or garbled messages, due to life, or whatever we're doing, or where we're at. There are times we can't even hear because we're too far away from the station, or in a spiritual aspect, our obedience to commandments is so far out of whack that we can't hear what the Spirit, in his still small voice, is trying to tell us. Then, we only seem to hear when we're whacked on the side of the head, given explicit instructions, or we fall and hit rock bottom, closing out outside influence from our lives so that we can finally listen to learn what we need to do. I'm speaking from experience. I know what it is like to not listen, and then be kicked in the pants to finally get the message. Now that I am on the correct path, it's amazing how much clearer the messages from the Holy Ghost come to direct my actions, my learning, and He helps me make correct choices.

The difference in clarity is amazing. Before Tip and I began our religious transformation in our lives, we rarely heard. We heard the big pushes of the Spirit, regarding really important decisions, such as where to move, and major changes, but we, I especially, wouldn't hear daily inspiration. Now, I know what I was missing all those years. I get to hear and feel daily inspiration as I study. We just had the General Conference of the Church and I found for the first time, I was feasting on the words. I can't even say that I'd always listened to General Conference, but here we had the Living Prophet and Apostles speaking words of revelation meant for our time, and I feasted this time. I took pages upon pages of notes. I loved it. It was awesome.

As I reviewed my notes and what I studied this week, there was a definite trend to the counsel we were given. First, I want to talk about a portion of this world's history that has always fascinated me. As many of you know. I love swords. I collect them, I practice with them, when nobody is looking, and I admire the skill that is required to use them. Swords have been around for a long time. But it's not the swords but the knights that I'm thinking about right now. Throughout history, knights have been regaled as heroes, conquerors, warriors, and many other things. One thing always stands out when talking about medieval knights. That is the code of chivalry that knights followed. What is chivalry? We know a little. TV tells us it's this, that, or the other. But, basically the tenets of chivalry were thus: A knight was charged to protect the weak, defenseless and helpless. A knight was to fight for the general welfare of all. A knight was to be faithful to his cause, loyal to his Lord, courageous in battle and a knight's HONOR meant more than life. Additionally, knights were supposed to be courteous to all, and they were charged to continuously study and become educated, in the arts, in warfare, in science, basically, in all things. One last interesting tidbit, NO failure of chivalry was accepted. Knights who demonstrated behavior that was not in line with the code were either stripped of rank or outright killed.

This code, chivalry, embodies many aspects that are required of us as children of our Heavenly Father. This is what I noticed in General Conference. All the talks, centered on many different themes, but an overriding theme could be found throughout. The theme was character. In other words, what principles of character are required of a Disciple of Christ? We are all children of our Heavenly Father and as such have been charged to learn of Christ, learn of His mission, learn the Plan of Salvation, and obey the commandments. As we do so, we become disciples, or followers, of Christ and He teaches us the path we must take to return to our Heavenly Father. As disciples, I pulled out of the conference talks, all these character traits are traits we should aspire to. As I list them, see how well they fit into the code of chivalry. They are: Faith, Sensitivity to the Spirit, Nobility, Honesty, Strengthen Testimony, Repents, Obeys, Serves Selflessly, Stands Apart from the World, Hopes all things, Has Integrity, Gratitude, Patience,

Humility, Steadfast, Immovable, Accountable for Own Actions, Seeks the Mighty Change of Heart, Prays Constantly, Studies, Endures, Forgives, Works Hard, Has a Broken Heart and Contrite Spirit, Sets an Example, Fasts, Lives the Gospel, Serves Others, Submits to God's Will, Diligent, Cleaves unto God, Ponders, Receives Revelation, and Embodies Love.

While there are many more things written here than are listed in the previous code of Chivalry, many of them are embodied by the code. The charge of the knights to be courteous, courageous, and to study constantly, not to mention protect the helpless, embodies a majority of these character traits as a Disciple of Christ. I'll cover just a few that stood out especially, both during conference and during my weekly study. The three traits that stood out to me this week are patience, gratitude, and service.

Patience-we live in a world where everything comes at the speed of light and sound. We are a ME generation--an "I want what I want and I want it NOW" generation! Why? When our parents were growing up, they had to work hard to accumulate what they have now, and yet so many of our generation think that when they get married, they have to have what their parents took twenty years to accumulate. This has led to a debt crisis in our country; even our leaders have fallen prey to the gottahaveititis. Tiffany and I for years have struggled with money. We absolutely sucked at budgeting and we figured we should get what we want, when we wanted it, and we went into debt to do so. Our parents both know the struggles we've had and how we dug ourselves into bondage. It's all a part of the same pattern. Before our choice to change our lives spiritually, we were both very much selfish, and into ourselves, not caring so much about the holes we were digging, the graves of our finance and spirit that we dug. Since our transformation, we've come to the realization that the chains of bondage were wrapped around us, and now following budgets and sticking with them is allowing us to see the end of the road for our debt ridden grave that we dug. I use this as an example of impatience. How many times have you been told to have patience, as the Bible says, for every time there is a season...In Elder Robert E. Hales' book "Return" he states, "When we have patience and faith, God truly provides better things for us, line upon line, through the suffering and experiences of life we submit to God's will, each experience will prepare us for the next step in our journey, and our journey will eventually help us realize our full potential as sons and daughters of God." Again he said, "So often we want the world records without the practice." and "I also fear that too many of us are vulnerable to get-rich-quick schemes because we have succumbed to a short-cut mentality. We want wealth without doing the work....we can't get something for nothing and we reap what we sow." These quotes are poignant reminders that the world thinks it knows best, that it thinks we DESERVE everything right now. When in reality, we need to learn to have patience, and work for our benefits, and then the Lord will provide.

Second- gratitude! President Thomas S. Monson, Prophet and President of the Church of Jesus Christ of Latter Day Saints, gave an amazing talk about gratitude, which I think goes along so well with the chivalric code of courtesy. Who are we? What are we? Are we better than others? No! We need to learn to be grateful, thankful, for those things we have, even when we don't have much or when we are going through trials. One quote I like from his talk was, "love overpowers jealousy, light drives out darkness, pride destroys gratitude." The two things don't mix. Pride, thinking we're better than others, destroys our ability to be grateful for the things the Lord gives us. Grateful living is a sure sign of a disciple of Christ. In Matthew it states that "In nothing doth man offend God" except when he doesn't recognize HIS hand in all things. We're getting close to the Thanksgiving Holiday in the United States. It was developed and set aside so the pilgrims could have a day to give thanks unto God for SURVIVING another year. We need to recognize that God is in control. He knows the choices we will make and He provides us opportunities to grow and "survive another year", hopefully getting stronger and more spiritually capable each year. We can't be negative and be grateful. We can't be prideful and be grateful. We can't be disobeying the commandments and be grateful...True gratitude is developed as we learn to feel the Spirit, and let it influence our lives, changing us, making us different people. I'm grateful for my wonderful wife and family. I'm grateful for the love that Tip has for me. I'm grateful that I've had this opportunity to be in an austere environment, going through the changes and growth I'm going through, so that I can honestly say, I'm grateful for my Savior, for what he did for me. I can't wait to see Tip again and hold her in my arms, even though it'll only be for two weeks and then I'll have to return to this dirt infested lump of a land, but I'm grateful for the opportunity to do so. Having her love me and having her as my best friend means the world to me. I love that silly girl! And I'm grateful that all those years ago while barely knowing each other, when I asked if she'd marry me, she said YES!

Lastly, I want to talk about service. This is one of those topics that is so important to the Gospel of Christ and to me in particular. I love serving and giving of myself to others, helping, counseling, etc. It even drives Tip insane because I'm always trying to save people and sometimes I've been the one that's been hurt, or fallen. I see the joy of helping others. As Tiffany has had hard times with me being gone, the best weeks she's had, have been when she's been able to forget herself and her troubles and serve her friends and family. She is my hero and a perfect example to me of selfless service. True, it's not easy, and we don't always WANT to serve. After all, it's hard, it takes us out of our comfort zones, but the Lord said, the two greatest commandments are to love God with all our heart might mind and strength and to Love our neighbors as ourselves. We do this by helping others. All the commandments are encompassed in those two. I learned some good lessons from the movie "Forever Strong". One quote, "It's not just about winning, it's about winning in life." We win as we learn to serve others and forget ourselves. Pride cometh before the fall, but service comes before growth. We learn to love others as we serve them. Loving others isn't always easy. In fact it drives me nuts sometimes, because there are some tough people to love in the military. Especially, when you're stuck with them 24 hours a day 7 days a week! It's tough to want to serve them, when they drive you nuts, but it's a requirement...I'm working on it. (Hey! I'm not perfect.)

Here are a couple other quotes which I find apropos to this week's blog. From the movie *Forever Strong*, "Practice doesn't make perfect, practice makes permanent." So we need to practice those things that we want to make permanent, such as the character traits of a disciple of Christ or the code of chivalry...However you slice it, it'll become part of you. A second quote, "You just need to learn to listen to that spirit inside you. Learning to listen, that takes discipline." We all have the light of Christ in us. Additionally, those that have received the laying on of hands for the Gift of the Holy Ghost have the promise of constant companionship of the Holy Ghost through obedience, and we need to learn to listen. That spirit tells us what to say or do, what is true, what is right for us, and will guide us through life if we let it....but we have to learn to listen and that does take discipline. I'm working on that. “Kiyakaha...Forever strong.”

Lastly, while reading in the Book of Mormon this week, I was struck by certain phrases. The disciples of Christ have their hearts "pricked continually", they "cleave unto God", they "search the scriptures" and they "ponder the revelations". These are not passive things. These are active desires. We must go and do likewise. I am striving to become a Knight of Christ, a disciple of Christ, and a changed man from my years of passively living. What do you want out of life?

Tip is the coolest most awesome wife on the planet and I get giddy just thinking about going to see her in just over a week.

I watched the movie Armageddon today, and it gets me every time, I cry!!!! I cry because of the selfless service, the love that Bruce Willis' character has for his daughter that he sacrifices his life! The changes in people are amazing. I know changes are possible, sometimes it takes earth shattering events, like in the movie to make us realize this! Such a good movie to watch on my birthday!

A scout is trustworthy, loyal, helpful, courteous, kind, thrifty, brave, clean and reverent! - Scout motto...sounds very much like a code of Chivalry doesn't it!

C-27 Squadron building on Afghan base; (below) the muddy walk to work

Chapter 32

THERE WILL BE A PART TWO

On the road again, I am getting on the road again….and I love it that I'm on my own again, away from work and on the road again…I am commencing operation go home for Rest and Recuperation. I just departed from Kabul today and am on my trek back home. First stop, midnight briefing to see if I can get on a flight! Ahh, the joys of military travel when not taking your own airplane! It's been an intriguing week because I haven't wanted to do anything. I've been busy and done stuff, but I haven't wanted to because I've been concentrating on the fact that I get to go home!!! Even though it's only for two weeks and then I'll still have five and a half months left after I get back…it's worth it. I'm excited and nervous and excited and actually I lied, I'm not nervous, just excited!!! I only flew once this week and it was a fun flight. I'll tell a little bit about it because it's fun to do different types of flying and that's what this was.

I took one of our better Afghan copilots, who also tends to be wild, having been trained in America and being a cowboy, he is like pretty much most American copilots – cocky, naïve, sure that they're indestructible…you know, how I always am! Anyways, our commander and I took him and taught him the basics of airdrop. We're slowly building a program to include everything. We flew out at 20,000 feet and dropped down to 300 feet to ingress into the drop zone. I chose an abandoned airfield and our point chosen was the intersection of the taxiway and the runway. I digress. We flew at 300 feet inbound to the drop zone and he had to run the checklists. The first pass was funny how quickly it came and we weren't even complete with anything….but that's the nature of training. We did multiple passes and eventually they were going pretty good. Each time we'd climb up to 3,000 feet and return to our initial point and do it again. The best part was that upon reaching the Initial point we had to make a 180 degree turn, and descend two thousand feet. The commander was flying so each time we'd roll the airplane to 90 degrees of bank and haul back on the stick coming around at 2-3 g's and then let the nose drop like a rock and we'd be back on our checklists, getting things done. It was a lot of fun. Then, following the last pretend drop, we boogied out of there as quickly as possible. I loved it.

One thing I'm noticing, as I sit here in Bagram, is change. Change is, change does, change happens and change is good. The last time I spent the night here was six years ago. I'm literally a stone's throw from the building I stayed in then, which is still here, but everything around has changed. The base is basically 5 times bigger than it was then. It's huge. Everything changes and everything stays the same. It's an intriguing concept, but change is good. I've always been a proponent of change. Changes of heart, changes of destiny, changes of location, changes of home…after all Tiffany and I have moved 19 times in our 14 years of marriage and only 12 of those were caused by the military….I know crazy, but If you ever need someone to help you move, or help you de-clutter to make a move possible…call my wife, she is the queen of getting rid of stuff and getting packed to move. We enjoy it; we enjoy change, though we miss the friends that we always seem to get close to right before we move. Isn't that just the way of it? Oh well.

I'm excited to go home…have I mentioned that? These first couple weeks of October have been great. Not only did I pin on

Major, but I had my 36th birthday, and I get to travel home. It's been a busy couple weeks, but I wouldn't trade it. The Lord works in mysterious ways. A year ago, if you would've asked me how I'd be feeling after being away from home already for nine months, plus an additional four where I'd been commuting home to the family on weekends because I was SUPPOSED to have deployed in Oct, not January so we moved the family…if you would've asked how I would feel…I don't think I'd have given the same answer. I'm a different person than I was a year ago. I'm still me, but my attitudes have change, my values have gotten more secure and fixed and my love for my family and especially my wife has grown by leaps and bounds. It's amazing what deciding to change your life and your heart can do for you. I'm so thankful for the Gospel which has wrought this change in my heart. I'm happier, freer in spirit, more settled in body and spirit, more peaceful than I have been in 10 years. It's nice. I'm calm. I'm calm with the calmness that comes from the Spirit, the Comforter who lifts and directs us. Life is good.

Now, my studies have been different this week too, due to the nature of my days, my attention span decrease due to being excited to go home etc. I've had some good lessons this week. First, I wish I had it with me to quote, but one of the main things I have focused on and learned this week is the family. Family is everything. Family is important. We can only be saved with our family. It's a unique doctrine of the church that we preach the salvation of the living and the dead. Genealogy is an important aspect because we teach the doctrine of Christ as He said in the Bible, "if the dead rise not at all, else why then should ye be baptized for the dead?" (1Cor 15:29) He was referring to the practice of Baptisms for the dead and other ordinances are done in proxy for those who are dead. We stand in for our ancestors during sacred ordinances of baptism, the laying on of hands for the gift of the Holy Ghost, the endowment and the sealing ordinances of the temple, so that they have the opportunity in the spirit world to accept or reject those ordinances. After all, when Christ died on the cross, before His resurrection He went to the spirit world and organized the spirits of the righteous saints to go to the portion of the spirit world known as spirit prison to teach the gospel to all those who died never having the opportunity to hear or learn the Gospel of Christ. The spirits in the spirit world have the opportunity to hear the Gospel and accept or reject it. If they accept it, they still need to have their ordinance work done for them here, because the priesthood authority to oversee the ordinances resides here on the earth. They are temporal ordinances, in other words they require a physical body to accomplish them. How then is it accomplished? One who is worthy goes to the temple and completes the ordinances for their dead ancestors or others, standing in proxy for them. Then, that person in the spirit world has the opportunity to accept or reject the ordinances.

Do we know if they accept or reject it? No, though there have been times when the Spirit has overwhelmingly testified that people have accepted. It's one of those things we take on faith. But, the Lord said that EVERYONE will have the opportunity to accept or reject the gospel. He's a God of love and compassion. He loves the Christian, the heathen, the pagan, the Muslim, the Hindu, the whatever…He loves us all. That's the point. Justice will be served and mercy will have her own. Justice can only be served if everyone is given the same opportunity. How then can people accept the Gospel? It's been said that the Lord knows people's hearts and their thoughts and if they would've accepted the Gospel had they heard it here, then their accepting it there is enough! He is nothing if not a merciful God. Think of him as a Father. Of all the epithets He could have chosen to be called, He chose to be called Father, our Father in heaven or our Heavenly Father. I love it. I think of my kids and want the best for them and He's the same way with us. He wants the best for us. He provides us with the opportunity.

This is going to be short. I don't know when I'll be able to send it, hopefully tomorrow in Kuwait enroute home, but I'm just excited. I love my family, and this deployment has done more to strengthen that love than anything else. I have the most wonderful wife, who has for this past week watched a total of 8 kids, four of ours and four of a friend. She's amazing. They stayed up late having girls night, they've played, watched movies together, joked and fought and ran around crazy together. What fun!

When I get home Tiffany and I are spending the first few days without kids on a semi-honeymoon, then we're going to pick up the kids and have some fun for Emma's birthday. Sadly, she's turning twelve this year, but it's only the sixth or seventh birthday that I've been there for her. That's the main reason I picked this date for my R&R, so I would not miss her birthday again.

My love to all, my spirit goes out to you. I hope and pray for your continued safety, change and growth since in my eyes if we all learn and change and grow together, we're helping each other out. As always, thanks for listening to my week's lessons. I love sharing them. I love teaching. I miss my gym girls in NC because I miss TEACHING them, even though it was gymnastics, I love teaching and sharing and giving. I know I know I talk about myself and say I a lot, but I say that I don't care because I enjoy sharing of Myself to all of you. Smile, this is only half the size of last weeks.

If you haven't read the "Proclamation on the Family" by the Church of Jesus Christ of Latter Day Saints…you should. The world is trying to tear families apart and the family really is the most important element of this life! Especially your spouse, or parents if you don't have a spouse. I absolutely adore mine!

I've really enjoyed having Croatian helicopter pilots move into our unit there in Kabul….I've gotten to speak a little Croatian every day and it's slowly coming back….though I trip over myself all the time. But I love it. I need to work more on my languages, because I love to share in people's personal language.

In preparation for going home, I had my back waxed at the salon on base…it HURT, but only for a second and it was fun, I laughed the whole time as I carried on a Russian/Serbian/English...Ukrainian, conversation with the worker…who didn't speak English, but it was fun. Each time the three inch long back hair (I've been told the longer it is, the more it hurts) was yanked out of my skin, I involuntarily jumped and my knees kicked up and then I'd just start laughing because it was funny. It was so painful it was funny!!!! But, I don't like back hair so I got rid of it!

Chapter 33

BE A CHAMPION IN LIFE

It's been a while since I've put fingers to keyboard and flexed my poor little brain in an attempt at wry humor, dry wit, and blatantly obvious spiritual discussion, but I've always enjoyed a challenge and the opportunity to share. I might've said that once or twice. Obviously from my last blog email from a month ago you understood that I was getting to go home for a couple weeks and I must say that was an awesome, special, wonderful truly amazing time and I actually managed to get three days more than I was supposed to thanks to the army method of moving people around. Do I feel the need to tell all about the trip home or what I did....Yup, but not too much, this isn't my journal, even though Tip would argue after she read my journal I've been keeping, that I put a lot more detail in the blog than I do the journal.

One thing that can be said about the trip home is it's long and tiring. It takes three days to get home from Afghanistan and it's all via Army methodology which means...HURRY UP and WAIT. Sleep is pretty much out of the question. I hitched a ride to Bagram, stayed up till midnight for a briefing and found out I got on the flight in the morning. The briefing ended by 0100 or 0200, I can't remember, but we had to be ready for a 0400 Roll call for a 0500 roll call then once the roll call was done, we waited and waited and finally went out to the airplane...at 0930 in the morning. The Army likes to make you show and be ready 4-6 hours early, just in case. I understand this in a way because many times flying in and out of Iraq, I would get a couple hours ahead of schedule, yet the army was ready for us regardless of when we show. But being on the other end....it's very long and BORING...except that I finished reading several books on the trip. Once we got on that flight we got to Kuwait and began the 24 hour process of getting a rotator flight out to Atlanta...It's very official and very organized and very long and tiring and hot in Kuwait. It was worth it to be going home, so bring on the boredom. I was ready to see Tip and the kids. I missed them terribly. Following a long delay and many roll calls and lack of sleep, we got on a plane and finally arrived in Atlanta. Now, this was where I got my first extra day. See, you get 15 days of leave, but it's all based on the itinerary they give you out of Atlanta. I was flying to Chattanooga and there wasn't a flight they could get me on the day I arrived, so they had me on a 24 hour delay in Atlanta. However, I was told in Kuwait that if I got a standby flight or whatever, I still would return on the same day as my itinerary so it behooved me to get an earlier flight. We got through customs and I got a flight...that left in twenty minutes. I ran to the gate and was informed that the seat they had changed my flight to...didn't exist, so I had to go change it again. There were no more flights to get on...to Chattanooga, so I finally got put on one to Huntsville. I called Tip to inform her of my change in plans and she informed me that she was waiting for me at baggage claim and to get my butt up there, she was waiting. So, I went and verified that I'd still get my flight back even if I missed my flight out of Atlanta and then I booked it up the escalator to where Tip was waiting with all the people from the USO. She looked gorgeous. I love it when she wears heels!!! OH baby! We got some pics and then left. Her sister was watching the kids and we had the next four days to ourselves. We went to Knoxville and got a room there since the cabin we rented didn't start for two days because I was two days early....ahhhh, the good times. It was so nice to just spend time with the love of my life. It was like a second honeymoon. We loved it.

The cabin we went to was in Gatlinburg and it was perfect. Secluded, just the right size, relaxed, all very needed. We spent two days just resting and relaxing and then went and picked up the kids and went back to the cabin. It was soooo much fun. Mack took a pair of my sunglasses and became a pool shark, since there was a pool table and Emma was a little Bond girl whenever we took pictures of her shooting the air soft guns we brought. She always has to pose. TJ spent most of his time shooting the air soft guns and Savannah had fun putting the little green army men all over the cliff out back and trying to shoot them. Everyone enjoyed the Hot tub and the sun and the peace and just spending time together. It was needed. It was perfect. Tiffany and I really enjoyed spending time together and with the kids. What more can I say? It was time much needed to spend together as a family and as a couple. My favorite part of the whole thing was reading scriptures together, praying, and doing things together. So much fun!!!

After the cabin we returned home and got back to living. I'd never actually lived at the house so it was new to me. It was comfortable, it was home. I was very sad to leave after two weeks. However, this is where I got my couple extra days. I had to fly out of Chattanooga and I had an afternoon flight. Thanks to maintenance delays, my plane took off three hours late. Tiffany and the kids drove to her sisters, halfway to Atlanta just in case. I got into Atlanta and found out I'd missed the rotator for that day and they put me up in a hotel near the airport....so Tip and the kids came to the hotel and spent the night. The next day, when we THOUGHT I was supposed to check out, the hotel informed me that they were informed we were staying one more night. I went to the military liaison office in Atlanta and found out that Yes we were staying one more night due to the fact that the flight wasn't until the next evening. I asked if I could save them money and just have my wife take me home for the evening, since it was only a three hour drive...they said that was fine, so I got my 18th day and it was awesome. Then Tip brought me to Atlanta, we got to see her dad and Mike and Laura and Tip's sister...all in all a very productive couple days and it was just a nice time. I love the spirit that exists in our home now. The Spirit of the Lord is so strong and evident especially since we changed our lifestyle and our lives. So cool!

I made the standard trek back taking three days to get back and only getting about 4 hours of sleep total during those three days...needless to say, my first week back I was exhausted. But I knew I was back when I walked in my dorm room at 0720 in the morning and the light was off and my roommate was still sleeping.

I've begun a couple things since I've been back. One, I've begun a heavy workout program and I am soooooooo sore. I've never lifted weights before but I want to lose my belly fat and so building muscle is the way to go, and I'm really enjoying it, even though I am in a lot of pain, but it's a good pain. Number two, is a Christmas project that I'd started before leaving and am working hard on it now. Of course I won't tell because I hate ruining surprises...But it'll be cool, at least I think so and Tip agrees with me. So, I've devoted a lot of time to it.

I've also been continuing my studies. It was so nice to be able to play piano again. It's awesome to study and learn and grow, mentally, spiritually and physically. As always, I'd like to share some of my insight with you. I love watching good movies with good messages. I love reading good books and filling my mind with uplifting information. Joseph Smith said, "Search ye out knowledge from the best books!" Some good quotes this week from the movie *Forever Strong*, "God doesn't make a 'no good' anything. Learning to listen to the Spirit inside of you takes a lot of discipline....Don't do anything that would embarrass you, the team or your family." I really like that, especially the last part. I coached gymnastics before coming out here and many of the girls from my team are reading this. I also am a father and you, my kids, are reading this. As a father and a coach I love that and have now adopted it as a personal slogan and lifestyle..."Don't do anything that would embarrass me, the team, or my family." I haven't always followed such good advice, but learning and growing from our mistakes is part of life. I want my team and family to know that challenges will come, choices will have to be made, life will give us lemons and we choose what we do with it. "Good decisions don't make life easy, but they do make it easier." (Also from Forever Strong) Be your best self, I'm striving to be my best self. I'm striving to learn and change and grow. Life is much more difficult when one is making poor decisions. From *Evan Almighty*, "we change the world through one act of random kindness at a time." As it says in the Bible, "Choose ye this day whom ye will serve, but as for me and my house, we will serve the Lord."

There is order in all things. I've seen it. I understand the wisdom in the Lord's church; the need for order, discipline, justice, mercy. Our Heavenly Father is a God of order. He knows all things; He sees all things; He understands all things; and he loves us unconditionally. I really want to talk about our Heavenly Father for a minute. After all, I've delved into this subject a few times, but never too deeply. I want to quote a couple paragraphs from the book Doctrine of Salvation by Joseph Fielding Smith. He was once the prophet of the church, around a hundred years ago, and he wrote clearly about the nature of God. I love the simplicity and the truth of the doctrine. I love the order that it expresses. I also have complete faith in the truth of the doctrine. As such, I'm translating it from Spanish so it might not be the most perfect translation ever. If you have questions, ASK! I enjoy discussion, I enjoy sharing. I enjoy the simple truths of the Gospel of Jesus Christ.

"God is a glorified man. Some people are upset because of the declarations made by the prophet Joseph Smith, those which are found in the sermon given in Nauvoo, in 1844 during the funeral of King Follett. The point that seemed so mysterious was the declaration that our Heavenly Father at some point went through life, death and is a glorified (exalted) being. This is one of the mysteries and for some seems to contradict other declarations given in the scriptures. Naturally, there are things that we won't understand while we are in this mortal state and we won't be able to disentangle all the difficulties that are before us. Our understanding is limited and we judge according to that which we know and that with which we are familiar. We won't understand all that is related to Eternal Life until we accomplish the goal of receiving Eternal Life, during which opportunity all will be clear.

In the scriptures we read that God is 'infinite and eternal, from eternity to eternity the same immutable God', (D&C 20:17) that He is 'the same yesterday, today and forever', (Mormon

9:9) and that he is unchanging from eternity to eternity. (Moroni 8:18) In what way is this in accordance with the teaching of the prophet? 'God at one time was as we are now; He is a glorified man!!!...At one time He was a man like us, yes, God himself, the Father of us all, lived on an Earth, as Jesus Christ himself also did...!' (Smith, op. cit. pages 427-428)

Christ was born, nevertheless He is Eternal. And I suppose that we all understand the fact that Jesus Christ was Jehovah, he that guided Israel in the days of Abraham and Moses, and also since the days of Adam. Also that Jehovah or Jesus Christ manifested himself as a person of spirit to the brother of Jared, that He was born as a baby in this world, and in this world grew until adulthood, and that therefore he didn't always have a tangible body. However, Jesus says that He is the same that was 'the beginning and the end', (D&C 110:4) and that He is the same that 'contemplated the vast expansion of eternity and all things under heaven, before the world was'. (D&C 38:1; Mi 5:2)

The Prophet Joseph says: 'If Jesus Christ is the son of God, and John the Revelator discovered that God, the Father of Jesus Christ, had a Father, we can suppose that He also had a Father.' Later he asked, 'has there ever been a son without a father? And has there ever been a father that wasn't first a son?' He stated that the Savior declared that He only did the things which his father had done, that is, give his live and take it up again. (Smith, op. cit page 381)

Let me ask: Don't we teach that as children of God we can become like Him? Isn't this, then, a glorious concept? It is imperative that we pass through this mortal state, are resurrected and later continue towards perfection as did our Father before us. The Prophet Joseph Smith taught that our Father had a Father and on and on...Isn't this a rational idea, especially if we remember that He made us the promise that we can become like Him?

In what manner is God from eternity to eternity? Nevertheless, the point that appears most enigmatic is the declaration that God is 'the same yesterday, today and forever'; and that is 'from eternity to eternity'. Is this certain and does there exist a contradiction with the idea that he passed through the same states that we have to pass through (birth, life, death, resurrection)? From eternity to eternity means from the existence in the spirit world, passing through this state of probation in which we are in and returning to the eternal existence that is to come! Certainly this signifies (means) eternal, because once we are resurrected, we will never die again. We all existed in the first eternity. I believe I can say for myself, and for others, that we came FROM eternity; and we are headed toward eternal life without end if we receive exaltation. The part of man known as Intelligence was not created, it has always existed. This applies to each and every one of us, and it also applies to God. Nevertheless, we have been born sons and daughters of God in the spirit and we are destined to always exist. Those who are able to become like God will also be from eternity to eternity."

OK, that's a lot to digest. To sum it up, "As man is God once was, as God is man may yet become." Our Heavenly Father wants us to become like Him. Christ stated He was doing that which He'd seen the Father do. I know this is actually deep doctrine, but I know it to be true. God our Father has a body of Flesh and Bone. HE is a glorified man. He is all-knowing, infinite and eternal and omnipotent. He knows all things. He sees the beginning from the end. He is a God of love and compassion. He is a God of justice and mercy. He wants us to become like Him. It's our choice. As I said already, "choose ye this day whom ye will serve, but as for me and my house we will serve the Lord." Thanks for listening. I love the Spirit that fills me as I read and study, watch wholesome movies, and teach my friends and family. I may not be perfect, far from it, but I'm now on the road, striving to improve and become the person that My Heavenly Father wants me to be.

What are you striving for? Do you know?

Chapter 34

A GIFT OF THANKSGIVING

I don't even know where to begin this last week. It seems like it's been a whirlwind and has, literally, flown by. I have stories to tell, embellish, extort, or just plain make enjoyable as the case may be. I've been meaning to write for a few days now, wanting to write before I had too much information that my brain is drowning in the experience that is my life…

OK so is that dramatic enough. In summary, I flew a bunch, even on Thanksgiving, had a good week and enjoyed hearing Tip's shopping experiences.

There you have it!

Seriously, though, No Seriously!! I have a hard time being serious, but my brain is fried and everything is all mushed up. I think it must be tryptophan induced even though it's been two days since I had turkey….Oh, it was good turkey too. I guess I'll do my usual, start at the end work to the beginning and then talk about the middle. If you aren't confused at the end, then you need to go back to the middle to find the beginning then work your way to the end and the start over to finish and it'll be clear as mud! Got it? Good. Now try and keep up, I don't have all day, actually, it is night over here, I work much better at night. It's that not wanting to get up in the morning thing. Oh well, such is life.

I was going to write this thing yesterday, but that didn't work out so well for me. See, we normally get a half to a full day off on Fridays since that's the day of the Afghan weekend. We usually have a short meeting and call it a day, allowing us all to vegetate in our own unique ways. Most tend to watch TV, play violent video games or sleep. I tend to read, read, read, and watch a movie or two, talk to Tip for hours, and basically recharge my batteries via my connection with my wife…Yeah! That didn't exactly happen yesterday.

First, we had our staff meeting. It was a record breaker as far as staff meetings go. I've found reality seems to take a back seat to many people's agendas over here. This is sad since it's our taxpayer dollars that are paying for all this, but se la vie. It is not my place to question….Actually, it is my place to question, that's kind of my job, to question premises, to try out ideas, to be a sounding board to leadership, and to put my foot in my mouth whenever possible. I love being in the middle of all the chaos. I thrive on KNOWING what's going on and why!

Again, I digress. So we had our little meeting, shoulda, woulda, coulda only been an hour, but instead it morphed into a 3 hour debate. I finally, got back to my room to put on my headphones and worked on another song. It's a pretty cool one with violins and violas and other really neat stuff like that!!! Just as I sat down to work on it, the DO (Director of Operations) told me that the plane that flew to Bagram that day had broken down and I needed to work the issue and generate a rescue crew and mission to go get them … Ahh, the joy … Normally we don't fly on Fridays, but it was a special day, we sent some people to go meet with the Chief of Staff of the Air Force…He's kind of a big deal…But anyways, we sent a plane and they broke; minor thing like the fuel leaking all over the ground when you turn on your fuel pumps, what's up with that? To keep a long story long, they weren't going anywhere until maintenance could figure out what the heck was going on. At this point, I was cell phone guru, making calls and figuring things out…the only problem being that 1. Since coming back from leave my work cell phone works for 30 seconds then shuts itself down. It has a false charge and it's a piece of junk. 2. We get a very poor signal in our building. 3. There were only three people that weren't flying the next day available to fly and I needed two instructors to go. I asked one, and he declined (not really a surprise there) so it was one of the other guys and me. Due to that fact, I ended up missing church and I was not happy about that, but it's the job, must rescue and everyone (lots of leadership on the broke airplane so kind of important for me to pick them up.) We finally flew in and our maintainers started looking at the plane. When we got back from lunch, the maintainers informed us that we needed to take everyone, because the other plane had blown a fuel line, not a simple fix. It wasn't going anywhere that day or possibly for a couple days. We loaded up and flew back.

Now this cast and comedy crew was a sight to see. We were flying on our day off. The three of us that made up the crew are pretty laid back and like to have a good time. It was a comedy circus on the flight deck. We joked, we laughed, we sang and eventually we took off and landed back at Kabul. The important thing to remember here is that we're (cough cough) professionals!!! ☺ Alright, we ARE professionals, we just like to have a lot of fun while doing what they're paying us to do. I mean, we get to fly around this beautiful country, star gaze at night, occasionally listen to the radio when they want us to do something like takeoff or land or turn or whatever…The sad thing is, Afghanistan is a beautiful country. I love the mountains and it's a mountain climber/lover's paradise here…or would be if it weren't one of the most heavily mined places in the world, and people weren't constantly trying to kill each other. But, those are just minor drawbacks that you don't see that from the air. You just see pretty mountains that Heavenly Father created.

Now, at the beginning of the week I flew, or attempted to fly a couple times. Seems like every mission I was put on this week changed, became a comedy of errors, or was cancelled. The maintenance reliability of the C-27 is somewhat suspect. Not because we have bad maintainers, but because we can't get parts to fix the broken airplanes. They built this cool program, stocked it with Afghans, set up some airplanes…………and somewhere along the line forgot that the planes need parts to continue flying, especially in a harsh, sandy, dusty environment. The airplanes have not liked the dust here. Airplanes are women. They are! Ask any pilot and he'll tell you about his plane and how much he loves "her", but they're fickle women. These spoiled planes rested comfortably for years in Italy, nice tropical climate, cool sea breezes, beautiful beaches…and we send them to one of the dustiest places on earth that makes it hard for us humans to breathe because of the crappy air quality, let alone our planes filters. So they pout and fuss and just quit when they're unsettled…and we don't have the medicine to fix em. OK, I'm exaggerating now. There is a supply line of sorts in place, but it gets us the wrong parts and it takes too long to get them, and they (the ubiquitous they) didn't exactly work the supply line plan well in the beginning.

In the last 8 days I've flown 4 times, and cancelled once so I was scheduled five times. I ended up bringing people and things all over this country. I've worked with some new instructors that just arrived from Italy to replace those that finished their year and went home and it's been a wild ride, because with broken planes, mission changes, and cargo instead of training missions, these new instructors are taking forever to finish in country qualification to instruct. I, on the other hand, have been having a marvelous time flying and flying and basically flying.

That brings me to the middle. I took off the day before Thanksgiving as the General's pilot. We flew to several places, sat around waited and finally ended up in Shindand for Thanksgiving Eve. I love flying into there, because right now it has a really, really short runway and it's a challenge. We stayed the night and the British at the camp had a massive bonfire going. That, in and of itself, was pretty cool. We also raided the chow hall and brought back tons of snack foods that our chow hall doesn't provide since the have a different contract. (They had a lot that wasn't getting used and gave it to us.) The best part was departing out of there the next day. Why? Because I got to be at the controls! As an instructor, many times I barely get to fly the plane due to training going on. I just let others fly. However, on Thanksgiving Day, I took the controls and departed Shindand. I pulled the gear up, flaps up and accelerated, while climbing to only three hundred feet. We invited the General to come up and stand on the flight deck to see the scenery. At three hundred feet the rolling hills are pretty cool; we passed over one saddleback ridge nice and low. I love flying low level out there. Eventually, we had to climb and let Radar Control know that we were around. After that we had an uneventful flight back to Kabul, got a Wing photo made, and then had a massive Thanksgiving Day feast.

I overate.

Speaking of Thanksgiving, I guess it's my prerogative to take this opportunity to tell all of you what I'm thankful for. I'm thankful to be a husband and father to a wonderful woman and great children that love me and accept me as I am with all my faults and with a job that takes me away from home for long periods of time. I'm thankful that they are watched out for by family, friends and church members that make sure they're doing well. I'm thankful that 14+ years ago my beautiful wife said yes when I figuratively asked if she'd marry me while at Amicalola Falls in Georgia, which it took me 13 years to actually get around to seeing the falls. I'm thankful for smart, caring, helpful children that accept change easily. It's not easy being a military brat, especially when you move as often as we have.

I'm thankful for this opportunity that I have to serve my country, to be over here making a difference, even though it seems small as we go through it, I know it is helping. I'm thankful for leaders (mostly church leaders) that guide us in wisdom and love. I'm thankful for the abilities that I've been blessed with. I've loved speaking other languages to people from the many countries deployed here, and making music on my computer, writing it, composing it, playing it…I love music, it soothes me and opens me to hear when the Spirit is trying to let me know something. Music can be such an instrument for good…or evil as the case may be. Music is powerful and I'm thankful for good music that keeps me sane. I'm thankful for family and friends, who accept my insanity, enjoy my spirituality, accept me as I am, and are true friends.

I'm thankful for my Heavenly Father, for his Son, Jesus Christ. As we now pass from Thanksgiving to Christmas season I can't help but think and study about Jesus. In fact the majority of what I've studied is about our Savior Jesus Christ.

Again, I'm not trying to negate anyone's beliefs. I'm not trying to say I'm right and anyone else is wrong. I'm just stating what I know to be true and what I've studied and what feels good to me. I love to share and this is my medium of exchange since I'm kind of in an austere environment. I believe it was President Hinckley that stated something to the effect of "we're not asking anyone to discard their beliefs, but to bring them with them so we can enhance and add to them." I know that many of the things I've learned, studied and delved into are deep doctrine. All are simple concepts that are hard to understand unless they're prayed about, because we do believe in modern revelation. I know that the Lord answers prayers and guides us when we let Him. I know that many things I've said may seem too detailed, since many details are missing from the Bible. I believe the Bible to be the word of God. I also believe Book of Mormon, the Doctrine and Covenants, the Pearl of Great Price and the words of Modern Prophets to be scripture as well. I know that by abiding by the precepts taught by our Lord and Savior Jesus Christ we will make it back to live with our Heavenly Father and grow to eventually become like Him.

Jesus Christ. I'd like to take a moment and just think about Him. You see, He was a real person. He lived. He walked the streets of His home town. In fact, once He began his ministry, He walked all over Judea. Crowds gathered to hear Him. He performed miracles; He healed the sick; the dead He raised; water turned to wine; and then He spoke all those parables. The question I want to ask and I ask this of myself constantly as I have been reading and studying, is this: How would I have responded had I lived during that time?

At that time period, the Israelites were looking for the Messiah, but many had a different view of what that Messiah would be. Many expected him to be the literal "King" of the Jews, to throw the pesky conquerors, the Romans, out. Judea had been a vassal state of Rome for a couple hundred years. The Israelites were looking for the king, the conqueror that would free them and place the Kingdom of God on the earth. If I were there and I'd been looking for that kind of Messiah, how would I have responded to the quiet spoken, humble, teacher from Galilee who also claimed to be the literal offspring of God the Father and a human mother. That's the key. Jesus Christ was no ordinary man. He looked like an ordinary man, but his father was Heavenly Father, Elohim. His power and priesthood were gifts of the spirit from his father. But, how would I have responded? There were many, who believed him to be a great teacher. This humble carpenter's son, from a small village in Galilee, has brought peace and war to many nations. He taught a higher law that was, and is, not easy to follow.

How would I react? Would I be one of the believers? Would I believe only because of the miracles? Or would I truly have known He was the Son of God, the great Jehovah, the Messiah, and the Prince of Peace? Would I have taken the time to try to understand His teachings? He often taught in parables. Why? Why not just come out and say what He meant? I understand and believe He taught in parables to teach us to think. We too are children of God. He wants us to become like Him. How does one become learned? Do we learn if everything is spelled out for us? No. Learning comes through study and prayer. You all know you've prayed before a final exam, even if it was only a "heaven help me get through this" type of prayer. ☺ We study, we struggle to understand and eventually the light bulb comes on and we understand a principle which sticks with us much easier and for longer than if we are just given the answer. When Joseph Smith was translating the Book of Mormon, Oliver Cowdery – his scribe, wanted to have the opportunity to translate. He was given the opportunity. He failed. In D&C 9:7 he was rebuked by the Lord when he was told, " ye have not understood; you have supposed that I would give it unto you, when you took no thought save it was to ask me…But, behold, I say unto you , that you must study it out in your mind; then you must ask me if it be right, and if it is right I will cause that your bosom shall burn within you; therefore, you shall feel that it is right." How often do we ask for things when we shouldn't because we haven't put in the work?

Back to parables; Jesus spoke in parables so that we would study things out in our mind. He wanted us to seek understanding, work at it, and then ask if our understanding is correct and we will be blessed with answers. This is Him helping us to learn, helping us to grow, weeding out those that don't want to learn, those that only want the easy road, with everything given to them. Our Heavenly

Father is a God of Love. He's also a God of Justice and Mercy. He abides by Celestial laws and cannot break them.

Now, back to our question, it's a personal question, would I have accepted Christ as the Messiah at the time? It's easy to say, "of course I would've", but in reality, at times, the teachings of the Master would have seemed very difficult and maybe too difficult to bear. Even with the miracles, many turned away. I'm taking this time to read the Gospels in the Bible, beginning with Luke. I've learned some great things and had new insights that I hadn't had before. Each writer wrote many years after Christ's resurrection and ascension into Heaven. They wrote what they remembered, which is why some things are in different orders and some books speak of things that others don't. We realize that each author of the Gospels was a man, an Apostle, a disciple, probably married, with families. How did their taking up their cross affect them? Jesus said that His yoke was not easy, but that if we take our yoke and follow Him, He will give us rest. In today's world, that is dumbed down, simplified, neglected, or just plain ignored.

We live in a world of "Eat, drink and be merry and tomorrow we die, and perhaps god will beat us with a few stripes and all will be well…." That's the lie that Satan has cast out into the world and has been caught and pulled in by a majority of even Christian believers. Can we justify sin? Can we say that Christ atoned for us so we don't have to do anything but accept him? That's not taking up His cross! That's the great challenge thrown down. I see many that profess to believe in God and Jesus Christ that take their names in vain and do everything under the sun believing that they are saved. That just doesn't jive with Christ's teachings as I read them in the Bible, nor with modern day revelation.

I am not casting stones. I'm venting. I get frustrated with people. I've said it before and I'll say it again, the military is a microcosm where everything is exaggerated and in many ways sin is revered. It's not an easy life. It's understandable that people seek ways to vent their stress; the possibility of death is always a real threat when you're at war and so people deal with that stress in different ways. It can be frustrating though to try to live a Gospel centered life when there is so much vulgarity around you. OK, I'm done venting.

I'm thankful for the military though. In spite of the issues it has, it also teaches military personnel that trust, honor, duty, and valor are important and to be revered…things that are often lacking in today's society. This is one main reason I am in the military. The military, just like the government, needs good people, willing to do what's right, to say what's right, and to stand up for what's right.

Finally, getting back to my discussion on Christ; I've only just begun and over the next few weeks before Christmas my studies are going to center around Christ. I know He's my savior. I know He's the great Jehovah. I know that He's taken upon Him my sins, my infirmities, my challenges, my stresses, my frustrations, everything…so that He can know how to succor us when we're down and out. We have a song we sing in church that goes, "I know that my redeemer lives, what comfort this sweet sentence gives, he lives, he lives who once was dead, he lives, my ever living head…" He lives. That's the key. He has a body of flesh and bone. Immortalized and glorified-the first fruits of them that slept. He's our older brother, our Redeemer, our Savior and wants to be our friend. I want to know him well enough so that when I meet him I'll already know him.

On that note I'll end. This has been a note of introspection. I'm asking you, as I'm asking myself, to answer those questions of "What would I have done had I been there?" It's not an easy question to answer, at least, not easy to answer deeply. Smile and know you're all cared for, missed and that I hope you all had a Merry Thanksgiving and as we go into the Christmas season….how about we spend some time thinking about Christ.

Chapter 35

EXCERPTS FROM A LETTER TO A FRIEND

I completely understand trying to let God direct your path as I am doing the same thing.

We both agree on the method of learning truth. We could ask others for their opinion, we could ask a pastor, or teacher, or bishop, for their view, but in the end it's the Spirit that's tells us truth. As it says in Moroni 10: 3-5 in the back of the Book of Mormon, and I'm paraphrasing - Ask God and he'll tell you what is truth, through the Spirit of the Holy Ghost. And the Holy Ghost can tell us the truth of all things. I mention here a statement of the Prophet Joseph Smith: "A person may profit by noticing the first intimation of the spirit of revelation; for instance, when you feel pure intelligence flowing into you, it may give you sudden strokes of ideas … and thus by learning the Spirit of God and understanding it, you may grow into the principle of revelation, until you become perfect in Christ Jesus."

I'd like to answer some of your questions too. First, you asked, "what does it mean to be the "only begotten son?" – Read these scriptures: Bible- John 1: 14, 18; 1 john 4:9; Book of Mormon - 2 Nephi 25:12; Jacob 4:11...

These all speak of Christ as the Only Begotten, both the Bible and the Book of Mormon. I know you understand the concept that we are all children of God the Father, as we call him our Heavenly Father, also known as Elohim. Jesus is our Elder Brother, He earns the title Only Begotten because He was the only begotten child of God with on earth...or to say it another way, all the rest of us are born of Earthly parents...our parents got married (hopefully) and bore children. But Jesus was different. His earthly Father was not Joseph. Mary conceived Him through the Spirit of God the Father, hence her being a virgin and fulfilling prophecy, so while Christ had a mortal mother, he literally was the ONLY child conceived by God the Father on the earth (Adam and Eve were created, not born). Jesus was mortal and human because of his mother, but he was immortal at the same time because of His father. This is what gave him the ability to overcome death and become resurrected giving each of us the chance. He was not killed on the cross. He GAVE His life for us. That's the difference. Through His father Elohim, He could have gotten off the cross, He could have not perished, He could have prevented His death, but as we read in the Bible He states, "into thy hands I commend my spirit" and he "gave up the ghost". He couldn't have been killed unless He let it happen. That is why He is the "only begotten son". We're all children of God, since He created our spirits, but Christ was His literal son on the earth.

"As man is, God once was, as God is, man may yet become!" That was the quote I used and I've used it several times in my latest messages. I'm including an excerpt from an LDS church magazine that best describes where the teaching came from and why. I know it to be a true doctrine. President Lorenzo Snow, to whom the statement is attributed, was one of the prophets of the Church of Jesus Christ of Latter day Saints following Joseph Smith.

“Is President Lorenzo Snow’s oft-repeated statement—“As man now is, God once was; as God now is, man may be”—accepted as official doctrine by the Church? (Gerald N. Lund, "I Have a Question," *Ensign*, Feb. 1982, 39–40)

"Gerald N. Lund, Teacher Support Consultant for the Church Education System. To my knowledge there has been no "official" pronouncement by the First Presidency declaring that President Snow's couplet is to be accepted as doctrine. But that is not a valid criteria for determining whether or not it *is* doctrine."

"Generally, the First Presidency issues official doctrinal declarations when there is a general misunderstanding of the doctrine on the part of many people. Therefore, the Church teaches many principles which are accepted as doctrines but which the First Presidency has seen no need to declare in an official pronouncement. This particular doctrine has been taught not only by Lorenzo Snow, fifth President of the Church, but also by others of the Brethren before and since that time."

In her biography of her brother, Eliza R. Snow explains the circumstances which led Lorenzo Snow to pen the famous couplet: "Being present at a 'Blessing Meeting,' in the Temple, previous to his baptism into the Church; after listening to several patriarchal blessings pronounced upon the heads of different individuals with whose history he was acquainted, and of whom he knew the Patriarch was entirely ignorant; he was struck with astonishment to hear the peculiarities of those persons positively and plainly referred to in their blessings. And, as he afterwards expressed, he was convinced that an influence, superior to human prescience, dictated the words of the one who officiated."

"The Patriarch was the father of Joseph, the Prophet. That was the first time Lorenzo had met him. After the services, they were introduced, and Father Smith said to my brother that he would soon be convinced of the truth of the latter-day work, and be baptized; and he said: 'You will become as great as you can possibly wish—EVEN AS GREAT AS GOD, and you cannot wish to be greater.' " (Eliza R. Snow, *Biography and Family Record of Lorenzo Snow,* Salt Lake City: Deseret News Co., 1884, pp. 9–10.)

"Lorenzo Snow was baptized a short time later and began his service in the Church. In the spring of 1840 he was called to serve a mission in the British Isles. Before his departure he was in the home of a Church member who was preaching a sermon on the parable of the laborers in the vineyard. (See Matt. 20:1–16.) According to Elder Snow, "While attentively listening to his explanation, the Spirit of the Lord rested mightily upon me—the eyes of my understanding were opened, and I saw as clear as the sun at noonday, with wonder and astonishment, the pathway of God and man. I formed the following couplet which expresses the *revelation,* as it was shown me, and explains Father Smith's dark saying to me at a blessing meeting in the Kirtland Temple, prior to my baptism. …"

> *"As man now is, God once was:"*
> *"As God now is, man may be."*

"I felt this to be a sacred communication, which I related to no one except my sister Eliza, until I reached England, when in a confidential private conversation with President Brigham Young, in Manchester, I related to him this extraordinary manifestation." (Eliza R. Snow, pp. 46–47; italics added. Brigham Young was President of the Quorum of the Twelve at the time.)

President Snow's son LeRoi later told that the Prophet Joseph Smith confirmed the validity of the revelation Elder Snow had received: "Soon after his return from England, in January, 1843, Lorenzo Snow related to the Prophet Joseph Smith his experience in Elder Sherwood's home. This was in a confidential interview in Nauvoo. The Prophet's reply was: 'Brother Snow, that is a true gospel doctrine, and it is a revelation from God to you.' " (LeRoi C. Snow, *Improvement Era,* June 1919, p. 656.)

"The Prophet Joseph Smith himself publicly taught the doctrine the following year, 1844, during a funeral sermon of Elder King Follett: "God himself was once as we are now, and is an exalted man, and sits enthroned in yonder heavens! … It is the first principle of the Gospel to know for a certainty the Character of God, and to know that we may converse with him as one man converses with another, and that he was once a man like us; yea, that God himself, the Father of us all, dwelt on an earth, the same as Jesus Christ himself did." (*Teachings of the Prophet Joseph Smith,* sel. Joseph Fielding Smith, Salt Lake City: Deseret Book, 1938, pp. 345–46.)"

"Once the Prophet Joseph had taught the doctrine publicly, Elder Snow also felt free to publicly teach it, and it was a common theme of his teachings throughout his life. About ten years before his death, while serving as the President of the Quorum of the Twelve, President Snow incorporated his original couplet into a longer poem. He addressed the poem to the Apostle Paul, who had written the following to the Philippian Saints:"

"Let this mind be in you, which was also in Christ Jesus:
"Who, being in the form of God, thought it not robbery to be equal with God." (Philip. 2:5–6.)
Part of the poem reads:
The boy, like to his father grown,
Has but attained unto his own;
To grow to sire from state of son,
Is not 'gainst Nature's course to run.
A son of God, like God to be,
Would not be robbing Deity.
(As cited in LeRoi C. Snow, p. 661.)"

Numerous sources could be cited, but one should suffice to show that this doctrine is accepted and taught by the Brethren. In an address in 1971, President Joseph Fielding Smith, then serving as President of the Quorum of the Twelve Apostles, said:
"I think I can pay no greater tribute to [President Lorenzo Snow and Elder Erastus Snow] than to preach again *that glorious doctrine* which they taught and which was one of the favorite themes, particularly of President Lorenzo Snow. …

"We have been promised by the Lord that if we know how to worship, and know what we worship, we may come unto the Father in his name, and in due time receive of his fullness. We have the promise that if we keep his commandments, we shall receive of his fullness and be glorified in him as he is in the Father."

"This is a doctrine which delighted President Snow, *as it does all of us.* Early in his ministry he received by direct, personal revelation the knowledge that (in the Prophet Joseph Smith's language), 'God himself was once as we are now, and is an exalted man, and sits enthroned in yonder heavens,' and that men 'have got to learn how to be Gods … the same as all Gods have done before.'

"After this doctrine had been taught by the Prophet, President Snow felt free to teach it also, and he summarized it in one of the best known couplets in the Church. …"

"This same doctrine has of course been known to the prophets of all the ages, and President Snow wrote an excellent poetic summary of it." (Address on Snow Day, given at Snow College, 14 May 1971, pp. 1, 3–4; italics added.)

"It is clear that the teaching of President Lorenzo Snow is both acceptable and accepted doctrine in the Church today. "(End of quote)

Your third question dealt with "Original Sin" of Adam and Eve...In the Garden they were given two commandments, 1. to multiply and replenish the earth and 2. to not eat of the fruit of the knowledge of good and evil lest they die.

There are two key points and I'll point out the scripture in the Book of Mormon that supports this. First, In the Garden of Eden, they were not mortal, they couldn't die. Because of that, they also couldn't accomplish the first commandment to multiply and replenish the earth, because they were immortal, had physical bodies, but no blood. They couldn't have children at that time. The second command was that they not eat of the fruit of tree of knowledge of good and evil or they would die and be cast out. Heavenly Father knew that Adam and Eve would be tempted by Satan; He also knew that the fall was necessary to carry out the Plan of Salvation. If they had not eaten of the fruit, they would still be sitting happily in the Garden of Eden, but they couldn't have fulfilled the other commandment to multiply and replenish the earth.

Eve, when she was tempted by Satan to eat of the tree to know good and evil, she recognized the necessity of the fall and the joys that would come because of the redemption...so she made a choice and Adam made the choice as well. So, "Adam fell that men might be, and men are that they might have joy." It was counted unto them as transgression, not sin, because they broke the commandment to not eat of the fruit, but in the church we teach that "man will be punished for his own sins and not for Adam's transgression." (That's the second article of faith in the Pearl of Great price) "After Adam fell, the whole of creation fell and became mortal. Adam's fall brought both physical and spiritual death into the world upon all mankind. (Read about this in Helaman 14: 16-17) The fall was no surprise to the Lord. It was a necessary step in the progress of man, and provisions for a Savior had been made even before the fall had occurred. Jesus Christ came to atone for the fall of Adam and also for man's individual sins. Latter-day revelation supports the biblical account of the fall, showing that it was a historical event that literally occurred in the history of man. Many points in latter-day revelation are also clarified that are not discernible from the Bible. Among other things it makes clear that the fall is a blessing and that Adam and Eve should be honored in their station as the first parents of the earth." - Quoted from the Bible Dictionary

Significant scriptures: 2 Nephi 2:15-26; 9:6-21; Mosiah 3:11-16; Alma 22:12-14; 42:2-15;

Your last question is regarding the fact that the book is Abridged. That is a true statement and nobody has read the unabridged version. That's actually where the book gets its name. Mormon, the second to last Prophet and abridger (or compiler) of most of the book, took the records of the prophets that had been handed down among the Prophets and Kings of the Nephites for a thousand years, and following the guidance of the Spirit, abridged all those writings into one book and when it was translated it was given the name of the Book of Mormon, since he was its principle author. The Book of Mormon was translated from Golden plates, but only the first third of the golden plates were translated because the other two thirds were sealed and it was not the time for them to come forth. Your question was actually the first time anyone's ever asked me that, but if you look at the title page (this was part of the translation as well, not written by Joseph Smith, but an actual title page written by Mormon) where it says - the title "The Book of Mormon - an account written by the hand of Mormon - upon the plates taken from the plates of Nephi," then stating in the opening paragraph

"Wherefore, it is an abridgement of the record of the people of Nephi, and also of the Lamanites-written to the Lamanites, who are a remnant of the house of Israel; and also to the Jew and Gentile...." Best to just read it yourself, but it's written to us, in our day. The prophets of that time, Mormon and Moroni (his son and the final prophet of the book) SAW our day, saw what we would be going through and wrote it for us. They abridged the books and teachings of a thousand years of prophets and history of their people, for our day so that we can find out what is important for us today and to clarify many teachings that are lost and missing. That's what I know to be true. I know that as you read it you'll gain an understanding, not only of the people, a broken remnant of the house of Israel, but also of how what happened to them applies to us in our day. A recurring theme, in the Book of Mormon, is that they are blessed, get prideful, get smacked down, are humbled, repent, get blessed and begin the cycle over again. We see the same cycle happening in our day...

My friend, thank you for your prayers, they are much appreciated and you are in mine as well. It is hard being gone, but the Lord watches over us and in all time passes quickly. As for our dialogues, I will always be open with you and accepting even if we disagree, because who am I to judge another when I walk imperfectly...You are and always will be my friend regardless of what happens. If you decided to suddenly become Muslim, we'd still be friends (I don't see that happening, but I'm just letting you know where I stand.) I enjoy our discussions and hopefully Tiffany, the kids and I will make it that direction sometime and you can meet them all. We have to sometime go that way to visit the Sacred Grove in New York where God the Father and Jesus Christ appeared unto Joseph Smith. I've been there and it is an amazing peaceful place that I'd like to take the family to see sometime, preferably sooner rather than later. As always, may the Lord bless you and may all your endeavors meet with good outcomes.

Chapter 36

IS DESIRE ENOUGH?

Is desire enough to get things done? Are good intentions enough to progress? How's it go, the road to hell is paved with good intentions! I'm thinking about some of my students right now. Some of them are earnest. Some of them are studious. Some of them are lazy. We had one pilot student that I flew with often that had an earnest desire to fly, he just wasn't very good. He had the best intentions to do well, but wouldn't study, until it was too late and he's not flying anymore.

I ask myself, if desire alone isn't good enough, what is required? Not just in my flying program, but in life!

Before I get around to answering my own introspective question, let me tell you a couple stories that really illustrate this principle especially from a pilot and instructor's point of view.

I only flew once this last week, which was kind of nice because my commander loaded me up with lots of work this week and I was working long hours which would've been even longer if

I'd been flying on top of that. The one flight was memorable, especially since I was completely worn out by the end of it. Being worn out, completely drained and only logging 2.8 hours; that takes a lot and makes for a memorable experience. Let me paint you a picture. Two students, one instructor (me) and an airplane. Before we ever left the ground, I knew it was going to be a long day. I put one of the students in the copilot seat and I took the other. As we made our calls for engine start, got the engines going and then prepared to taxi, I noticed a glitch in the matrix...actually, I noticed a problem with our radio. It was doing the funky chicken. What I mean to say is that in order to hear on one radio you had to punch up a different frequency on the other radio and then you could hear. If you selected the same frequency instead of hearing from both radios (we have two) they blocked each other and nothing would come out. Weird, never seen anything like it! We had maintenance come look at it and they pulled circuit breakers, reset them a couple of times and it appeared to be working. We made the choice to take the plane and proceed. We taxied out, lined up and took off. Then, wouldn't you know it, on climb out, after getting some vectors to continue our climb, our radios got really, really quiet again...not cool when you're in an area that's known for being very busy. I played around with the radios, trying different things, for about ten minutes. Meanwhile we're trucking out at 14,000 feet over the valley. I had my loadmasters and copilot looking outside clearing for traffic as I messed with the radio. Finally, by shutting one radio off completely, I was able to get a hold of Air Traffic Control. They were happy to hear from me, because we'd had a stuck mike the whole time and NOBODY could hear ATC because I was blocking all radio traffic, and didn't know it. I immediately requested a return to Kabul and they were more than happy to be rid of me. We landed, flying a precision approach and my student was a bit behind the airplane, but that was understandable considering it was his first official instrument approach. It was his second "instrument" training sortie. We taxied back to parking and maintenance in their infinite wisdom at first tried to tell me it was my headset's problem.....except that it wasn't. They replaced the radio transmitter and it worked fine after that. I do not recommend going NORDO (no radios) in a busy traffic environment. It's not fun for the pilots, nor the controllers. That is the point when my stress level began to rise a little bit.

After getting fixed we proceeded to start again and repeated the scenario. Departure and everything went fine after that. My student in the seat was well prepared for this portion of flight and understood instrument procedures, navigation, etc. which made it a nice relaxing trip up north to Mazar-e-Sharif. Then the fun began again. My student was going to do a non-precision approach at Mazar-e-Sharif. He briefed up what he was going to do, how fast he was planning on descending, to what altitude he would descend to begin the approach, and then threw it all out the window when he actually began to fly it. After briefing a 1,500 foot per minute descent rate to arrive at his starting point for the approach on altitude, he began to descend 1,000 feet per minute, 1,500 feet per minute, 2,000 feet per minute, 2,500 feet per minute, then 3,000 feet per minute. I let him do this for a couple minutes and pointed out to him he was going to reach his altitude far out from where he wanted to be. He acknowledged this, was surprised since he hadn't realized it, and didn't slow his descent at all. I was working radios and he blew right through the altitude he had briefed and kept going down. At this point I had switched from Approach control frequency to Tower frequency and the radio went from clear communications to ridiculously bad jamming on the radio, so bad that Tower couldn't understand anything I said. A helicopter on the airfield decided to shut down and wait for the jamming to go away since it was so bad you could barely hear anything.

Through the static, I heard Tower send me back to Approach controls frequency. Meanwhile my copilot was doing the proper turns and everything as he had briefed EXCEPT he was 2,000 feet lower than he'd briefed. (I need to point out that he was at a safe altitude, just not one that he'd planned - when flying instruments, if you brief something to the crew, you need to fly that.) He was still descending, and I got a hold of Approach control who informed me they were kicking us out of the area and sending us back to Kabul. Too bad, so sad, thanks for playing, now go away! They were actually very polite about it, but my student's training still suffered. At that point I told him to stop descent and proceed on a certain heading. He was confused, since he hadn't been listening to the radio chatter....He should have, but he didn't, he was concentrating on flying...something we have to work on with our students, they only want to do one thing at a time. We leveled off and then proceeded back to Kabul.

At this point the story should be over....it's not! I put the other student in the seat. The other student has good intentions, studies hard, and has one of the greatest attitudes about training of anyone we've trained. However, he takes a long time to understand things and gets sucked into monotask mode. When flying you have to multitask. If you can only do one thing at a time...you're giving the other guy, in this case me, a headache and being quite dangerous. We flew back to Kabul and an immediate difference was noticed between students. The previous student held heading and altitude really well. The new student in the seat was “rocking and a rolling, rocking and a reeling Barbra Ann ba ba ba ba baran.” We were 10 degrees either side of centerline and 300 feet above and below our altitude...in other words, not straight and level. Finally, after letting him battle with the plane for a while to get his hands warmed up to the flying I let him put on the autopilot and we discussed things like all the instruments that are there to help get us on the ground safely if we were flying in the weather. We discussed this in length and by and by we arrived over Bagram. Hoping to salvage some training for the day, I requested to fly a precision approach into Bagram, followed by radar vectors (or directions) to Kabul for another instrument approach. My luck was not holding for the day!

You could hear in the controller's voice that he had ZERO desire to have me there doing training at that moment. And he let me know without telling me. Radar controllers will give us turns and descents to line us up for a straight in approach to the runway, following our course guidance on our instruments. We are required to follow their directions, especially altitudes and headings. This controller was really nice. He turned us for a short final and put us on final approach, 11 miles from the runway...........at 16,000 feet, in other words, 8,000 feet high. There was absolutely NO possibility for my student to get down to the approach glide slope, let alone the runway from that altitude. I took the controls, put on the brakes and shoved the nose over to about 20+ degrees nose low. Lucky for us our airplane comes equipped with methods to descend very steep, while flying very slow.....I call it the drop out of the sky like a rock approach. It was a lot of fun, but was negative training for my student. I leveled off over the field at 500 feet and executed a missed approach. My Afghan loadmaster hadn't finished the checklist, and while I could've landed half way down the field and the runway was plenty long enough, I didn't want to teach bad landing habits to my student, so I went around and we cleaned up the gear and flaps then I gave the plane back to him. At that point, approach control gave us vectors back to Kabul. He flew the vectors fine, but had a tendency to move the plane wherever he'd look. If he looked right the plane moved right etc... He was fighting the controls so much to try and continue straight and level that he was miles behind the airplane. He missed calling for the flaps, the gear, the checklists....I called them for him and made sure all was well and then he ended up having a nice smooth landing....go figure. He'd been behind the airplane all day, and I had the makings of a great headache at that point!

Safely on the ground, we parked and since it was late, sent them home and debriefed them the next day. That was good because instead of telling him he sucked at flying I was able to analyze his problem and give him ideas to fix it.

This goes back to my original question...Is desire enough? Are good intentions enough? In the flying world, the answer is definitely not. In life it’s the same ... definitely not. But it is a start.

During the time of Christ there was a group of Israelites called the Zelotes, or the Zealous. They were warriors and their goal was to be zealous for their religion and get rid of ROME. They thought that the Messiah would come as a warrior and king to beat back the enemies of Israel and throw off their yoke of bondage as they saw it and set the kingdom of God upon the land. They were zealous, but they didn't understand who or what their Messiah would be. Zeal, or Zealous.

What is it? What does it mean to be zealous? It is defined as "ardently active, devoted, and full of devotion". Being zealous toward gospel things is not a bad thing. Being "ardently active and devoted" to the gospel of Jesus Christ is something to be admired and even to strive for. So, where did they go wrong? They went wrong in misplacing their zeal. Not only that, but desire, devotion, zeal, while good qualities, in and of themselves are not enough if we don't act, and do everything that is required. Just like my student that had good desires, but because he couldn't perform the required actions, he had a bad flight. In life, we should have zeal, we should have devotion. We should take the time to learn and do those things that we need to in order to follow our Heavenly Father's teachings.

Do we worry too much about what others think? I know I worried sometimes when I first started writing this book about what some people might think. I wondered if I was being too self-righteous, or talking too much about my spiritual quest. I wondered if I was sharing too much of my thoughts and feelings about God the Father, Jesus Christ, the Holy Ghost, Joseph Smith, the Living Prophet and Apostles, the church....and then I realized that I was writing this for my own growth and to share my testimony as it grows and changes. This week as I've studied about Christ's life and teachings one thing that really stood out to me was when He was asked which of all the commandments was the greatest. He responded in His typical way with a question. I noticed and learn that He talked in questions and parables to make us think. If everything were given unto us because we desired it, we would never learn and change and grow. That was an eye opener. It's in striving to understand complex issues that we develop our mind and our spirit to understand even more complex issues. Heavenly Father wants us to understand and to grow, line upon line, precept upon precept, until we can ultimately become like Him. I know this to be true. Now, back to my insights! He answered with a question, asking what the law said. The petitioner responded, "Thou shalt love the lord thy God with all thy heart, might, mind, and strength, and the second is like unto it, thou shalt love thy neighbor as thyself." He then asked "Who is my neighbor". Christ responded in typical fashion then with a parable...the parable of the Good Samaritan.

How often have we heard the story? How often have we asked who was the better neighbor? We condemn the priest and the Levite as unfit neighbors and assume, or at least I used to, that the

Samaritan was the neighbor. But, in reality, the brother that had fallen to the thieves was the neighbor and we should be willing to help, even when it is not perhaps the best time, or whatever. I know I've digressed, but it's such a good point. The Samaritans and the Jews Hated each other. Many, perhaps most, of the Jews would take a day's extra journey to avoid travelling through Samaria to Galilee from Jerusalem. I find this fascinating. And yet Jesus showed that the Samaritan was a better friend, brother, and neighbor to his neighbor who had fallen than any of the others. The point was to show us that in those two commandments lay all commandments. The order of the commandments has meaning too. We are told to Love the Lord our God above all things. To me, that speaks of zeal, of devotion, of honor, of family, of everything. If we put God first in our lives, everything else will fall into place. We're never told it would be easy. In fact we're constantly told to "take up our cross and follow him". That doesn't depict an easy road. It depicts one that will be difficult. The world is constantly showing us the easy road and multitudes are those that head that direction. I was one of them. I was not zealous. I still have a long way to go. I'm learning and growing and trying each day. One foot in front of the other, sometimes leaning on my wonderful wife, sometimes she's leaning on me. Together we're making this pathway and growing together.

Is it easy to put love of God first? No, it's difficult. So many things keep vying for attention, attempting to divert our thinking into diverse paths. I notice that pride or embarrassment is one of the many ways that we keep from being zealous as the Lord would have us. Alma 27 in the Book of Mormon, talks about the Ammonites. They were converted and the description of them is amazing. In verse 27, in chapter 27, it says, "And they were also distinguished for their zeal towards God; and also towards men; for they were perfectly honest and upright in all things; and they were firm in the faith of Christ, even unto the end." I want that kind of description said about me and my family when I'm no longer here. In verse 30 it continues, "and they were a zealous and beloved people, a highly favored people of the Lord." How cool is that? And here I sit and find myself having short prayers at times with Tiffany, being quiet, because my roommate is standing 3 feet away at his wall-locker in his underwear. Am I being quiet and saying it quickly, because I fear man more than God and don't want his ridicule? Or, am I doing it because I find it sacred and end up speeding through it because I don't want him, my roommate, listening in. I think it's both. As I said, I've got a long way to go. Tiffany says some of the most amazing prayers, because they're so thoughtful and contrite and deep and I love listening to her pray. I want to, and often do, pray like she can, but only when I'm alone. I've found I have a hard time when my roommate's around, because it's distracting to have someone listening in, so here I try to follow the advice of Jesus to "retire to your closets" to pray, and I find I can have so much more meaningful, spiritual prayers when I am hidden behind my wall locker on my knees talking one on one with my Heavenly Father. I know He hears and answers my prayers. He's answered them too many times.

I want to finish off with one last story. This came from church today and I thought it was pretty cool. Many facets of the Gospel of Jesus Christ teach us about how to deal with our fellow man. Love your neighbor, service etc...Well, the teenagers of a couple guys that I go to church with have done some pretty cool things in the last couple weeks. Apparently they've been gathering school supplies, clothes and money and shipping/or shipped it to Afghanistan for some of the schools and people here. When you realize the average yearly income here is something like 1,200 dollars a year....you realize that there is a lot of need. These teenagers collected boxes and boxes of stuff on their own and with help of family and sent it here. That is so cool. A few times we've been involved in Humanitarian aid movements of just that sort of thing around the country here and it is one of the coolest missions we do. That is exhibiting zeal and effort, doing and living the Gospel.

Life is not meant to be easy. The cross of the gospel that we carry with us at times can be difficult to carry. But the interesting thing is in the same breath we are told, "Come unto me all ye that are heavy laden, for my burden is light and I will give thee rest." I've found that living the gospel is easy and restful at the same time it's hard. Christ talked about his teaching dividing families and that he "brought a sword" This is due to the fact that there has developed much contention regarding the doctrines of Christ. I testify that I know that Jesus was the Christ, the savior, the Prince of Peace...That he is the First-born of God the father and the Only-begotten son in the flesh. He is the Messiah who came in the meridian of time to publish glad tidings, to teach the Plan of Salvation and to rescue us from physical and spiritual death. Through him we will have the opportunity to be judged and if we repent, pass by those angels guarding the celestial kingdom and be able to live eternally with our families and with our Heavenly Father, learning to become like him. I know this. This is the "Cross" we're asked to bear. We're asked to stand as witnesses of God in all places where we're at. I didn't understand that before. I didn't live that before. Now I know and understand and hope to be that "light set on a hill that cannot be hid." And that my friends, is why I do not worry about talking about spiritual things. That is why I freely tell what I know to be true. That is why I council everyone to read the Book of Mormon. That is why I recommend studying the Bible. That is why I know that if you pray about what is truth, you will get an answer. I may be many things, but this much I know. My testimony is stronger now than it ever has been in my life. I'm glad that I can share it with you. People will fail, the Church and the Gospel of Christ is true regardless of the members of the church that may not always act and do what they should. I pray that the lord's blessings will be upon each and every one of you. We are counseled in the Doctrine and Covenants to "stand in holy places" in preparation for the second coming of Christ. Those holy places don't have to just be temples and chapels. They are also our homes, our rooms and even just our little cubicle if that's all we've got, if we're striving to Take up our Cross and Follow. I love learning about the teachings of my Lord and Savior, Jesus Christ.

ANSWER to Question One

The Question:
- How do you know that the Spirit is talking to you? Do you see the Spirit, like Joseph Smith did or do you feel something like 'energy' (for lack of a better word) flowing through you? My Gods spoke to me only once via a 'conscious vision'. I believe that this 'energy' may not always be felt but signs can point towards the answer to your question if you look carefully enough.

The Answer:
- Every person is unique and therefore the Spirit talks to everyone differently, in the way that suits them best, enabling them to recognize the Spirit when it is talking to them. The spirit, as tiffany said, is a person, a member of the Godhead, also known as the Holy Ghost. He is a personage of spirit, having the form of a man, but not the body, that allows him to influence us directly, talking to our spirit that inhabits our bodies. As I said, the Spirit converses with every man in its own way. Tiffany told you that she often gets the chills. Many times the Spirit gives us gifts, i.e. enables us to learn to play music or learn a language easier...These are some of the gifts of the spirit. Others are listed as follow (after the list, then I'll go through the ways that the spirit manifests himself to us.): In the Bible in 1 Corinthians chapter 12 verses 8-11 it states, "For to one is given by the same Spirit the word of wisdom; to another the word of knowledge by the same Spirit; To another faith by the same Spirit; to another the gifts of healing by the same Spirit; to another the working of miracles; to another prophecy; to another discerning of spirits; to another divers kinds of tongues; to another the interpretation of tongues: But all these worketh that one and the selfsame Spirit, dividing to every man severally as he will." This is stating that every man is given many gifts of the spirit. This is not a comprehensive list. Another list in the scriptures is found in the Doctrine and Covenants Section 46 verses 11 through 26...It states, "For all have not every gift given unto them; for there are many gifts, and to every man is given a gift by the Spirit of God. To some is given one, and to some is given another, that all may be profited thereby. To some it is given by the Holy Ghost to know that Jesus Christ is the Son of God, and that he was crucified for the sins of the world. To others it is given to believe on their words, that they also might have eternal life if they continue faithful. And again, to some it is given by the Holy Ghost to know the differences of administration, as it will be pleasing unto the same Lord, according as the Lord will, suiting his mercies according to the conditions of the children of men. And again, it is given by the Holy Ghost to some to know the diversities of operations, whether they be of God, that the manifestations of the Spirit may be given to every man to profit withal. And again, verily I say unto you, to some is given ...to have faith to be healed; and to others it is given to have the faith to

heal. And again, to some is given the working of miracles; and to others it is given to prophesy; and to others the discerning of spirits, and again it is given to some to speak with tongues; and to another is given the interpretation of tongues..." I like to think this has been a gift given to me to learn languages and music etc....it comes naturally, a gift from God...

Now these gifts are just a portion of what the Spirit does for us. You asked how we know that he is teaching us truths. Christ has said many times, "Ask and it shall be given, seek and ye shall find, knock and it shall be opened unto you." This is a literal promise. And as it says in the Book of Mormon, through the Holy Ghost you may know the truth of all things. So....How do we know he's speaking? Personal experience first....then scriptures. Personally, many times I feel chills like Tip. I also at times will feel a comforting presence as I hear a soft voice that sounds like me talking to myself, usually reciting scriptures or other information that answers my prayers or questions and I feel calm, and knowledgeable about the answer. Very, very rarely with me, I'll cry. I have also on a couple occasions had personal revelation ... through dreams or just knowledge put in my head...I can't explain it, it just is ... and at that point I KNOW!!!

Here are some ways the scriptures say the Lord talks to us. In John 14:26 it states, "But the Comforter, which is the Holy Ghost, whom the Father will send in my name, he shall teach you all things, and bring all things to your remembrance, whatsoever I have said unto you." (this shows two things. 1. He's a comforter...gives feelings of comfort. 2. He brings things to your mind, remembrance....The scripture that follows is one that he always sends me...Peace I leave with you, my peace I give unto you: not as the world giveth, give I unto you. Let not your heart be troubled, neither let it be afraid.)

In Acts 2:37 - Now when they heard this, they were pricked in their heart... - Key phrase "pricked in their heart" it is a feeling, a sentiment maybe, a warm feeling, a moment of knowledge...many ways one may be pricked in their heart...

In 3 Nephi 11:3 it states, "And it came to pass that while they were thus conversing one with another, they heard a voice as if it came out of heaven; and they cast their eyes round about, for they understood not the voice which they heard; and it was not a harsh voice, neither was it a loud voice; nevertheless, and notwithstanding it being a small voice it did pierce them that did hear to the center, insomuch that there was no part of their frame that it did not cause to quake; Yea it did pierce them to the very soul, and did cause their hearts to burn." - This has many good points. 1. It is a still small voice that we need to listen for. 2. It can cause us to quake and pierce us to our center. 3. It causes our hearts to burn...

D&C 8:2 - Yea, behold, I will tell you in your mind and in your heart, by the Holy Ghost, which shall come upon you and which shall dwell in your heart... - it makes sense doesn't it.

Then in D&C 9 verses 8-9 we learn, "But, behold, I say unto you, that you must study it out in your mind; then you must ask me if it be right, and if it is right I will cause that your bosom shall burn within you; therefore, you shall feel that it is right. But if it be not right you shall have no such feelings, but you shall have a stupor of thought that shall cause you to forget the thing which is wrong;..." This shows us the importance of our own efforts to understand. The Lord is willing to bless us and reward us, but as in the original statement, ask, seek and knock...they're all actions...It's not just asking, but it's thinking about it, studying it, asking questions about it, then finally asking Heavenly Father if what we "think" is correct, or true. If it is, he can cause that our bosom will burn, or if it isn't, we could have a stupor of thought.

Again there are many ways to receive answers. Before I left to serve a mission, I questioned why I had never had the BURNING that these previous scriptures talk about. I was praying for an answer and the quiet still voice came to me and let me know that I DIDN"T NEED it, because I already knew the Gospel and the Church to be true....And I never doubted. I may have made mistakes in my life and at times forgotten, but I've never doubted because one of my gifts of the spirit is to KNOW.

One thing we're constantly warned about is seeking signs. This is because Satan can mimic the signs of God. That is why we are asked to study, think, ponder, pray....so that we can then have our heart and our minds awakened and in tune. Satan can even mimic an angel of light and this of course is a whole different discussion, but the meaning is that signs, while good indicators of truth, should not be the only indicator. We read in the Bible, the Book of Mormon, even history, that many people have seen signs, and then turn away from God...Because their belief wasn't internal, it was external. God our Father wants to change our hearts, not just our minds. Have I ever seen a Heavenly vision? (You mean besides Tiffany???) In all seriousness, I've never seen an Angel like Joseph Smith, but I've felt the Spirit, and I've heard him, especially the last several months, talking to me and giving me knowledge and visions (for myself and my family - the Holy Ghost won't give us a vision for someone that's not our responsibility!) I've definitely felt His inspiration as I've written my blogs, knowing what to say, and when I've been writing music. Things, notes, words, just come to me from the spirit as I write. I hope I've been able to make this clear.

Lastly, the Lord has told us to ask, with sincere heart, with real intent, desiring to know, and by the Holy Ghost we can know the truth of all things. I know this to be true. And I know you can KNOW it too. That's my earnest desire that you can find out for yourself what is true and what is not.

Chapter 37

A MUDDLE OR A MESS

The week is a muddle; it's been full, filled, set to with changes and challenges. BUSY!!!!!!! I had the honor of flying twice and I'll discuss that at length. Additionally, I've been occupied helping get things going on a project. It's been going on for the past two weeks as I and others have crunched numbers and gone to great lengths to figure out a completely unrealistic plan….Actually, it was a realistic plan…just not bloody likely to happen due to the assumptions that we have to make and the likelihood of the assumptions actually coming to fruition. If you're confused, that's ok, because as we worked everything out we were confused too, so you can join the club. ☺

The flights this week were unique. I had two separate and distinct missions. One was a training mission with a single student, I haven't gotten many of those, but they're really nice to have since we can spend the time one on one and teach some important things, like how to fly instruments in the weather; how to follow a radial; how to make an approach safely to an airfield; how to fly and not kill themselves and everyone else…you know the little things. Usually we go to many different locations, or we just go to one location about an hour away to practice instrument approaches.

However, for this flight we decided to see if it were possible to stay local and fly instrument approaches. The fun thing about this plan is that it's very aggressive. You don't have an hour of drone time to get your hands and head warmed up before you're suddenly required to be all over the instruments and preparing to land. Needless to say, it's a very intense time, especially if you're new to instrument flying as my student was. It was only his second ride. But, he'd been through training in the states and on our wonderful instrument trainer known as Microsoft Flight Simulator … We spare no expense to train—actually we could really use a simulator, but it's not scheduled to arrive for a couple years … some minor thing like having to build it from scratch.

The flight was intense … for my student … I had a blast and it was fun to watch him struggle. I know that sounds mean, but it's not. Our Afghan students tend to want to do things with the least amount of effort, so by forcing him to struggle and push outside of his comfort zone he got a decent introduction to instrument flying. The thing is, without a simulator, we can't push them too far because they can always cheat and look outside at the clear sky. So, my theory is that by increasing their stress load, by having things happen faster than they want or are used to, they'll be forced to learn, at least a little bit. It WAS stressful. It WAS difficult. He WAS sweating. But he LEARNED a lot. After all, I heard that on his next flight, when he had all the time he wanted, he did well. There was one nice little anecdote. After our flight, which only lasted 1.8 hours, instead of the normal 4, he went to one of the other instructors and complained about how tough I'd made it and how he didn't want to do that again. I made him fly a program that was tough but doable and he did a good job, he just wasn't happy about the effort required.

The second flight I went on turned out to be a LOOOOOng day, with not much going on. We got tasked to fly an Afghan DV around and had to get up at 0445 in the morning. Not fun. I don't like getting up early. I'm a night owl, not a morning person, but I got up, went to work and flew. The airplane suffered all sorts of issues that day. We ended up writing up several problems, including a cracked window. It's not recommended to fly with a cracked window, but it was not found until we were on the way back so, oh well. We got to our location with no problems. Then, we began our wait. We had to wait for their meetings to be over, or whatever. We were told 1430 would be their return time to the airplane. But that was an Afghan 1430, which means that they didn't show up until they were two hours late. Our long day got longer and we finally made it back to Kabul after a 13 hour-plus work day. Yeah, that was a lot of fun. (Insert Sarcasm Here!) The fact that I then had some other work to look at when I got back made it real interesting.

As I said, I've had a lot of things going on at work. I took over as the ADO, or Assistant Director of Operations, and have been the squadron commander's go-to guy for small projects. Well, a couple weeks ago, a small little question was asked about how long it'll take for our airplane to take over the mission of another airplane the Afghans have that is going away. Apparently my original assumptions weren't accepted because they were too realistic. Leadership doesn't like bad news. We ran numbers to generate numbers that showed what a BEST case scenario would be assuming we had unlimited hours, planes that didn't break every flight etc…and that's what we worked on for the last two weeks. We created a nice profile of the possibility, should all that happen, and we found out we can work ourselves to the bone and get a lot done….except that the assumptions are biased, the airplanes are NOT working right and the supply system for the airplane is broken, which is why the airplanes break a lot. Therefore, we made this briefing, spent probably 40-80 hours over the last two weeks, myself, and a couple others, and briefed it to leadership. Here's the funny thing. The general got back early, and wanted the brief early. Sooooooo, guess who got to brief all of our portions of the slides….yup, me! I think I managed to interrupt the General a couple of times and I told him straight up what I thought. No, I didn't get in trouble for it. Some very good things have started to happen because of all this. We're getting rid of the ambiguity we had with a couple Afghans. We had a meeting and decided to move two DANGEROUS copilots that had qualified in both the left and right seats, to just the right seat, until they're not dangerous anymore. I don't think it'll go over well with one of them because he has an entitlement personality, and he'll be definitely offended, but that's the way it has to be. Better that than place others in danger because we don't trust him. We're making changes to make sure that we don't sign anyone off to fly that we wouldn't want our mothers to fly on the plane as a passenger.

Among the many other things that happened this week, I had a day of being upset, followed by a day of being excited…And then Tip, my wonderfully impatient wife, spoiled my surprise. She's a doll and it was quite funny to make her wait to find out what it really was all about. OK, to make a long story longer, on Wed, I received an email from Pope AFB asking me to sign a document and return it. It cancelled my PCS, otherwise known as a move, to Germany. It gave no explanation; it had no data, and the people at Pope that got me my C-21 assignment to Germany were as confused as I was. I was a little bit peeved and frustrated to not be able to get any information. The next day, I emailed my Wing Commander back at Pope and asked a simple question, "Did he know what the heck was going on?" Surprisingly he emailed me about 5 minutes later and told me what had happened. I apparently was picked up for a Selective Service Assignment as a Regional Affairs Strategist. This is a highly selective assignment that only takes about 60 per year in the Air Force. The majority of the assignments are in the Embassies around the world; working with the governments and military's of the country I'm assigned. Before you ask, I have no idea yet where we're now going to get assigned. I do know that this summer we'll be moving to California for training, the program pays for finishing my Master's in International Relations, and I'm super excited.

Tiffany and the family are excited too. What's fun is that where we do our training is the same place that TJ was born, our first assignment in the Air Force. Crazy! But, I'll be involved in this program for several years. After training we'll move to whatever region/country I'm assigned to and hopefully work in an Embassy. I love it. It's the unique career path I was hoping for and I was praying that the Lord would guide us to the correct assignment. While I really wanted to go to Germany, THIS feels right. This feels like what I was meant to do and it feels like we're being pushed in the right direction.

Throughout my life, even when I wasn't the most spiritual and committed plenty of mistakes, I always have had faith that the

Lord would guide Tiffany and me in the assignments I get as a member of the military. Faith, I've spoken a lot about that over the past eight months. But, faith is such an important aspect of life. Faith is the seed that grows a testimony. I love hearing about Tiffany and the kids bearing their testimony of truths they've learned about the Gospel. It's inspirational to see the changes that have come about in our lives as we live the Gospel and attempt to be examples to our children on how to live and what to do. In the introduction to Elder Russell M. Nelson's book *HOPE IN OUR HEARTS*, he states, "We also know that truly faithful people are produced not by fleeting flashes of exuberant effort but by continuous consistency in keeping the commandments of God." This is how our faith grows. Faith is an action. When Alma describes faith, he describes it with words like, exercise, experiment, etc. Faith requires action. If we're trying to get an answer about what is right or wrong, or what is true or not, what do we do? Do we only pray and wait? Sometimes we are given answers easily, other times we must work at finding out through study, through prayer, and through fasting.

Why fasting? Jesus fasted 40 days in the wilderness before commencing his work. What does fasting do for us? Fasting promotes spiritual growth as we exercise control over our appetites and allows us to grow closer to our Heavenly Father and be more in tune to receive information from him. Fasting is important especially when we're searching for hard answers. Fasting can help heal, fasting can bring the spirit. Fasting is a law of God.

As we continue in this Christmas season, I've enjoyed learning more and more about Jesus. I've had several questions asked this week and I have really enjoyed answering those questions. Jesus was born of Mary, through a virgin birth, the only begotten of Heavenly Father in the flesh. Jesus was also the first born spirit, hence His high place in the pre-mortal existence. He was there; He offered Himself as a sacrifice for us. But what does that sacrifice mean? What all did He do for us? We don't understand everything, and we don't know HOW it worked completely, but we do know the reasons He did what He did. We know those things that His Sacrifice and Suffering did for us. Here are a couple things that we're told in the scriptures. Isaiah saw Him and said that He was a "man of sorrows, acquainted with grief". In the Book of Alma chapter 7 we read, "And he shall go forth, suffering pains and afflictions and temptations of every kind; and this, that the work might be fulfilled which saith he will take upon him the pains and the sicknesses of his people. And he will take upon him death, that he may loose the bands of death which bind his people; and he will take upon him their infirmities, that his bowels may be filled with mercy, according to the flesh, that he may know according to the flesh how to succor his people according to their infirmities."

This remarkable description highlights that He not only took upon Himself our sins and our afflictions, but He took upon Himself our sickness', our pains, our frustrations, our transgressions, our desires, our temptations, our death, our life, everything. He fulfilled His part so He knows what we go through, EVERYTHING. In order to fulfill His roll He not only had to suffer death and pain for our sins, but He had to know what it is like to be tempted, yet He never gave in. Satan tried to tempt him. Satan tried to destroy him. It didn't work. He executed his mission and broke the bands of death and took upon Himself our sins and our infirmities so He may succor us and guide us and teach us and lead us and ultimately, judge us. He, as arbiter of our souls, asks a lot of us, without forcing us. The most important truth is that we are given our free agency to decide for ourselves whether we want to obey and learn all required to follow Him. He tells us to "take up his cross" and follow Him. He tells us to "bear one another's burdens". He tells us to "follow me and I will give thee rest". But He doesn't ever say it'll be easy. He doesn't ever say it doesn't require anything from us but our hearts. No, we have to learn that which He wants us to do. I love my Savior. The more I learn, the more I grow, the closer I feel and the greater love I have for the sacrifice He made. I'm 36 years old. He began His ministry at 30 and was, according to our learning, was crucified when He was approximately 33 years old. I am nowhere near to being like Him, but I'm trying. He asks the impossible of us, but then prepares the way for us to accomplish all that He requires. "Be ye therefore perfect, even as I and your Father in Heaven are perfect."

Tiffany and I have spent a lot of time learning and growing over the last 8 months of me being gone. I love the changes we've gone through. I love how close the Gospel has brought us. I love being able to have Gospel discussions. I love the fact that some of you have asked questions and I've been able to provide answers to those questions. I love sharing my testimony of the truths I've learned. In the General Conference of the Church of Jesus Christ of Latter Day Saints this last October, President Thomas S. Monson, the Prophet and President of the Church stated, "Our Heavenly Father did not launch us on our eternal journey without providing the means whereby we could receive from Him God-given guidance to assist in our safe return at the end of mortal life. I speak of prayer. I speak too of the whisperings from that still, small voice within each of us, and I do not overlook the Holy Scriptures, written by mariners who successfully sailed the seas we too must cross." We are not alone in our quest for righteousness. We are not left to our own devices. We are told that we can know our purpose. We can know the truth. We are also free to choose.

President Monson compares our life and our choices with the story of Alice in Wonderland. I'll quote him since it makes it easier, "You will remember that she (Alice) comes to a crossroads with two paths before her, each stretching onward but in opposite directions. She is confronted by the Cheshire cat, of whom Alice asks, 'Which path shall I follow?' The cat answers, 'that depends on where you want to go. If you do not know where you want to go, it doesn't matter which path you take.'" Our decisions determine our destiny. How sad is it to see people, and we may all be some of them, I know I was for a long time, that don't know "where they want to go". I've studied a lot and talked a lot about the Plan of Salvation because it talks about "where we want to go". If we don't know where we want to go, we're wandering and "it doesn't matter which path we take", because we'll get somewhere eventually, but we might not like where we get. The world is falling apart. The world is enticing us to NOT follow the savior. The world is teaching us that we should, "eat, drink and be merry for tomorrow we die, and the lord will beat us with a few stripes and we shall be saved." But the truth is that if we follow the world, we'll be thrust down to hell.

Now on that happy note!!!! We are the captains of our souls. No one else can make our choices for us…unless we give away our choices. We are the determiners of whether we're going to live a life that may not be easy, may be ridiculed by the world for the standards we choose to uphold. I, for one, would rather, especially now that I am on the correct path, be ridiculed for doing what's right, rather than follow along with the world and be led away down to hell. You know when I was in Instructor upgrade for the C-130, my evaluator pilot thought I was cocky because I laughed at life and enjoyed the tough training … and then jokingly told him to "bring it" the night before my check ride. He humbled me during the check ride, but I wasn't cocky. I was enjoying the challenges. In life we need to be humble and teachable, but also enjoy life. "Adam fell that men might be and men are that they might have joy." The joy found in living the gospel is so much better than the fleeting feelings of worldly pleasure. And since it's now midnight and the witching hour…I think I'll call Tip and go to bed. I love praying with her before I rest. It makes for a much better day.

Chapter 38

"MY PLANE!"

A common enough phrase, spoken by us instructors here; thoroughly, and well used! This week was no exception. I wish our students would learn the following words of wisdom by Kenny Rogers, "You gotta know when to hold em, know when to fold em, know when to walk away, know when to run. You never count your money, when you're sitting at the table; there'll be time enough for counting, when the dealing's done." This week I got to fly a couple times, once was a continuation flight so that my commander and I could get time practicing since we don't get to be hand's-on that often when instructing and we want our skills to be up to par to be able to demonstrate correct principles and procedures if we need to. That was a fun flight. The boss and I worked hard and flew for 3.5 hours getting a lot of flying done, practicing instrument approaches, single engine patterns and go-arounds, and I even gave him a simulated emergency to keep him on his toes. That flight was uneventful except we were flying the Pig. The Pig is the VIP configured aircraft that is very nose heavy and though it flies the same as the other aircraft, because it is nose heavy, you can feel it. Therefore, I've termed it the Pig!

The second flight this week was with a student that is struggling. It was graded as a "No-Grade" sortie because since he was struggling we decided to send him out to the area to practice climbs and descents, constant rate climbs and descents while turning, and my favorite - unusual attitudes. I ended up logging 5.2 hours that day since I had two students and gave them a full profile and a long day of instruction. Out in the area, my struggling student nailed all the turns and climbs and descents and was spot-on with his airspeeds and altitudes. That was weird, because he usually can't hold altitude and airspeed to save his life. But, he did better than my other student who has been doing well. As I said, my favorite part is the unusual attitudes. I make my student close their eyes then I twist and turn the airplane, going up, down, and sideways finally telling the student to open his eyes as I've got the airplane in a twenty degree nose high attitude and 45 degree bank. He is supposed to add power, roll the wings level and bring the nose down to the horizon. He did everything, just very slowly and not at the same time. It's supposed to be a coordinated maneuver. It wasn't, so we kept doing it. I'd give him the airplane after throwing it around the sky in either a nose low or nose high position, and always with a high bank angle. (Just so you know, we're doing this over ten thousand feet in the air so that we have room to maneuver.) He eventually got it and started to move the yoke and the throttles together, still too slow, but better than it was....plus I was getting to throw the airplane all over the sky, that was just a fun little bonus. Then, to keep things going on the profile we had to fly, we headed back to the training base and set up for several instrument approaches. On his first approach he did fairly well. I was coaching him on everything, but the area work helped him out to maintain his headings and altitudes and courses to fly. Later, the issues turned up.

For the second portion of the instrument flight, during the second approach, I told him I wasn't going to coach him through the approach, especially since it was going to be the exact same approach that we had just flown. He said OK. Right off the bat I knew we were going to have problems. We started the approach by holding over a fixed point along a radial (this is a radio transmitted signal that is represented by compass headings/bearings to the station or away from the station). This is an important skill especially during bad weather. I knew it was going to be a long hour when he flew to the holding point and didn't put the course in that we're supposed to fly. I let this go to see what he was going to do....he didn't do anything. Somehow he was flying by just flying headings, not bothering with the actual courses we were supposed to be flying. He got lucky because he was actually more or less on course, and I wanted to see what he would do next. He flew the whole bloody approach without setting in his course at all. He was within a mile of his course centerline out of sheer luck. After fussing at him and explaining what he'd just done, we went to go out on another approach, flying the precision approach (tighter limits) and darned if he didn't do the exact same thing again. I let him go until about three miles from the runway until I couldn't take it anymore and made him dial in the course. He flew fine down the glide slope and then we entered the normal traffic pattern. Here's where my initial quote came into play. He's been in the program for several months now and already passed the "visual" portion of flying which includes airport traffic patterns with both engines and one engine out and no flaps...in other words simulated emergencies to teach them how to handle the airplane should an actual emergency occur. I won't add that every flight with them is like an emergency from an instructor's point of view.

He flew a normal pattern, touch and go. At that point I gave him a simulated engine failure. Now, safety dictates that we don't actually shut down the engine. This is smart on our part. I pulled his power to idle on his right side engine. Proper technique is to increase power on the left engine, raise the right engine to 5 degrees above the horizon, and step on the left rudder to keep the plane flying straight. He did none of these things. He raised the left wing 10 degrees and bank was increasing, and then stepped on the incorrect rudder which caused the plane to begin to roll to the right. That's when I took the airplane from him, added power, kicked in left rudder and rolled out of the bank. In the second that it took me to do that we'd rolled 30 degrees of bank, which isn't much in the grand scheme of things, but that was only one second and I was prepared for him to do something stupid....If the sortie had been graded, he'd have failed it at that point for safety. Needless to say, that generated quite a bit of discussion when we got back to base and I sat down with him to debrief the next day. It also caused him to look at his procedures again. As always, it's always a memorable experience every flight with these students.

My other student, while he didn't do near as well in the practice area, understood instrument work and did a fairly decent job flying his approaches, though he has a fear of pushing the nose over when he gets high. When you switch from instruments to the visual for the last 1/2 mile, you need to keep the same aim point on the runway. He tends to let it drift and gets high and will require a steep drop to get back on a normal glide slope to the runway. I love to get high and drop like a rock. That's fun, it's exciting and it's just bloody good times. But, he gets nervous and just doesn't want to pull off his power and let the nose drop down, even though that's the way that you get the plane back on track without getting super-fast. It's a challenge to break them of these habits and fears or whatever they're called...I like challenges and I find I really do enjoy these instructional sorties, even though I'm worn out mentally by the end.

Poor Tip, she's spent the last three days driving across country to Utah for Christmas and yesterday was in whiteout and blackout conditions thanks to a storm that decided to dump snow on NEW MEXICO...I mean, we planned her route to go the southern way so she wouldn't get hit with snow and ice...and then a winter storm dumped on her...figures. But she's a trooper and will get to Utah today; actually she just crossed the border as I write this and get to have Christmas with my family.

I must say too that I am very proud of my wife. I know you're not supposed to brag about your accomplishments, but I'm going to brag about my wife because she's such a good person. Christmas is the season of giving, the season of sacrifice, the season of helping. I find it sad how the world has soooo commercialized Christmas and taken away the true meaning of the season. It's become a commercial holiday. But, this year, we decided to do something different. While we bought a few gifts, most were crafted or made and additionally, Tip took the time to help others. Right before leaving on this trip she did some things for at least one family if not more, gifting food and supplies on their porch and leaving. She didn't ask for recognition, though I'm giving it to her because I'm proud of the giving spirit I see in her. She truly is happiest when she's doing things for others and I love watching, hearing about it even from these 7,000 miles away. She's an amazing woman and I'm thankful to be married to her.

Tiffany's example exemplifies the whole reason we celebrate Christmas. Today in church we talked about sacrifice. The Lord no longer requires sacrifice of animals, and I believe it's true to say that he never condoned human sacrifice. :) However, he asks us for a broken heart and a contrite spirit. What does that mean? Do you know? This is one topic I'm always trying to understand, because it's a prerequisite to entering the kingdom of God. Nobody gets through the gates into the Celestial Kingdom except they have a broken heart and contrite spirit. For all intents and purposes, this means humility. It means we become humble. King Benjamin, in his discourse about how to live and return to God talked about this in Mosiah 3:19. He said, "For the natural man is an enemy to God, and has been from the fall of Adam, and will be, forever and ever, unless he yields to the enticing of the Holy Spirit, and putteth off the natural man and becometh a saint through the atonement of Christ the Lord, and becometh as a child, submissive, meek, humble, patient, full of love, willing to submit to all things which the Lord seeth fit to inflict upon him, even as a child doth submit to his father." There it is in a nutshell. We need to become meek, submissive, say we're sorry, be humble, mild of temper, not easily irritated, nor easily angered. We need to be lowly of heart, modest, not arrogant, nor proud. We need to be able to apologize, be patient and be able to endure when evil comes against us without murmuring. We must be full of love...in essence put off the natural man. Is this easy? NOPE. In fact it's the work of a lifetime, the work of our life following this. After all Christ told us that we must love God the Father and we must then love our neighbor as ourselves. There's no equivocating there. There's no second guessing. It's a challenge to overcome our petty differences. It's the challenge to be DIFFERENT than the world. The world still teaches an "eye for an eye, and a tooth for a tooth." I've been watching a show this week that shows how awful that philosophy is. Until we learn to turn the other cheek then we'll never grow to our full potential.

Our deepest hunger should be to do the will of the Lord. If the first and greatest commandment is to "Love the Lord our God with all our heart, might, mind and strength", then this doesn't call for us to love anything greater, nor hunger for anything more. It took me 36 years to figure this out. And I still have a long way to go. In the book *RETURN* by Elder Robert D. Hales he states, "Through prayer, fasting, obedience to the commandments, and priesthood blessings, we then qualify ourselves for the strength, comfort, and hope that comes through the Savior's atoning sacrifice." Additionally, in D&C 130:20-21 it states, "there is a law, irrevocably decreed in heaven before the foundations of this world, upon which all blessings are predicated--and when we obtain any blessing from God, it is by obedience to that law upon which it is predicated." We answer to the Lord our God, our Heavenly Father, as to how we are fulfilling the first and greatest commandment. This is not something where I can say how someone else is doing. This is an internal question. Ask yourself, am I fulfilling my responsibility? Am I living up to this commandment? I wasn't. I freely admit that and have admitted it many times in these chapters. I didn't, but now, more than anything else, I desire to do what HE wants me to.

I started out talking about sacrifice and there are some sacrifices that are greater than others. Sacrifice helps us prepare to live in the presence of God. Becoming humble, sacrificing our pride to know God, that is how we learn to grow to become like God. Sacrificing of ourselves for others, developing charity, which is the pure love of Christ, this is how we grow. This is how we learn. This is how we become worthy to live in God's presence. In our Gospel Principles class lesson today there was a good, though poignant quote about sacrifice. "We may not be asked to sacrifice all things. But, like Abraham, we should be willing to sacrifice everything to become worthy to live in the presence of the Lord. The Lord's people have always sacrificed greatly and in many different ways. Some have suffered hardship and ridicule for the gospel. Some new converts to the Church have been cut off from their families.

Lifetime friends have turned away. Some members have lost their jobs; some have lost their lives. But the Lord notices our sacrifices; he promises, 'Every one that hath forsaken houses, or brethren, or sisters, or father, or mother, or wife, or children, or lands, for my name's sake, shall receive an hundredfold, and shall inherit everlasting life' (Matthew 19:29)." This isn't an easy requirement.

Why would the Lord require so much from us? We see the world growing more and more wicked. We see the principles of righteousness trampled and disregarded. That which was abhorrent is now common. "Eat, drink and be merry for tomorrow we die" is the common theme of the world. But of those that would follow the Lord, more is required. "Mine elect hear my voice and harden not their hearts." This is the season when we should turn away from our petty desires, our commercialized overconsumptionized Christmas and become disciples of Christ, helping others, loving and giving of ourselves to those in need. It's been said, it is better to give than to receive and that is true. Give something of yourself this week, this month. Take time to listen to someone that needs a listening ear, a shoulder to cry on, a helping hand, a lift up out of the gutter. Be there for someone. That's the challenge for this season. Then, keep that feeling throughout the year. Make it a lifestyle. Choose to be different. Choose to grow this year. Choose the Lord. Choose to find truth. Choose to build a testimony of the Gospel of Christ and live His teachings so that when we walk out of this life Our Lord and Savior will be there to greet us and will say unto us, "well done thou good and faithful servant." Don't be afraid to be different. Don't be afraid to have higher standards than those around you. Don't be afraid to be a lighthouse to the world.

Tiffany shows the young women she works with that you can still be fun loving, righteous, and that as an adult you can still have that kid in you. This ability helps her associate well with them, and our kids.

I'm not trying to be on a soapbox. I'm preaching to myself as much as anyone else. These are things I've been learning and things I need and am striving to work on. Life is an adventure through which we learn and grow, if we're amenable to that growth and learning. I wrote another song today, called Epiphany; because that's the way my life has been the last while. I've had the epiphany that if I truly want to be happy, my Heavenly Father comes FIRST in life, not second or third or thirty-eighth as he'd been.

I share my testimony that through the eternal Plan of Happiness, the Plan of Salvation, we can return to live with our Heavenly Father, as we put off the natural man and become as a child, meek, submissive and full of love for all men. I know that my Savior Jesus Christ made it possible for me to repent and grow and change. I know that the Book of Mormon is a true book of scripture and that it teaches about Christ and how we can become nearer to him. I know there's a prophet on the earth today to guide us in these dark times as the world heads toward destruction. I'm thankful that I have the opportunity to hear his words, or read them, and apply them in my life. And finally, I'm thankful to my Savior for His atoning sacrifice and I want to take this time at this Christmas season to give back what little I can in sharing my testimony with all of you.

Chapter 39

MERRY CHRISTMAS 2010

Merry Christmas from the war! War, such an ugly term, and yet there have been wars raging on this planet non-stop almost since time in memoriam. Wars, rumors of war, contentions, incidents, actions, conflict…all ways to describe something that man wages to right wrongs, resolve disputes, take power, overwhelm, and to promote peace. Interesting how often war is used to promote peace isn't it. War is grotesque, war is ugly. War is people dying. So why do we do it? Why am I here? Why do we put ourselves in harm's way? Why? Because we feel the urge to stand up for what is right. We feel the need to do that which is necessary. We acknowledge that sometimes you cannot continue to turn the other cheek. Now, my war has been different. I'm not a frontline soldier, though I am here in Afghanistan. I've not had bullets firing at me (that I know of anyways). But I've seen a lot of the effects. I've carried the bodies out of the combat zone. I've flown the Medevac missions with wounded soldiers. War is, that's all there is to it. We do it out of a sense of duty. I do it out of a sense of duty. I do it out of a sense that sometimes good people need to stand up and be counted and do the right thing. While I'm not out pulling triggers,

I'm helping Afghans to stand on their feet and do their duty for their country.

Did I say Merry Christmas? I did. It's Christmas Eve here. Funny, the places you don't expect to be on Christmas. Most of you are probably home with family, going through the traditions handed down from generation to generation. Or maybe you're not. Maybe like me, you are alone this holiday season, maybe for a different reason than mine, but still we're alone. And I've found out that that's OK. See, being alone and away from family makes me appreciate them more. It makes me cherish the times when I am home more. It makes all this worth it. Family, it's important, it's special, and it's a blessing.

Before I get into my weekly topic, or my weekly lessons learned, of course I must regale you with this week's adventures. After all, what's a pilot's book without the flying right!!! This week I had one extremely intense and special flight…and it wasn't that big of a deal up until the last hour and a half of the day. We flew down to Kandahar on a regularly scheduled Aeromedical mission. The idea is to move people from the smaller field hospitals to the large hospital in Kabul. Everything that day had gone smoothly. I was a standing instructor, letting two of our qualified Afghans fly. They did a good job, handling everything professionally and successfully throughout the first half of the day. We loaded the airplane to head back to Kabul and I was informed that we had 6 patients on litters (also known as stretchers) and 15 walking wounded. No problem. The lead Aeromedical technician informed me that two of the patients were critical, meaning we had to watch them carefully. We took off and proceeded to head back to Kabul.

About halfway back to Kabul, the lead Aeromedical technician asked me to make sure we flew as quickly as possible because one of our critical patients was having problems. I ensured that our two pilots were flying at max continuous power, and thankfully we had a tailwind as well, and we proceeded. Turning around from where I stood on the flight deck I could see the technicians working with the patient. They were stressed, putting in IV's and giving him as much oxygen as they could get to him. I've been on several of these types of missions in the past, but this one took on a whole new meaning. They were fighting for this man's life. I watched and worried and hoped we could get there quickly. I would turn from watching my guys to make sure they were flying safely and correctly to watching the med techs work on the poor guy. As we got to the Kabul area I had the copilot notify control of our intentions. We were put on a vector away from Kabul…I didn't like it, it didn't feel right. We were informed that Kabul had just opened up again, and that we were being given delaying vectors. I told the copilot to declare an Aeromedical emergency to get priority vectors to get on the ground. We were put on a new vector towards the ILS approach, but as we flew along we were informed that Kabul Airport was closed again. Trying to talk through an Afghan to relay information to Approach control was very frustrating because he wouldn't or couldn't say what I was telling him to say. I was getting frustrated because I could see them working to keep this guy alive and we needed to get him on the ground ASAP.

Finally, after attempting to have the copilot tell the controllers what the problem was, and watching him butchering it so they didn't understand, I told the copilot to get out of his seat. I was nice about it, but he had to go. I jumped into the seat and quickly summed up the situation for the controllers. I informed them we were declaring a medical emergency and if they couldn't get us on the ground immediately at Kabul then I wanted an immediate divert to Bagram. They informed us Kabul was closed, so I declared our intentions to divert. They sent us direct to Bagram. Enroute I told the controller to inform Bagram to have an ambulance waiting for us when we arrived. We were cleared to do whatever we needed and cleared to land. The Afghan pilot did a passable landing considering the winds were strong and he had a 20 knot crosswind. He was too slow putting the plane in reverse and getting on the brakes so I grabbed the throttles and put them in reverse myself, told him to get on the nose wheel steering and we got off the runway and taxied to parking.

The ambulance was pulling up as we stopped and the patient was hurriedly taken off the plane. Our Aeromedical tech had been ventilating him for 45 minutes straight. His vitals had dropped from a 68 which is not good to a 15 which is really not good. We got him off the plane and waited for the Aeromedical tech to return from the hospital. Winds at Kabul were bad. They were in and out of our crosswind limits. At this point I was glad I had taken the seat. I trust the two guys to fly on normal clear day conditions, but I still don't trust them when you get outside normal conditions. When things are going to hell in a hand basket, as was happening to us, then, I really didn't trust them to put us on the ground safely. I know, I know, I like being in control and when it comes to flying, you bet, I'll stay in control, even when someone else is flying, I'm still in control because it's my, and everyone else's life on the line and I'm the one that is responsible for everyone because I'm in charge on the plane. On a normal day, that's not too much responsibility. On a day like this one, it was a lot of responsibility. So, since the pilot had gotten to do the flying on one leg, and the copilot had gotten the flying on the first leg, I decided to stay in the seat and I flew the final leg from Bagram to Kabul. When winds are THAT strong and almost or out of limits….yeah, I'm going to be at the controls. At that point we took off and flew back to Kabul. I was cleared for a visual approach and the winds I was given were right at the edge of our limits, but still within, so I flew the approach and landed. The whole time I used it as an instructional opportunity to teach crosswind controls and how to fly sideways while flying straight. I find when I'm explaining and demonstrating, even difficult maneuvers like this; it's easier to be explaining while I fly. All in all, I must say, I had a beautiful landing, nice and smooth on centerline….and we taxied to parking and called it a night. That last hour and a half of the day was draining, very draining.

This story is a classic example of the challenges we face. The events could have gone many ways. I've since found out that the guy survived. He's off the ventilator and moving to an Afghan hospital. He had a fractured skull, bruised lung, mucous blocking a lung, malaria, you name it, he seemed to have it, but he's alive thanks to the skilled work of our Aero med folks and I was proud to be just a little portion of that, getting them on the ground safely and making timely decisions. That's what it's all about. That's what life is all about. Making the correct decisions at the right times! How often do we get second chances? Sometimes more often, sometimes never! The truth is we don't know when we'll get second chances, so our decisions need to be right the first time.

That's where the spirit comes in. The spirit envelopes us, fills us, guides us…if we let it.

I was reading in *Return* by Elder Robert D. Hales and he states, "We don't know the end from the beginning. That is, we don't know what opportunities, adventures, and trials we have ahead of us. For example, we don't know whether our greatest test will be morality, an attitude about a doctrine, losing the Spirit because we refuse to forgive someone, or the illness, injury or death of a loved one. But we do know that as we press forward each of us will be tested in some way. To recollect Nephi's vision of the pathway through life, all of us will find ourselves in the mists of darkness—forging ahead through experiences and circumstances that can deceive us, distort our perspective, and make it easy to wander off into broad and strange roads. Only when we hold on to the word of God, including the promptings of the Holy Ghost in our own hearts and minds, will we be able to stay on the path, take our rightful place, and receive our eternal reward."

I think about that. I know it's true having lived it and while living through it every day. Every day is a new challenge. Every day is a new adventure. Every day the adversary attempts to draw us away, discredit our feelings, destroy our sanity and lead us off into sad strange roads. I find my life has been one long adventure and I hope it will continue to be so. The Lord has blessed me to see and do many things throughout the world. I'm learning to grow and increase in spirituality, finally. It took some hard lessons to learn that. I wandered in strange roads; I was deceived; I had a distorted perspective, all those things Elder Hales was talking about. I found my way back through repentance and with a second chance that I didn't expect, I am taking each day as an opportunity to change and grow and live according to the Gospel, to be that city set on a hill, to be the light on the candlestick. Will I make mistakes again? I'm human, of course I'll make mistakes, but each new day gives me an opportunity to learn from them and grow.

Another quote from the same book, "There will be times in our lives when things don't go as we plan, but the Lord's plan is greater than we can even dream. When disappointments come into our lives, it is well to remember that we should learn from our experiences, both successes and failures, and be grateful for being able to move joyfully forward with faith and hope." Things will happen; people will not do the things you expect. Life will not always go the way we hope. Often we want something that just isn't in the cards. I've always said, and until now didn't realize how true, that we play the hand that we're dealt. Yes, I know it's a card game reference, but it's true. Last week I quoted Kenny Rogers "The Gambler" song. It's a true statement about life that we can only play the cards we're dealt. We can choose to accept it and make the most of it, or we can wallow in self-pity at the grievances that are done to us. I don't know. I've heard several things this week about people choosing to enjoy the time they have while on vacation regardless of what tension or pride may be causing problems in everyone's life.

Pride, the big downfall, the big sealer of man's fate! Pride is a curse. It is insidious. It is "all about me", not thinking about others. Pride was the cause of the downfall of the entire Nephite nation in the Book of Mormon. Pride destroys. Our pride wants everyone to feel sorry for us. Pride makes us think that we're better than others. Pride makes us only see our petty concerns. Pride essentially is the root cause of most evil. We are continuously warned to beware of pride. Pride destroyeth. Pride is worldly. Pride seeketh not the Spirit. Pride destroys the influence of the Holy Ghost. Pride is essentially telling God, not thy will but mine be done. Let's contrast that with the Savior.

As we concentrate tonight and tomorrow on the Savior's birth, let's think about what He did for us. We know that He was actually born in the spring and that Christmas was celebrated as His birth when the Roman's adopted Christianity. They just took a day that was already being celebrated as I believe it was the birth of their Sun God and they changed it to be the celebration of the birth of Christ. Be that as it may, Christmas is a time for us to reflect. It's a time to think of others before ourselves. It's a time to forgive. It's a time to share, to love, to give of one's self. Can pride fit in there? I think not.

What was it Christ did for us?

Handel in his mighty work "Messiah" quotes Isaiah 9:6 – "For unto us a child is born, unto us a son is given: and the government shall be upon his shoulder: and his name shall be called Wonderful, Counselor, the Mighty God, the everlasting Father, the Prince of Peace." Unto us, a son is given….how true a prophetic statement there ever was. Jesus Christ, firstborn of God the Father in the Spirit world, Only begotten son of God here on earth. He was given unto us to suffer for us, to provide the way back to the Father. The Plan of Salvation hinged on Him accepting that bitter cup and drinking. It hinged on Him being tempted in all things and not falling. It hinged on Him being lifted up on that cross after shedding His own blood in great drops because of the pain of our sins in the Garden of Gethsemane. It hinged on Him commending His spirit unto our Heavenly Father after He'd passed each test, and then three days later taking up His body again, glorified, resurrected, immortal and perfect. He paved the way for us. He made it possible for us. That is His mighty work. That is why we celebrate His birth. That is why we should strive NOT to think of ourselves at this time and season. That is why we are to be humble servants, not masters.

"When you have done it unto one of the least of these my brethren, you have done it unto me."

Last week I reiterated how sad the commercialization of Christmas has become. I urge you to do something for someone without them knowing. I urge you to not seek for glory, but to seek first the Kingdom of God. I know I'm not one to talk as I share my stories of adventure each week. I enjoy sharing my adventures because I know I live a unique life. I want to share that with you. Life is meant to be lived, savored, cherished and loved.

I've been sick for the last 24 hours with a head cold and it's amazing how much clarity you don't get when you're sick. It's also amazing how seemingly simple things suddenly take on a whole new picture. Life is stressful, life is engaging, and life is a mystery that's meant for each of us to find our place in. When we don't know our place we feel lost, hollow, like we're missing something. Tiffany and I were in that place for a long time and we're glad to be out. I love my wife. I love the fact that we're growing together and seeing where we were hollowed out before. The amazing thing is watching as we both fill that void with the love of Christ. He is there for us. I've been having a Battlestar Galactica marathon as I've been sick. There are some good lessons to be learned about trust, loyalty, truth, honor, and you see how people that lose their way, have to struggle to find out who they are. There are many points about the show I have issues with, namely it's too worldly, completely too worldly. I miss the original series. Interestingly enough the original series was written by a member of the LDS Church and many gospel lessons were taught in it. The new series kept many things from the old, but added in a lot more negative. The one thing that has stayed true throughout the series though has been the search for truth, and that honor and trust are absolutes. Searching for truth…that goes back to everything I've been saying today. We search to know the truth of who we are, why we're here, what we're supposed to do. I spoke of pride getting in the way. Pride is a killer. It's silent. Often we don't even realize how proud we've become. We don't realize we're only thinking about ourselves. We wallow in our self-pity and don't realize that if we'd reach out to others, then we'd find our peace and happiness.

Peace. That's the yearning of every soldier, airman, marine and sailor. Peace is a hope that is evasive. Peace, my favorite quote from the Savior, "Peace I leave with you, my peace I give unto you: not as the world giveth, give I unto you. Let not your heart be troubled, neither let it be afraid." Peace. There is no greater hope when you're at war. Peace, there is no greater symbol to a warrior. The peace of the Lord is infinitely greater than anything else we can aspire to. I am at peace as I do what the Lord commands. We joke about beauty pageant contestants always saying they want world peace, but the only way we'd truly get that is for everyone to return to their Savior and feel the Lord's peace.

Lastly, I started talking about family. Family means everything. First, we're all part of Heavenly Father's family. Second, we are all part of an earthly family. Ask yourself, "How have I treated my family today?" A song going through my head goes like this. "Have I done any good in the world today? Have I helped any one in need? Have I cheered up the sad, and made someone feel glad? If Not I have failed indeed." Let's start with our families. Let's enjoy the wild children. Let's care for the brothers and sisters, mothers and fathers and grandparents. Let's demonstrate Christ-like love so that they can say, wow, they really do love me. This is a time when people feel alone in a crowd. This comes through pride. May the light of Christ shine in us and help us to be the best people we know how to be and directly show that to our family and friends. That's my message and my lessons learned for this week. We only get one chance in this world. Let's make ours count.

"And it came to pass in those days, that there went out a decree from Caesar Augustus that all the world should be taxed. And all went to be taxed, every one into his own city. And Joseph also went up from Galilee, out of the city of Nazareth into Judea, unto the city of David, which is called Bethlehem, to be taxed with Mary, his espoused wife, being great with child. And so it was, that, while they were there, the days were accomplished that she should be delivered. And she brought forth her first-born son, and wrapped him in swaddling clothes, and laid him in a manger; because there was no room for them in the inn. And there were in that same country shepherds abiding in the field, keeping watch over their flock by night. And, lo, the angel of the Lord came upon them, and the glory of the Lord shone round about the: and they were sore afraid. And the angel said unto them: Fear not" for, behold I bring you good tidings of great joy, which shall be to all people. For unto you is born this day in the city of David a Savior, which is Christ the Lord. And this shall be a sign unto you; Ye shall find the babe wrapped in swaddling clothes, lying in a manger…." – Luke 2

Merry Christmas!

Chapter 40

Happy New Year

You know, it's New Year's Day, can you believe it? Twenty eleven is finally upon us. That means…I go home in a few months…Yeah! This shall be a day long remembered. (If you caught the Star Wars quote, give yourself a cookie!) What a week! A lot happened and yet at the same time it's the same-same, every day monotony that changes and yet does not. I had a couple of things that were accomplished this week. For one thing, I'm one of the few people that seemed to accomplish missions this week. I don't say that to brag, I've just gotten lucky on being able to say nyah-nyah-nyah-nyah-nyah-nyah to weather and broken airplanes and though I've brought the airplanes back in a broken condition, I've brought them back after my mission was completed.

For my first flight this week I took a student on one of his final flights prior to his checkride. He still has not completed his checkride yet! It was one of those flights that, as an instructor, you hope for throughout the whole program. Everything went smoothly. We took off, went our way and I gave him multiple problems throughout the flight. Aside from some minor mistakes such as trying to turn left when he was supposed to turn right, and trying to turn right when he was supposed to turn left, it was a fairly benign ride. I even commented to him that it was well done and I thoroughly enjoyed it. My student was sweating profusely at different times during the flight because since he's nearing the end, I don't make it easy. He needs to be challenged. We don't have a simulator so I have to put him through the wringer and give him several different emergencies to handle, while having to fly the plane, not crash us into the ground, and get the plane safely to the runway while handling the emergency. It's amazing how many emergencies happen when students are in the middle of a calm regular briefing, which really throws them off their game plan, and that's the whole point. The idea behind this pressure is that we never know when something is going to happen, so we have to be ready. That's where his sweat glands kick in…it's kind of funny and fun at the same time.

The flight went well, we made it back safely, I even got to take a couple of landings and then we returned to Kabul…all in a day's work. For the rest of the week I pretty much worked on small office projects, like trying to figure out when students are going to be returning from their training overseas to enter our training program. Also, how many we'll have to train over the next few years, and how long it'll take to build up the squadron….reality bites sometimes, but I painted an accurate picture and I'm sure it wasn't what was wanted to be heard, even though it was what was needed. It's not popular hearing that it'll take a lot longer to get full crews built then they expected. Oh well, that's just the way it is. I won't sugar coat it. How can we function if we don't accept reality…I'll be back to this topic later.

My second flight of the week turned out to be an overnighter to Kandahar. They were hosting an Open House today, so we sent an airplane with crew and I ended up being the volunteer instructor to go. I took two of our qualified Afghan pilots. One of the pilots is approved to fly with a standing instructor, so he can fly with the other Afghan pilot in the copilot's seat. This isn't that bad of a deal, except when there's weather or as in last week's "if I have to kick them out to get control to know what the heck the emergency is about" type of mission. Yesterday, it was an interesting experience going in to Kandahar. For one thing, it's a very busy airport with everything from airliners to jet fighters to transports to UAV's flying around constantly. I stood behind the pilot as we got vectors to a final approach course. We were routed farther out than normal and put on a 25 mile final…everything was working OK….except, that the pilot decided to configure the aircraft at 25 miles…this slows us down to a crawl, which isn't bad if you're the only airplane in the sky going to that airport, but when you have airliners coming up your tail at 80 miles an hour faster than you, it's kind of frowned upon. I saw the situation developing from the get-go but part of my job is to let them make mistakes so they can learn from them. Well, it began to get interesting. He finally got on course and began his descent…the only problem was that he wasn't watching his distance and he started too early, so he was a thousand feet low, and I had to tell him to stop descending. He had gotten on course, but the wind was blowing us left, then further left, then further left and he was just flying a heading, instead of watching the instrument needles that were telling him he was almost completely off course.

I ended up having to give him directions to get back to course, the copilot was trying to help, telling him the same things, but he would make a correction, then immediately turn back to his heading. This succeeded in moving him approximately 5 feet in the correct direction. This wasn't a recipe for success. Finally, after ten miles of this, approach control finally told us to break off the approach. (There were a couple big, fast airplanes coming up our tail) Neither pilot nor copilot heard or understood the radio call, so I quickly told them over interphone what to do, turning 90 degrees off our course to get away from the final approach course. We were then vectored around and eventually able to start another approach, this time from much closer to the airfield. Again, the pilot let the wind blow us until his instrument was fully deflected from the course, but that was about when the copilot declared the runway in sight and the pilot went in and landed….20 feet left of the center of the runway. You really can't make this stuff up. Reality is its own crazy story. That was my most recent adventure. The flight back today was uneventful and the other pilot did a very nice job. I was in the copilot seat today and was able to enjoy a nice relaxing flight back to Kabul.

The Open House was interesting as well. There were approximately 1200 people there. The Afghan base commander had invited a bunch of civic leaders and their families to visit, as a recruiting tool, and it was a big thing to have the families and kids there. It was very similar to airshows we have at home, without all the stunt flying. We had our airplane open and invited people to come on and take a look. The funniest thing was watching from the plane as the kids were let loose to go look at the planes. As a herd they would charge and run from one plane to the other, en masse. It was pretty funny and a little 9 or 10 year old Afghan boy summed it up when he was standing next to me in the cargo compartment watching as 20 of his friends and siblings climbed over each other trying to climb onto the flight deck at the same time. He turned to me and in very good English said, "they look like a bunch of monkeys!" They were hanging off the walls so it was a very accurate statement. I'd say the oddest thing for me though, culturally, was the luncheon afterwards. It was held in a big hangar, and tables were set to feed all 1200 plus people. The food was laid out. And then all the men went and got their food. The women and children were relegated to the back of the hangar, after the men were done getting their food, then the male children were allowed up, then finally the female children and then the women. It was a culture shock, and was difficult to watch, but the food was delicious.

I just don't understand a culture that puts women as being below men. I don't get it. But, that's part of our job here to try to understand, but I don't think I will ever understand that. The kids were fun to have on the airplane, to make them laugh and to joke around with.

Back to my previous comment about sometime reality biting and our need to accept it; it's a fact of life and nature that things happen that we don't have control over. We can do our best. We can make our choices. Sometimes, though things just happen and we have to rely on faith. I finished the Book of Mormon again on New Year's Eve. I'd made it a goal and though I had to read over a hundred pages that night, I accomplished my goal. There was one thing that really stood out to me, that I've seen in other places in the scriptures, but had never noticed how clear this teaching was until this time through. In 3 Nephi, when Jesus Christ was teaching the Nephites (for those that don't know, the Book of Mormon contains the account of when Christ came to the American continent after his resurrection and ascension into heaven; he came to America and taught the people that which he'd taught in Israel) we are taught about faith. In 3 Nephi 26 verses 9 to 11 we are told, "And when they shall have received this, which is expedient that they should have first, to try their faith, and if it shall so be that they shall believe these things then shall the greater things be made manifest unto them. And if it so be that they will not believe these things, then shall the greater things be withheld from them, unto their condemnation. Behold, I was about to write them, all which were engraven upon the plates of Nephi, but the Lord forbade it, saying: I will try the faith of my people."

We are given many things. We are asked to do many things. Often things happen to us that we don't understand. The Lord has many mysteries that we are not told. Yet, as we are given more knowledge, then more is opened and unfolded unto us. But we're not given that knowledge until after we've exercised faith. I've talked about faith before. Faith is believing that which you can't see, but which is true. Faith is believing the words of the Lord without having to be shown signs and wonders. Faith begins with a desire to believe. But, further knowledge isn't bestowed to us until AFTER our faith is tried. How can our faith be tried? Oh, there are myriad ways that our faith can be tried. There can be physical trials. There can be mental trials. There can be derision from the world. We can have personal problems blow up in our face, we can have anything that we consider a trial come upon us to make us question those things that we begin to feel in our heart is true. When we desire to learn what is truth, that is when we have contentions with neighbors or family or spouses, or problems with employment. Why? Why is it that when we desire to know the truth, to do good, to grow, that is when problems affront us on every side?

In a word – Satan.

The devil is miserable. He's had thousands of years of misery. He was an angel in heaven in the pre-mortal existence. He was highly favored of the Lord. And he rebelled and was cast out. His rebellion led to his being cast out with a third of the hosts of heaven and being sent here to earth without a body, without the opportunity to EVER have a body. He desires that we become miserable like he and his minions are. The Lord allows this so that we have the agency to choose good or evil, happiness or misery, and so that we can learn from our trials. When we go through trials, our faith can do one of two things; either it will grow, or it will diminish. The one thing it won't do is stay in the same place. "There comes no witness until after the trial of our faith." This is a true statement. Satan wants our misery. When we succumb to his enticements, our faith dwindles, we seek for momentary pleasures that don't last. We become numb to goodness; we find fault and try to bring others down. This is because we are slowly becoming miserable. Look at the world! It is miserable and tries to find humor in hurting others, dragging people down to misery, and it's thought to be funny. Satan laughs as the world slowly enters the gutter and gets on his level.

I've been amazed at all the reality shows that have become so popular in the last ten years. Gone are shows that teach healthy habits and good friendships. Instead we have reality shows where backbiting, double dealing, lying, cheating, slandering, jumping from bed to bed, and all other hideous practices are shown as the norm, and the way to be happy…all to get the money or the girl or whatever. It's disgusting that we find entertainment in others misery. OK, done with my soapbox. I just am amazed at how far and how fast the world is falling. We're becoming as Sodom and Gomorrah. Anything goes is the attitude of the day. Make yourself happy at others expense is another. Don't help others unless you get something out of it! Hypocrisy! We need some good old fashioned trials to make us look to our maker to realize that everything we have comes from him. When we see that, then we can realize our true potential. I've written now for 9 months about the changes that have come into my life. I'm so thankful for the changes. I love my wife and family and the changes that have come have blessed us immensely. Of course this is why I share these teachings and perspectives with all of you. They help me as I go through my trials. Hopefully, you're gleaning insights in your own trials.

There's been another aspect to my learning and since we're talking about trials today it fits in nicely. I spent a couple days watching some church history videos. Many of you know, or have heard about the Mormon pioneers. You've heard of Joseph Smith and the persecution the early members of the church of Jesus Christ of Latter Day Saints suffered. If you haven't then this will be new, if you have, then it's a nice refresher. Persecution of the church came about from the very beginning when Joseph stated that he'd seen God the Father and Jesus Christ and that they'd told him to join none of the churches of his day. When he received the golden plates to translate the Book of Mormon and received further teaching and counsel from heavenly messengers, there was further persecution. There was persecution right up until he and his brother were killed in Carthage Jail. But the persecution did not stop, and neither did the work of the Lord. The path had been set up and the keys of the priesthood had been restored. Brigham Young as chief Apostle, having been called as a prophet, seer, and revelator, became the president of the Church and in vision saw the move of the Church to the Rocky Mountains. The pioneers faced hardship, storm, loss of life, as they walked and moved handcarts and wagons across almost 1500 miles of rugged terrain. They bore their afflictions and lifted their voices in song…Now the question to be asked is … WHY?

And we come full circle to the answer – Faith. Their faith was tried. Their faith was tried in the wilderness, in the cities of Ohio, Missouri and Illinois, as they were kicked out of one home or another, as many were persecuted and tarred and feathered. Their faith was tried as the Prophet Joseph Smith was killed and as they were forced to leave their homes, their land, their newly built temple and move across the plains through the mountains to a home in the Rocky Mountains. When gold is refined and made pure it is smelted and made hotter and hotter until all the impurities are burned out. The persecution and the trials were a refiner's fire for the saints of the early church. They faced hardships that we can't even imagine. We face hardships such as "they're making fun of me because I don't drink or smoke and want to stay a virgin". There are many other daily trials we go through, some harder than others. But, each of us go through a refiner's fire so that we will either come out pure and clean, or we will be burned up, if we let our faith fail. It's a personal matter. I'm thankful that I've been going through my refiner's fire. It's been a tough road and I'm thankful that I'm able to share my learning with you.

I hope that my life will have an impact on your life. I'm not perfect, I've got a long way to go, but I have a hope in Christ that as I continue, I will make it through my refiner's fire and be welcomed home to live with my companion and help meet, my best friend and lover, my wife, and live for all eternity together. That's the promise. That's the blessing that we're promised if we make it through, be with our loved ones forever, become as our Heavenly Father and live with him. I open many things and many discussion topics in these chapters because it's amazing and beautiful doctrine to me. We are here on this earth to learn, to grow and to have joy. Joy is all encompassing. Joy is not momentary, not fleeting followed by pain or remorse. Joy doesn't wake up with a hangover or say to itself what did I do!!! Joy is powerful and constant when we find it. Joy comes from living correctly, learning the Lord's plan, and following it.

I'm working on finding and having that joy as a constant.

Life is a gift. Life is to be treasured. Life is to be lived, not vicariously through others, but in making our own proper decisions. We have agency. We have choice. And this is life eternal, that we might know thee the true and living God and Jesus Christ whom thou hast sent! What is the meaning of life? Is it an accident of nature? Is it a quantum shift in the cosmos? Is it a cosmic joke? NO! Life has meaning. Life has a purpose. Find out your purpose. I'm finding mine and I'm sharing it with you because you are my friends and family and I want you to know what I know. I love life. I love the insanity of it and the chaos AND the joy that comes as I find my correct path through the chaos and insanity. It's a sane life in an insane world. STARK RAVING SANE! That's the truth and crux of the matter. Find your own insanity and live it sanely. Find the truth and follow it. When you look for the truth, pray for knowledge and by the Spirit I promise you will receive an answer.

For myself, I know that God the Father and Jesus appeared to Joseph Smith. I know the Book of Mormon was translated from plates of ancient date written by prophets from the American continent. I know the Gospel has been restored to the earth at this time and that we have the opportunity to find out the truth for ourselves. I know revelation, having received many personal revelations from my Heavenly Father. I know the "Mountain of the

Lord's House was established in the Tops of the Mountains" as foretold by Isaiah when the pioneers moved to the Great Salt Lake. I invite you all to find out what is true.

Chapter 41

HISTORY LESSONS

"Those who don't remember history are destined to repeat it." Edmund Burke – 1750 This quote is much utilized and is apropos to those things we are doing here in Afghanistan as well as things going on throughout the world. There are so many things I've studied and worked on this week. But, I wanted to start this week with a philosophical debate of things that we do here, that tell me we haven't learned the lessons history has taught. Nor do our students seem to remember well the lessons they're taught. It's a catch 22 sometimes. Many years ago there was both a book and a movie entitled catch-22. It was an intriguing kaleidoscope of futility matched by rigor. The premise is that whatever you do, you're stuck. It was a satire against war, but at the same time pointing out that without it, we would have been in a state possibly worse. To sum up the premise, a catch-22 is when you're darned if you do, darned if you don't, between a rock and a hard place. Etc…

We find ourselves in that situation often here. We're told to produce an Afghan Air Force and do so in a timely manner, but produce a western style advanced fully capable air force. Those two things don't exactly go together. In order to build a fully capable air force, it's going to take time, and to try to do so in a timely manner .... won't build a fully capable air force. So we're in a Catch-22 scenario here. Ahhh, the joy of trying to figure out which is the lesser of two evils! Oh well, mine is not to question why...and all that jazz.

In keeping with my history lesson, this week's history is one of busy meetings, trying to inform leadership of actuality without presenting information in too cold of a manner. While at the same time I've been handling personnel issues and even managing to squeeze in a couple of very important flights. Ahh, yes, the flights are the real meat of the story anyways. This week didn't disappoint. I flew two days in a row, and actually flew three times this week. The first, I was just returning from the open house in Kandahar, which was the subject of last week's blog. But the third and fourth were both very important flights. Both were the "recommend ride" for two of our three students. A recommend ride is the ride just before a check ride to have an experienced pilot say that yes! They're ready for their check ride. The lot fell to me to do it since the other instructors that have been here as long as I were either on leave or going out of town for different reasons. I'm not complaining, because I tend to think that I give a pretty tough instructional sortie comparatively speaking. I figure if I'm harder on them than their check ride will be, then they'll do well on their check ride.

On the first flight I took a student and it was a good flight. We flew a traditional sortie to up north and enroute I simulated a fire coming out of the instrument panel. I made my student put on his oxygen mask and pointed out how difficult it is to communicate with it on. Then going through the proper checklists we saw how difficult it is having the Afghan Loadmasters that don't understand the checklists very well, at least for emergencies and I found myself having to unbuckle, turn around in my seat and show the loadmaster where the circuit breakers were that would need to be pulled to stop the fire, should it be a real occurrence. All this in preparation to fly into the terminal area and begin our training! We got to our training airport and prepared a speedy arrival. My student made the mistake of beginning a descent early, but he recovered nicely and after several patterns the real fun began. First I told him to fly a mid-flap approach, but when he called for flaps, I simulated that they wouldn't move. It's always funny how, when you change something on students, they panic or get all flustered. Such was the case here as well…It took a few seconds for him to wrap his head around it and change to the correct procedure. Then the fun continued. I simulated engines failing a couple of different times for multiple different reasons, making him use correct procedures, and then calling out aircraft on the runway, making him go around on one engine. Now this is not that difficult low weight, but we were flying the heaviest airplane in the fleet and we were loaded with fuel, so we were a pig in the air…It made it very interesting indeed. But, thankfully, he's been learning well and his procedures were correct. (They'd better be we've been beating them up on using correct procedures for 6 months.)

We flew some different types of instrument approaches and again had simulated engine problems, after which we returned to Kabul. Along the way of course he let his guard down and thought he could relax. As we entered the Kabul airspace and were being turned onto an instrument approach to the Kabul airport…wouldn't you know it but one of our engines failed again. This time it through him for a loop and it took him 15 miles to not only get it under control, but to get control of his approach as well. Nonetheless, he did a good job and I recommended him to go to his check ride, which I hear he passed even though he made some mistakes, happens to everyone!

The next day I followed the same profile with the other student, this time I got to be in the left seat instead of the right seat, which gives me more control. This other student was getting a copilot check ride so his skills didn't have to be as polished as the other guys'. What's funny though was that the other student's flying skills were better, his general knowledge suffered. The second student's flying wasn't as good, but his knowledge was better. Having just done the exact same ride the day before, I could have a lot of fun with it and we had multiple issues. We had simulated fires in our electrical panel. We had engines simulated flameout; we had multiple simulated problems and go-arounds and all in all it was a very tough ride. He did ok. Again, I recommended him for check ride and I believe he passed as well, though I was in meetings all day when he took it so I didn't get to ask.

All of this brings me back to the beginning. History! If we don't learn from it, we'll repeat it. History here in Afghanistan is mixed. They've been at war for thirty years. I find we keep doing things reminiscent of the way things were done in Vietnam, which held lots of opportunities to learn from. But such is life I guess. When it comes to life, though, we have many opportunities to learn and change and grow and if we learn from our mistakes and/or others mistakes we won't be destined to repeat them.

A big source of my study this week has involved debt. Personal debt, national debt, etc… I'm not going to get into any sort of debate about national debt. I've been reading the latest Glenn Beck book about it and suffice it for me to say that I believe that our country has been awash in bad judgment for years. But the reading has been in line with my personal studies and plans. See, for a long while now I've been trying to get out of debt. I finally figured out that I've been wasting my income paying someone else, essentially being a slave. Debt is a curse. It's not a blessing to help a starved economy. Debt is a wicked task master that is encircling our nation, the world, and all people and laughing all the way to the bank. It's crippling.

One thing I've learned, over this past year especially, is that there's a way out. There always is, you just have to develop the gumption and the resolve to do it. Therefore, in line with my previous year's growth and learning my first resolution for the New Year is to get out of debt, completely out of personal credit and loan debt. I know it'll take longer for the house and the cars, but that's the goal. Be done with it! Why! Because I will not live another moment chained to that burden and curse that I'd bought into for years. I robbed Peter to pay Paul, stole from Mary to enable Jane…etc…what a pathetic excuse. But this last year I saw, the issue. Another thing that I saw was the absolute need to test God. What! You say, "How can that not be blasphemous?" Well, it is one of those miracles that we are taught. In Malachi 3:8, 10 it states.

"Will a man rob God? Yet ye have robbed me. But ye say, Wherein have we robbed thee? In tithes and offerings. Bring ye all the tithes into the storehouse, that there may be meat in mine house, and *prove me now herewith*, saith the Lord of hosts, if I will not open you the windows of heaven, and pour you out a blessing, that there shall not be room enough to receive it." (italics added) This year we have definitely put that to the test. This is one of the only times that the Lord commands us to test Him. His blessings are innumerable and in this instance we're blessed not just spiritually, but temporally as well. Now, I'm not going to go into any details about what I pay, or not, or whatever, because that isn't the point, the point is that Tiffany and I have tested this principle and have found that it is one hundred percent true. The Lord truly does open the windows of heaven and bless us. In that regard, we should be out of debt soon. I thank the Lord that He offers us this opportunity, because this is a blessing that is offered to all, and it doesn't matter how much or how little one makes. The Lord provides. It's been a constant blessing this past year that I've been gone. All our needs and wants have been met!

Now, I don't feel the need to go further on that subject now, maybe at some later date, but this week, today actually, one of mine and Tiffany's friends asked us a question that went along with the majority of my study this week and it's a subject that is not an easy one to bring up just in casual conversation, because the answer makes a bold statement which I make with all the assurance of one that has received a witness from God the Father of its truth. The paragraph, question and then my answer follow:

"I was reading Facebook and I 'like' a page from the actress Fairuza Balk and she posted a couple of hours ago a message saying that she had watched the documentary called 'Jesus Camp' and that she was quite taken aback by the message. Now, my question is the following: Until I came to the US, I had only been aware of 2 divisions of the Christian faith: the Catholics and the Protestants. Then I went to the US and stayed with a family who was following the Baptist practices and met another family who were following the Evangelist branch. I've heard of the Jehovah Witnesses although I have the feeling that they tend more towards the Jewish faith (I haven't read anything on the subject, so it's a pure stab in the dark).

And obviously, I now know about your church. So I'm wondering how many 'sub-divisions' are there within the Christian faith and in laymen's terms, what is the difference between them? I hope I'm not opening a can of worms there... As you can see, I still don't know an awful lot about Christianity.... But I'm learning every day and I'm enjoying learning!"

The question of why there are so many different "Christian" religions is one that is as old as it is both difficult and easy to answer. So, I'll do what I enjoy doing, tell a story, start at the beginning, work to the end then cover the middle…in other words muddle it all up and hope you can sort it out!

During Jesus Christ's ministry, in fact predating Christ's ministry, Prophets were called, both in Israel and on the American continent, to establish the church of Christ on the earth. They taught the Law of Moses, it being a type, or an example, set to lead followers to a belief in Jesus Christ who would come as the Son of God to establish His kingdom upon the Earth. Now, when Christ came, that is exactly what He did. He called Apostles to be special witnesses for him, Seventy to be ministers of the word, teachers, priests, etc. were all called to teach and expound the scriptures and the words that He taught. He gave the Apostles authority to act in His name. All of this was set up so that after His crucifixion they would be able to continue spreading the Gospel to all the inhabitants of the world. The authority given to the apostles were called Keys of the Priesthood and were passed by the laying on of hands. However, after the death and resurrection of Christ, after the church began to grow, there were many disputations over doctrine, being one of the reasons there are so many epistles in the Bible. One by one the Apostles were killed in different parts of the world and they were unable to get back together to call more. Eventually a Roman emperor was converted and declared Christianity the state religion. The problem was that many of the truths that had been taught by the apostles, and the authority of the priesthood they'd held had been lost or misinterpreted. The Emperor called a council to decide on correct doctrine, The Council of Nice, was held and from there the Catholic Church developed. However, the authority, the full doctrine, and the priesthood itself had fallen away and was not found on the earth. Paul the apostle even talked about it when he spoke of the second coming of Christ, he stated that "these things shall not come to pass except there be a falling away first." He prophesied that the true Gospel of Christ would be missing from the earth.

That didn't stop the Gospel, as they had it, from spreading throughout the world though. A period of time known as the dark ages followed. Learning was disapproved of and eventually you had people who began to question the "Christianity" and the teachings they were receiving. They did not hold it as not being correct with what the Bible said. Martin Luther and others "protested" the teachings of the Catholic Church and were excommunicated, starting their own churches to attempt to put the teachings correctly into practice as they saw them. That's one reason you see so many "protestant" churches and really the majority of "Christian" churches are considered protestant because they were founded by someone protesting the teachings of the Catholic Church.

I liken the church that Jesus Christ built on the earth to a mirror. A true mirror is without blemish, is perfectly formed and is magnificent to behold. What happened after his death is that the mirror was smashed. Some gathered some pieces and stated, "here I have the original" or there is the original, yet all they had were pieces of the whole. If you've ever seen a broken mirror you can see that it is not perfect, even if you get most of the pieces, you're still missing some key things and there are broken lines running through. The only way to have it back together is to "restore" it or in other words, have it made anew.

Eventually you had Catholics, Protestants, Baptists, Evangelicals, Methodists, Lutherans, Episcopals, Seventh Day Adventists, Jehovah's witnesses, etc…all purporting to teach the word of God. Only NONE of them taught the same doctrine. None of them acknowledged revelation. All of them claimed that the Bible was it, that God no longer spoke to man. This is fact. I do not disparage any other religion. I believe that any religion that teaches a man to walk better and live a Christian life is a good thing. However, we are told that there would be a marvelous work and a wonder prior to the Lord's second coming. We are told that there would be a restoration of all things prior to his return. Restoration!

That means to rebuild, to place again, to restore to the way it was. There is constancy in the Lord's path. When God makes a promise to us, He will fulfill it. He promised that He would restore.

I've spoken of Joseph Smith before. The truth is that after he sought wisdom through prayer, as counseled by James in the Bible, he went to the woods to pray and once again the Lord called a prophet on the earth. God the Father and Jesus Christ appeared unto Joseph smith and told him to join NONE of the churches of that time. They were missing many important points of the Gospel including the authority to act in God's name. Revelation…Modern revelation…not revelation from two thousand years previously, but actual heavenly messengers again came to earth. John the Baptist came and gave Joseph and Oliver the authority to baptize. Peter, James and John the same apostles from the Bible, came and gave the keys of the higher priesthood that had been conferred upon them by Jesus Christ. Joseph was called as a Prophet and was directed to call Apostles to whom he passed on the keys of the priesthood. All the offices of the original church were restored. And today the Church of Jesus Christ of Latter-day Saints, restored to the earth through the prophet Joseph Smith, has a membership in excess of 13 million members worldwide and is continuing to grow at a rapid pace and will grow until it has reached every nation, kindred, tongue and people. That's the thing. The Second Coming of the Lord Jesus Christ is not far distant, though no one knows the day nor the hour, but as the Gospel is preached to all the world it is that much closer to His coming.

In keeping with my teaching about the necessity for all this I learned that "when you climb a ladder you must begin at the bottom and go step by step until you reach the top. So it is with salvation." We have a long way to go. I have a long way to go though I am no longer sliding backwards but moving forwards. I love the Gospel. I love teaching and learning the Gospel. There are so many wonderful truths that are waiting for us. I don't mean to offend, but I state unequivocally that the mirror that was Christ's church has been restored in these latter days and is encompassed by the Church of Jesus Christ of Latter Day Saints. I've prayed to know this for myself and I feel it burn within me. I've cried real tears this week as I've studied about the Restoration of the Gospel, especially today as

I read and studied Doctrine and Covenants, a book of modern revelations. This is saying a lot, because I don't cry. Ask Tiffany, there's very little that makes me cry, yet as I've studied, I've cried this week. (I think some music helped because I'm very sensitive to the Spirit through music.) Heavenly Father wants our happiness.

There you have a long answer to a supposedly simple question. The truth is that many churches were formed because people realized that things were missing from the church; that many truths were not taught as in the Bible and they tried to interpret through their understanding and they formed many, many different churches all under the name "Christian".

The Spirit tells the truth of all things. It speaks peace to our soul should we study out our questions in our mind. One last thing on this topic; one other thing I learned is that if we don't ask specific questions to the Lord in prayer, we can't expect the Lord to provide answers? The more specific we are the more specific He'll be with an answer. The Lord knows what we need before we ask, but He tries our faith by making us ask. That's why we are told many times, ask and it shall be given, seek and ye shall find, knock and it shall be opened…they are all action verbs, not passive. We need to make the effort.

OK, on a different topic altogether, here are my resolutions as I've come up with them for this New Year.

1. I will read the New Testament all the way through
2. I will seek the Lord every day to do his will
3. I will seek to have the Light of the Lord in my eyes
4. I will live what I believe
5. I will be a light to those around me
6. I will continue to reread the Book of Mormon
7. I will lose my gut (this is a temporal thing, but while I'm not fat…I don't like my belly)
8. I will live with my family again this year! (This is an important one, considering by the time I live with them again, it'll have been two years almost since I moved them for this deployment.)
9. I will make my weaknesses strengths and lastly
10. I will be out of debt!

There you have it. Those are my resolutions for this year. I've already been working on many of them for the past several months so I will continue to do so. What are your resolutions? What do you think? Where do you see yourself a year from now? Life has a purpose, have you found yours?

If you have more questions, ask! It gives me reason to study specific topics. I love studying the Gospel and sharing it, I'm sure you've figured that out by now. Anyways, have a great week and enjoy it. Take care and seriously, if you have questions, ask!

By the way I hope nothing I say offends. I try not to be offensive. I want to share my growth and learning and I love that I have this opportunity. Thank you for taking time to read, if you've made it this far! May the Lord bless you and the devil miss you, as my seminary teacher used to say. You're all in my prayers daily. Don't worry, as more Afghans try to kill me with crazy flying you will be the first to know!

Kandahar Open House

Piling on the plane at Kandahar Open House

Meal at Kandahar Open House

Chapter 42

LIFE'S A GRAND ADVENTURE

I don't even know how to start this week. It's been an insane week, and the main thing I have to say is that, "I'm tired!" My studies have suffered a little due to my being worn out. It's an interesting phenomenon, being worn out and tired, especially when you are constantly busy. The lack of energy stems from a very simple reason. This week has been a week of flying, flying, trying to fly, more flying and some more trying to fly, weather, winds, snow, broken airplanes, long waits, late nights, long days, and so by the time evening rolls around, I'm beat. There how's that for a chapter, the end!

OK, maybe I'm kidding about ending it there. When I tend to write thousands of words, writing a short little couple line chapter would just not fly. (pun intended)

I was scheduled to fly 5 out of the last 7 days. Yes, it's been busy. I flew last weekend. I can't even really remember what I did that day. It was an eventful day, obviously! I enjoyed the fact that I was flying a lot. On Sunday, I was asked to take a plane that had seen its fair share of problems out to fly and demonstrate the engine problems it was having to maintenance. The previous day they had attempted to run the engine to verify the problem the previous pilot had noticed, but they were unable to duplicate any of the problems. I don't know exactly why they couldn't; they just were unable to duplicate the problems. Now these aren't simple little problems, they're problems like the fuel being taken away for a second or two from the engine, then kicked back in which causes the airplane to pull to the right then back to the left. This is not good, especially when you've got an Afghan at the controls. The previous day the crew aborted their takeoff and turned the plane over to maintenance. However, like I said, they couldn't duplicate the problem, so they were sending an engine guy with us to check it out while we flew it to verify the problem.

I didn't mind doing this, because I prefer to show maintenance when there's a problem. Truth in advertising as you might say. Sometimes they just have a hard time believing us until they see it with their own eyes. We all tend to be like that though, don't we? So, I went to fly it, but we decided to do an engine run on the ground prior to going flying just to see. Immediately the problem showed its ugly face and we repeated it 6 times. This was good enough for the maintainer, so we just taxied back to parking and gave it back to maintenance. Duh! We told them there was a problem, but until they saw it they had trouble believing.

Monday I was scheduled to take one of our qualified pilots up to north to practice instrument work, engine shutdowns, and various other fun things to challenge his skills. However, as we sat for an hour at the end of the runway waiting for people to land, airliners to take off, children to play, cats and dogs living together (ok I exaggerate, but we really are the least priority for takeoff!) we finally were number one for takeoff. I was pretty proud because we'd been able to get ahead of our group commander in another C-27 and he'd gone to his plane half an hour earlier. We got in front of them because we're just cool like that. Finally, we were number one. We were ready….right up until the warning light for our engine popped on. A drive that runs our propeller and generators, was failing so we had to tuck our tail between our legs and request to go back to parking. I shut down the generator, but missed the special disconnect switch for the drive. The light comes on when the drive is out of oil and it's overheating. We got into parking and shut down and climbed up with maintenance to see if it was just low on fluid. When the steamy smoke from a burned out drive came out of the engine door after we opened it…we knew we weren't going anywhere. The drive had burned itself up, hence the light. Apparently, it was out of oil….something maintenance must've missed on their preflight. Oh well, such is life. We turned the plane over to them again and called it a day. Back to the grind of meetings, meetings, meetings, meetings! Had I actually flown, I would've missed most of my meetings that day, but since I didn't I had meetings all afternoon long and ended up being the last person to leave the squadron that day. My brain was drained from too many meetings! Ugh!

I walked back into the squadron after a long meeting and noticed on the scheduling board that I was suddenly scheduled to fly again the next day. I was scheduled with both of our special, awesome, most dedicated and experienced pilots (insert sarcasm here). Actually, it was with the two guys that we demoted to the right seat only due to their demonstrated lack of skill. We had an interesting flight though. We flew up to Mazar I Sharif and spent almost five hours flying around doing different skills training. When we got there the visibility was OK, not great, but dropping. Due to that fact we did all of our pattern work first. It's always interesting doing pattern work when we're told to fly our patterns to the left (known as the south of the field). I've mentioned many times the short hills there that you have to watch out for. Like every other time, there were several instances where I had to direct the copilots exactly what to do so they wouldn't hit the mountains because they get very task saturated when I shut down engines on them and make them fly single engine, heavy-weight and to the left. They all seem to sweat, and the stop looking outside. That's what makes it fun to challenge them. Both guys did OK. In fact, the one that flies horribly even managed to not try to flip us over by using the wrong rudder, though he was very tentative and slow making me prompt him to make correct inputs. At least he wasn't kicking full opposite rudder like he's done before. That can flip the airplane upside down and that's not recommended at low altitude.

We finished our pattern work and went on to instrument approaches, which was good because the weather had turned yucky, low visibility and misty--perfect for instrument training. Again, they did ok, but not great. At one point, for each of them, I had to take the airplane or give very specific directions to them about what they needed to do. With the one guy, again same guy with horrible habits, we had a problem. We were flying the approach and I let him go and go and go, until we were descending and departing the protected area of the approach. At that point I yanked the controls out of his hand and stopped our descent, turning so that we'd get back on course. Then I gave him the airplane back. Honestly, I don't know when these guys will really be qualified. They're just not! At least, the first guys aren't. The later students had a lot more emphasis on instrument flying after seeing where the deficiencies were in the first pilots. Things are going well, just slow! Slow because we have to reteach things every day.

After being worn out on that flight, I got back to the squadron, and noticed the scheduling board....yep you guessed it, scheduled for the next day to fly, this time with our current troubled student. He's the only student we have in the pipeline right now and he's difficult because even though his heart's in the right place, his memory fails him and his comprehension fails him, usually at the worst times. But, we went to go fly, and the weather was horrible. Actually, the weather was perfect for an instrument training sortie, but we were supposed to do a visual flying only sortie. We only flew for two hours, out and back, but it's keeping him flying. To keep things interesting, when we got back to the squadron, I just happened to check the scheduling board...and there was my bloody name again, this time scheduled for a nice long flight.

I just had to laugh. I was tired; flying will do that to you, even just attempting to do so can wear you out after a while. I came in and prepped to fly the next day. We were taking a truck to the other side of the country. No problem. The only problem was the weather was not being very nice. We got our first snow yesterday and it hit right as I got to the airplane. Snow isn't bad per se, just if it sticks to the airplane, and we didn't have any de-icing equipment on base. Amazingly enough, we managed set everything up. The weather forecast was such that I couldn't rationally decide to cancel so we went. We ended up being the only flight to go that day, the others ended up cancelling. For us it was a nice uneventful flight. I flew right seat on the way to Shindand and left seat on the way back. I had fun with the pilot that I was flying with. Since we didn't have any passengers, just a truck, when we got into the downwind pattern to land, without telling the other pilot, I took away one of his engines and he suddenly had to do a single engine approach. The point I explained later was that, you never know when something is going to happen so you always have to be prepared. I chose to fly the left seat back since Kabul was supposed to be getting snow dumped on it and the weather was intriguing. I flew the flight back, our autopilot was broken, and Air traffic control for some reason refused to give me an instrument clearance so I had to remain clear of clouds…so I got to do my favorite thing, cloud surfing. This is where you fly along the tops of the clouds, turn the plane sideways through arches that sometimes form, and make the one passenger in the back puke! Got back to Kabul and the weather was fun, low ceilings (low hanging clouds) and poor visibility, with random snow showers, like I said, fun! I enjoyed a challenging approach, landed and called it a day.

All this is really pointing to several things. One, I'm tired. Two, I've had fun this week. Three, I relaxed in the evening when I was worn out, but my Skype has been working great this week so I was able to talk to and see my beautiful wife every day this week and see the kids and chat and read scriptures with them. I love it. They've been pretty cool, making an igloo in the front yard, hollowing it out, building a fire and roasting marshmallows in the fire. So cool! It's also been hilarious watching them deck out to go outside, finding my uniforms and other clothing to stay warm.

I'd been thinking all week about certain topics and found that I have been learning from all the different things I've done. And my studies, and relaxation movies, and my week in general have pointed to a certain lesson that I, and we, and everyone really, can use. It stems from a question. The question is simple:

What is truth?

I've spoken for weeks, and months discussing many topics, discussing different ideas, many spiritual experiences, and acknowledging that through the spirit we can know the truth of all things. I've repeated many times that if we seek we'll find, if we knock we'll find it opened, and if we ask it shall be given. But really, do you know what truth is? Do I? I've spent a lifetime learning. I've spent this last year learning spiritually. Here are some things I've picked up this week and this year.

Truth is eternal. Truth doesn't change. Truth is real; it doesn't bend to the whims of a naïve or prolific public. It isn't subject to the winds of change or the whims of public opinion. Truth is! But again, how do we know? How do we find it? Truth is all around us. There is truth found in scientific exploration. There is truth found in astronomy, biology, sociology…in all aspects of life we see truth. Truth is eternal as I said. It doesn't change and allows us to learn and grow.

One thing I've noticed this week, and the last few weeks, is that while truth is eternal, we humans are fallible and subject to one of the worst and hardest to overcome problems, one that the devil uses with abandon. The thing that plagues us is perception. Perception doesn't care about truth. Perception makes truth irrelevant. Perception, at least in the eyes of society, often is more important that truth. I don't buy that. Truth is more important than perception, but our perception can mask truth so that we are unable to see it. I've had several experiences where our perceptions cloud what is true. I know that I have perceptions about how things are here in Afghanistan, how our students are, how these pilots are, and my perceptions cloud the truth. I've found that truth is usually somewhere in between different perceptions and we need to learn to see through the cloud and find the golden kernel of truth and hold on to it.

This holds true with all things, whether it is with human relations or with spiritual insights. Spiritual insight, human development, scientific discovery, is all governed by one fact. All that we have, all truths are eternal, given to us by God our Heavenly Father and we have the opportunity to KNOW the truth, to find the truth, but we won't find it overnight, we won't know all things even in this life. In John 8:32 Jesus stated, “And ye shall know the truth, and the truth shall make you free.” In some of my reading this week I learned another couple lessons regarding truth. Truth can never be defeated, even if people forget about it momentarily. Truth exists outside of us and it is imperative that we find out for ourselves what truth is and what fiction is; what is truth, and what are lies or deception.

Another interesting anecdote that coincides with this is that idleness gives time to despair, to complain, to feel pains and let ourselves be let down. Finding something to do that is worthwhile fills more than just our time, it fills our souls. As we spend time searching for truth, it fills our souls with a desire and a glow, a hunger to fill that void that worldly activities and knowledge just don’t fill. I earlier stated that a friend once told me that we all have a God-sized hole inside of us and we strive to fill it. We’re coming up soon to the “God of the world” time period, at least in the USA…known as the Super Bowl. It’s amazing to me how people get so involved in sports and teams and they LIVE for their team and the outcome of a game, millions of people, millions of dollars, and people worship the players, the teams etc… You see the same thing with the World Cup in Soccer. People are constantly trying to fill that void in their lives.

Why is it so important that we fill that hole with truth? I’ll tell you. After all, I’ve pointed out that truth is eternal, so when we fill that hole with spiritual truth, it LASTS. Heavenly truth isn’t momentary, it doesn’t fade, and it doesn’t fall victim to whims. Heavenly truth fills us and heals our spirits.

How do we find truth then? First, we must seek it. After all, we’re constantly told to seek and we’ll find. So the desire to seek out what is true is the first step. Then, we must act on that desire, study the scriptures, study the words of the prophets, and PUT IN PRACTICE what we learn. Once we’re trying to do what is right, and we’re open to the influence of the Spirit, then we are open to LEARN. In the book Doctrine of Salvation we’re told, “The man that is guided by the Holy Spirit and keeps the commandments of God, he that dwells in God, will have the most clear understanding and ability to judge in every moment, because he is GUIDED by the

Spirit of Truth. And the man that abides in his own abilities, or the knowledge of other men, will not have as clear a vision as that man will have that dwells in truth and is directed in his path by the Holy Ghost."

Before we get to that point where we can be continually guided by the Spirit of Truth, the Holy Ghost, we must learn how to recognize truth. "The Lord hopes that we use our faculties and He gave us reasoning as a gift to measure the truth under certain conditions. In the search for the truths of the Gospel there needs to exist, principally, the teachings by the spirit—The Holy Spirit, speaking to our spirit—and this occurs only through obedience to the Gospel." This is the key. If we want to learn the truths that the lord has prepared for us, we need to strive to live the rules and laws that our Heavenly Father set forth. As we do this we receive further light and knowledge. We receive further understanding. That's the whole purpose of this book. I've been attempting to live the Gospel and it has brought many changes to my life. It's been amazing to see the changes in my family, in my wife, in myself, as we've struggled to do what we know is right, and we've been abundantly blessed and that's what I hope you all see from reading this. It has opened the windows of heaven to us, and changed my perception. When our perceptions come from the Lord we can see truth more clearly.

In Doctrine and Covenants 93:27-28 it states, "And no man receiveth a fullness unless he keepeth his commandments. He that keepeth his commandments receiveth truth and light, until he is glorified in truth and knoweth all things." We won't learn all truths, nor all things in this life, but we are promised that if we learn and study and grow and abide by the commandments we'll continue to learn line upon line, precept upon precept throughout the eternities until we ultimately know all things and become as our Heavenly Father. We will, "grow in knowledge, in light and truth, until finally the perfect day of light and truth arrives." (Doctrine of Salvation)

One last comment from this section – "but man cannot determine, by the force of his own understanding, without the help of the Spirit of God, the power and saving grace of the principles of the Gospel, nor hope to find God. It cannot be done!" At times it will be necessary to walk in faith, as well as through sight to discover truth. Truth is all around us. We just need to open our eyes to the truths that exist. The Gospel has been restored. The Savior died and was resurrected for us. Prophets receive revelation today. The priesthood has been restored. Life is full of wonder, glory, majesty; all things are given us by our Heavenly Father. The greatest of all gifts was the gift of Agency, which allows us to decide for ourselves whether to fall for perceptions of the world, or to seek to see through those perceptions and find truth which can only be shown through the workings of the Spirit on our souls. One other way to note truth, truth brings forth good works. Truth brings forth good feelings of joy, even amidst pain or struggle. Truth at times is sharp, if we've been following the knowledge of the world, truth may even seem harsh or unrealistic, but we can always put it to the Lord's test...Ask, seek, knock! Then wait for a response. The Spirit will whisper to our souls the truth.

D&C 50:17-20,23-24 "Verily I say unto you, he that is ordained of me and sent forth to preach the word of truth by the Comforter, in the Spirit of truth, doth he preach it by the Spirit of truth or some other way? And if it be by some other way it is not of God. And again, he that receiveth the word of truth, doth he receive it by the Spirit of truth or some other way? If it be some other way it is not of God....And that which doth not edify is not of God, and is darkness. That which is of God is light; and he that receiveth light, and continueth in God, receiveth more light and that light growth brighter and brighter until the perfect day."

Chapter 43

HAPPINESS IS A STATE OF MIND

"Life is only what we choose to make it, let us take it, let us be free"...You have to love 80's lyrics from the TV cartoon Robotech. Life is an interesting manifestation of those things we learn, do and attempt. Life is nothing if not an attempt to find our destiny, our place in the world. This week, as always, was full, though for a change, I didn't fly--not once. There will be no stories of craziness, of attempts to take the airplane from danger, nor will there be stories of adventure of the flying type.

However, my week, as always, was busy, full, and exhausting at times. I've spent hours each day teaching ground school to a new student. We discussed important aspects not only of aircraft equipment, but how, why, and in what way we do things differently from his previous experience. I took him out to an airplane twice this week and we crawled all over it and around it, looking at the parts, at how different pieces work together to enable it to lift itself from the bonds of earth and throw itself into the sky, confirming Orville and Wilbur's declaration that man would be able to fly in heavier-than-air machines.

It is refreshing to go into class, initiate our lesson and realize that the student studied, took notes of his studies, and was prepared with questions for the lesson. This is different from the students we've had up to this point, and I feel it will be a wonderful change, although he is the exception, not the rule. Oh well! He's younger for starters, compared to others that we've taught. He's only 42. The majority of guys are mid-forties or older, a lot older, having spent twenty to thirty years in the Afghan Air Forces already. But, this student, comes to us looking younger, desiring to do his best, to learn, to excel at this new phase of his life. It's cool to watch, and to have a hand in molding his education. This next week, I'll have plenty of stories of flying with which to entertain since I believe I'm scheduled to fly 4 or 5 days out of the next week. Then, I'll be departing to pick up another airplane in Italy. That'll be nice, because I could use the break, short though it will be.

Today, Friday, I've happily not gone to work. For the first time in a couple weeks I had the opportunity to have a day off, so I took it and I've thoroughly enjoyed it. I've spent the day in contemplation and study, not to mention the fact that I got to sleep in and after talking to my wonderful wife, I went back to bed for another couple hours. I love talking to her and she really is the best woman ever.

This week has been full of meetings, and challenges. I had to figure out different answers to questions posed by leadership. Following that I had to prepare paperwork to get signed. A lot of what I dealt with this week had to do with the next year's and future year's Air Force structure and numbers of personnel assigned to the C-27 program. I made many changes to the planned force structure in order to make it more realistic and to set up the future of the program. The hard thing is looking at where the program is and where it needs to go. Therefore, I built a plan based on looking at where they need to go, not where they're at, because it's going to take a long time, several years, to get to the point where they need to be. You can't change the fact that it takes a long time to develop pilots and loadmasters. Not to mention all the aspects necessary to run a squadron, especially when you're pretty much starting from scratch. I must say that this is a unique and fun time to be involved in this work. Every day, every week we see changes and growth, or lack of growth, or even stagnation of growth in some areas. In reality, every week is new and exciting.

The hardest thing I've done all week, seriously, was try to get a good deal for my car rental in Italy. I have some issues with using the company that would probably get me the best deal. I refuse to use Europcar, since they stole, or sold, (at least someone in the company did) my credit card information and rented a car last September in my name. Not cool! Therefore, I won't use them, which made it difficult to decide how to rent a vehicle. I spent hours looking online. Finally, a little aggravated and frustrated at the pain in the neck it was, I just made reservations. That lifted a little weight off my shoulders since I'd been letting it bother me. Why? I don't know. Sometimes little things try to get us down, or frustrated, and we have to shrug them off and remember that life is more than the little things.

You know, I really have a good life. Even though I'm 7,000 miles from home, having already been gone for over a year, with a few months still to go, I really can't complain. Sure, there are problems and trials, struggle and frustration, like trying to find a good rental car! But in reality, I have a good life. I have a good woman that is my best friend, my lover and my wife, my help meet, my partner, my buddy and my better half. I've got good kids that are smart, cute, put up with a lot being military brats and all, that are able to take what life throws at them and keep going. I've got an understanding now of the Gospel that I never had before.

In all truth, I live in Neverland. You know; that mystical place second star to the right and straight-on till morning. I live a life that is blessed, and in true warrior fashion…I'm both kid and pirate at the same time. After all, if I'm going to live in Neverland, I need to ensure that it's properly peopled. Why do I say this? Because to live joyfully is to understand oneself; to live fully is to understand that life is that man might have joy. Life is a blessing, not a curse. There are many times that we are pulled down with the weight of the world on our shoulders, but I say BOOO! Not for me. I'd rather be looked at as being weird, being myself and enjoying every second of life that I have, not in a worldly way of momentary pleasure, but in the sublime spiritual happiness that comes from living a clean Gospel oriented life.

Tinkerbelle and Peter Pan would be pleased. Like I've said before, if you don't like Tink, you're weird… OK, I haven't really said that in these pages, but I like Tinkerbelle so sue me. Tiffany is my Tinkerbelle, my little pixie of a wife. She's cute and stubborn and I love it. I'm the 36 year old Peter Pan; I don't want to grow up. That doesn't mean I don't take responsibilities and life seriously, it just means that I can look at life and its myriad problems and laugh. It's not ego, it is just life! It is how it is! How's the saying go? "No use crying over spilled milk." OK, so maybe I should shed some light on this crazy little world of mine. Let me usher you into a minor glimpse of the workings of my mind. I warn you to please keep your hands and legs inside the ride at all times and refrain from standing so that you do not lose your head. That would be sad.

Life in a nutshell is life. It is how it is. I've talked about all the aspects of life, the meaning and purpose, the challenges posed by a tempter who just wants us to suffer, opposition in all things and all that jazz. Now, life is full of fiery darts and temptations. I'm honest in saying I've fallen to more than my fair share, many of which brought about sore repentance and have brought me to the point I am at and that repentance enabled my life to turn around. I've always been a happy person. It's in my nature to laugh at problems. I find that, for me, the more chaotic the better, I thrive on chaos. But I've found that as I made changes in my life my sense of joy and happiness has increased as I've put on the Armor of God.

What is the armor of God? How does it protect us? The armor of God is in short: Loins gird about with truth; the breastplate of righteousness, feet shod with preparation of the gospel of peace; the shield of faith, which will quench the fiery darts of the adversary; the helmet of salvation and finally the sword of the Lord's spirit. The Armor of the Lord protects us from evil. It is truth, faith, righteousness, preparation, learning the Plan of Salvation and fighting back with the Lord's Spirit which will dwell in us and lighten our loads. My favorite scripture is John 14:27 – "Peace I leave with you, my peace I give unto you: not as the world giveth, give I unto you. Let not your heart be troubled, neither let it be afraid." This comes to me often, especially when I am feeling alone or down and it lifts me up, picking up my spirits and renewing my faith and allows my childlike wonder to reawaken.

Life is fun. Life is exciting. Life is full of insanity, which makes it intriguing. We live in a crazy time. We live in the fullness of times when not only will the Gospel be preached to the entire world, but darkness will also cover the earth. There will be no middle ground. One will either grow or fall, there will be no quarter given, no time outs, no penalty box to sit in and wait things out…This time of our life, now, is the game. We are in the middle of the biggest battle ever waged, the battle for our souls. Too often I see people, including myself in the past, sell their souls for temporary pleasure. And it drags down more and more people. So many people look at this life as being all there is. Or, they look at life in a Darwinian way that espouses survival of the fittest, take what you can and leave everyone else behind. I don't aspire to that kind of thinking. I don't subscribe to it either. The Lord even claimed that "For whosoever will save his life shall lose it; and whosoever will lose his life for my sake shall find it. For what is a man profited, if he shall gain the whole world, and lose his own soul? Or what shall a man give in exchange for his soul?" Interesting questions don't you think? A man, or woman, that puts others first, losing themselves in service, finds joy and happiness unbounded. The Lord blesses and increases the joy.

I'd like to take a second to thank some special people that have sent some packages that bring cheer, though they don't always get thanked. While I've been here I've gotten packages from the VFW in Philadelphia, PA thanks to a good friend's family. I've also received a package from the VFW in Scottsboro, AR, thanks to the good brothers and sisters of the church there that participate in such programs. Additionally, my nephew Isaac's classes at his elementary school have sent me two packages filled with loving cards and pictures and food and other stuff. Those gifts come from the heart and I want to thank all that have sent things, because they are treasured and appreciated, because they come selflessly. That's a little bit of losing yourself to find yourself. I hope that all those that have ever sent something to a soldier, sailor, airman or marine that is out on the battlefield understand how much that love and support mean. Well done, thou good and faithful servant!

Happiness comes from within. Happiness comes from following the Gospel. Happiness comes from living a righteous life. Happiness comes from helping others. Happiness is an outer and inner manifestation of the Spirit of the Lord dwelling with you. I'm not talking momentary pleasure, or fleeting joy, but true lasting happiness that can be found wherever you are and in whatever circumstances you find yourself in. This topic has come up so much in my study this week. I love the discussion; I love the passion for life that it evokes. I love the truth, that inner happiness is more important or powerful than gold.

Here are a couple more things from my studies this week. I know, I know, it may seem like I ramble on and on, but I'm just excited. As I said, I love life. I love sharing these treasures I learn and I just can't find the ability in me to stop at a short story…I'm blessedly cursed with the joy of storytelling and the ability to be longwinded as my wife would say. I read a true story this week written by a member of the LDS Church about the loss of her husband and how she struggled, but also how his spirit was allowed to come back and give her glimmers of eternity and let her know that their temple marriage was eternal and enabled her to trust in the Lord and have faith that all was going according to the Lord's plan. The author offered words from her deceased husband that are so poignant to our discussion about how to find true happiness, as shown to her in vision she received while knocked out to have a C-section. "You must make Christ your foundation. As the entire structure of a house rests completely on a firm foundation, so the structure of your life must rest completely on Christ. He is the only foundation that will not crumble in the times ahead. And you must make his church your cornerstone. The Church is true. Live by its precepts and listen to the words of the prophet. Remember these things. Make Christ your foundation and the Church your cornerstone. Study God's word. Pray continually. The power of prayer is real. Attend your meetings faithfully, and have family home evenings. Follow the Spirit. It will lead you aright. These are the ONLY ways to overcome the buffetings of Satan and his forces." That in a nutshell is the key to happiness, regardless of what comes.

Listening to conference talks today, for most of the day, I was struck by how similar all the themes were. The talks all centered on our need to follow the commandments, and not be deceived. We are exhorted to keep all forms of pornography out of our homes and our lives; to teach our children to have faith and to lean upon our own faith in Christ. In other words, we're told to make Christ our foundation, and the Church our cornerstone. Not only that, but President Monson admonished us to be grateful, regardless of what comes our way, be a grateful people. Man is that he might have joy, joy comes from helping others and from doing what's right. Avoid foul language, it chases the Spirit away. Avoid any sort of immorality; the Spirit ceases to strive with man in those circumstances. Don't talk bad about others. There are many more rules we could follow, but really as we strive to do what is right, following commandments becomes natural and we feel happier than ever. I've felt happier in the last nine months, since repenting of my sins, and working hard to make the Spirit a daily part of my life, than I have ever felt my entire life. I attest that the Spirit brings joy. At times it brings tears as well, but those are happy tears.

The last thing to talk about this week is a final quote that always sticks with me whenever I talk about happiness in dealing with trials and how the Spirit can enable us to be happy no matter what happens in our lives. In D&C 122:5-8 it states, "If thou art called to pass through tribulation; if thou art in perils among false brethren; if thou art in perils among robbers; if thou art in perils by land or by sea; if thou art accused with all manner of false accusations; if thine enemies fall upon thee; if they tear thee from the society of thy father and mother and brethren and sisters; and if with a drawn sword thine enemies tear thee from the bosom of thy wife, and of thine offspring, and thine elder son, although but six years of age, shall cling to thy garments, and shall say, My father, my father, why can't you stay with us? O, my father, what are the men going to do with you? And if then he shall be thrust from thee by the sword, and thou be dragged to prison, and thine enemies prowl around thee like wolves for the blood of the lamb; And if thou should be cast into the pit, or into the hands of murderers, and the sentence of death passed upon thee; if thou be cast into the deep; if the billowing surge conspire against thee; if fierce winds become thine enemy; if the heavens gather blackness, and all the elements combine to hedge up the way; and above all, if the very jaws of Hell shall gape open the mouth wide after thee, know thou, my son, that all these things shall give thee experience, and shall be for thy good."

"The son of Man had descended below them all. Art thou greater than he?"

How sublime the teaching. We forget sometimes that Christ suffered all things so that we might not suffer if we repent. Nothing the world can throw at us equals what he did for us. Therefore, we can see peace through the tumult. We can find happiness amidst despair, and I can act like a kid in a candy store for my entire life, because happiness and faith are intertwined and as my faith increases, so too, my happiness and joy. I love life. I love my wife. I love the Gospel. I love the fun and joy and happiness that living the Gospel brings me. I may be in a war zone, doing a thousand different tasks, up to my eyeballs in crappy details and jobs…but I have joy!

You can too!

Pres. Heber C. Kimball once wrote, "There are many vessels that are destroyed after they have been molded and shaped. Why? Because they were not contented with the shape the potter has given them, but straightway put themselves into a shape to please themselves; therefore they are beyond understanding what God designs, and they destroy themselves by the power of their own agency, for this is given to every man and woman, to do just as they please…..It is that alone that will make you truly happy; to be perfectly limber in the hands of the potter like clay….you cannot be happy unless you submit to the law of God, and to the principles of his government. When a person is miserable wretched and unhappy in himself, put him in what circumstances you please and he is wretched still. If a person is poor, and composes his mind, and calmly submits to the providences of God, he will feel cheerful and happy in all circumstances, if he continues to keep the commandments of God." (talk given April 2, 1854)

Chapter 44

SITTING ON THE DOCK OF THE BAY

I sit at the brink looking into a long day tomorrow. I do not complain for there is no reason to complain about getting a break from Afghanistan. In fact, I am thrilled with my adventure that is about to begin. Tomorrow, I hop on a plane and fly to Italy for a couple reasons. I am going to be attending all next week a program management meeting for the C-27 program. There are many issues that need to be discussed as I'm sure you've gathered from previous blogs regarding our maintenance reliability rate etc. After that, I'll wait a couple days and my crew and I will (there are three of us going) pick up another C-27 and begin the trek back to Afghanistan. That should provide a lot of fodder for future blogs. After all, these planes haven't exactly been refurbished to like new conditions. The plane I'm picking up was built in 1978 or 79. In other words, it'll have problems, guaranteed.

This week has been another round robin week of adventure that emphasizes the need to have patience, especially in dealing with all things Afghan and this program. I ended up being scheduled five times to fly this week and I managed to fly four of those times. One of those flights will be, I hope, an interesting story of adventure and chaos….Always the best kind. As it was, I was scheduled to fly on Sunday, Monday, Tuesday and Thursday. Well, Sunday we didn't exactly get off the ground. We got the engines started, we taxied, but then this little thing called a Generator failed. We taxied back to parking and by the time we got back to parking, somehow it started working, but there was another problem, which I can't remember what it was, so we gave the plane to maintenance and they worked on it while we went to lunch, fair trade if you ask me. When we came back we went to start the APU, known as the Auxiliary Power Unit – used to start engines and power equipment etc., but if immediately flamed out. Not Good! It has a door that opens to allow air to enter to make it run. It's this little jet engine and on our instrument panel it was showing the door as being open….it wasn't. That was a problem. We told maintenance and it turned out it would be better for us to cancel since the airplane was supposed to fly again in a couple hours and if we took off without it being fixed, which was legal, we would hose the guys behind us. So I opted to cancel the mission and they fixed the airplane.

The next day was a sad, sad day….I flew again, and as I was getting prepared that morning, I got a phone call…….my roommate was back from his leave and needed a ride from Bagram to Kabul. The sad part was I was the one available to go get him. ☹ Ha-ha It's only sad because I've had the room to myself for the last couple weeks, so now we're back to no, or limited privacy. Ugh! Oh well, my copilot and I went and picked him up at the end of our training. I had an Afghan copilot and we went and practiced pattern work and one engine out patterns, instrument approaches, you know, the standard practice flight. He did a wonderful job, except for a couple minor things when flying precision instrument approaches. But I felt like he was improving. I like it when that happens; it makes me feel like we're accomplishing something. After we were done we went to pick up my roommate. This was a little funny. Normally when we go to Bagram they park us on the far end of the airport, at least a half mile from the passenger terminal, so we told him to wait for us there. He walked early to get there and watched us arrive, and then sadly watched as the ground personnel parked us right in front of the passenger terminal.

We waited for him! He had a LONG walk.

I got to fly the approach back into Kabul, which is nice because even though I fly often, usually I'm instructing so I don't get a lot of time on the controls. It's like being a race car driver, sitting in the passenger seat telling your 12 year old how to drive…sometimes nerve wracking, sometimes not!

I was scheduled to fly a night flight the next day with our Squadron Commander. We were pretty much doing the exact same profile as I just did the day before. Not bad. We got into the pattern and began our practice. The interesting thing about flying at night is you don't have the visual references you have during the day, which makes it more difficult to not lose track of your heading, altitude or airspeed. He, the commander, was getting frustrated with himself because he was having problems keeping himself on altitude and speed. I gave many pointers and techniques to use at night. In his defense, he's only been flying mission flights, not getting pattern practice for at least two months….like any other skill, if you don't use it, you lose it and it takes a while to get the skills back. I really enjoyed it because I was able to take several patterns and do my own single engine work and no flap work and practice short approaches. (That's where you get abeam the runway numbers and pull the power to idle and immediately turn to land instead of setting up for a mile final; you're in a constant bank until the last second. Very challenging!)

Well, after a couple hours of practice, we decided it was time to head back to Kabul. As we were climbing out to head back, I noticed a slight pressure on my ears. Looking at our cabin altimeter, I realized we weren't pressurizing. We were right at ten thousand feet and climbing. Regulations let us fly for half an hour up to 12,500 feet, but this wasn't good, especially since our air conditioner (which is used to pressurize the aircraft) was on. We immediately turned around and headed back to Mazar I Sharif and requested to hold at 9,000 feet while we troubleshot a problem. We were cleared to do so and began our overhead circles while we went through all the options, trying out circuit breakers, opening and closing switches, checking everything. Nada! We ended up having two options. Neither option was good. First, we could land at Mazar I Sharif and wait for a maintenance rescue. That was not optimal, and could take a day or so. We didn't know what was wrong other than the airplane wouldn't pressurize and we could hear a squeal, like bearings going out, in the background noise when we had the air conditioner going. Not cool! Our other option wasn't fun, but would get us back to Kabul and get us fixed. We went with option two. After exhausting all our possibilities we told approach our plan, got clearance to depart the area, and put our oxygen masks on. We turned off the air conditioner and began to climb. We climbed and flew the hour long flight back to Kabul while sucking oxygen through the masks, which I can now say are NOT comfortable to wear for an extended period of time.

We made it back and maintenance was happy that we'd made that choice. Turns out that a duct had blown out, so the air wasn't getting from the air conditioner to the interior of the airplane! Oh well, such is life! It was a fun night, what can I say, and the 100% pure oxygen being put into my system made my muscles feel much better the next day as I worked out hard while doing a leg workout at the gym…so my body thanked the airplane. ☺

That was the last day I was supposed to fly, since I gave my Thursday flight to my roommate because I had to get paperwork completed for this two week trip. Then, Thursday, the scheduler asked me at the last minute to go out on a short 15 minute flight to check out the gear on an airplane. No problem! The only problem was that we never got off the ground. It failed a ground check so we went back to parking and told them to fix it. We were nice though and said we'd fly it again on Friday since we didn't get it done Thursday. Maintenance was appreciative, since right now the airplanes are not faring well, only 2 out of 9 were flyable the last couple days of the week. We went out again today…and we got off the ground, flew for 25 minutes, long enough to be vectored around for an approach, and the plane failed the gear test it's been failing for 3 weeks or more…what a pain!

In a nutshell, it's been a crazy week. Hope my multiple pages of story about flying aren't too boring. It's an adventure every day. We sacrifice time and home to serve our country and I seem to always have something new to share.

Sacrifice. That's a thing that we as Americans really aren't used to making anymore. I think about our parent's generation and their parent's generation. They went through the Great Depression, two world wars and they sacrificed a lot to give us the prosperity that we have today. However, do we learn from that history? This week there have been a couple of topics that seemed to take prominence in my studies and have not only invaded my senses and sensibilities, but have really made me think.

We take so much for granted. We have become an entitlement generation. We so often think we deserve things just for being and living. We don't really understand sacrifice. A lot of my study this week was again directed to the debt and problems our country has faced and will face because of years of overspending. Whether it's a country or a family or an individual, we can't consistently spend more than we take in without everything falling apart. As I said, we give, give, give, and take, take, take without thinking about the cost. When you talk about a country's debt as being in the trillions, it's kind of hard to comprehend. I'll take it down to a more personal level. I watched and read a couple of great stories this week, true stories, about some of the pioneers. There was John Tanner, a man who was self-made, rich, but upon joining the church, learned to live the law of consecration to help make it possible for the church to pay for the first Temple in these latter days to be built in Kirtland Ohio. Over his lifetime he continued to give. He dedicated his life to helping move the work of the Lord along. He never looked back, in spite of giving everything and ending up with nothing, losing a child on the long trek to Nauvoo, having to beg for bread. He didn't look back. He served, he gave, he didn't think about himself…he knew what sacrifice was. He and his family weren't worried about the things of this world. They were worried about the world to come, raising the Lord's kingdom. What examples of faith!

Another story that touched my heart was the story of a stone cutter. He was converted to the Gospel of Jesus Christ in England and brought his family over to America to join the saints. (That's what members of the Church of Jesus Christ of latter day Saints are known as when not called Mormons.) They ended up being in the first handcart company to cross the plains. Now, I know many of you have never seen or heard of handcarts, but let me tell you, they're not easy to move. When I was a teenager we did a 30 mile, several day, handcart experience and it was exhausting and we only walked and pulled that thing 30 miles over 4 days. These pioneers pulled their handcarts two thousand miles to Utah. Well, this stonecutter settled in Alpine Utah. When the work began on the Salt Lake Temple, he was called to help. He had no horse. He had nothing but a pair of shoes and desire to serve. For twenty years he would get up at 2 AM on Monday, walk the twenty plus miles to the work site, and work all day, stay with his son and his wife during the week, and on Friday afternoon, walk back twenty miles back home to be with his wife and family for the weekend. Can you even imagine the sacrifice? I've done the weekend commute, for four months and it was a pain. And, that was driving from North Carolina to Alabama, that was pain enough…but twenty years…that's dedication. The story doesn't end there though.

He ended up getting kicked in the leg by a cow, receiving multiple compound fractures in his leg, such that they had to amputate his leg. It took him about a year to recover during which he built himself a false leg out of wood, and was able to limp around. Once he was able to get around the farm he picked up his stone carving tools, and told his wife he was going back to work. In all he worked on the temple for some thirty plus years, though he never got to see it finished, the Salt Lake Temple having taken 40 years to build. But his sacrifice and dedication can still be seen by all when you look at the HUGE declaration carved into the wall 150 feet up where it starts out saying, "Holiness to the Lord, the House of the Lord…" He wasn't sacrificing for himself. He was dedicated to serving his Father in Heaven, giving his all. There really are only two types of people in the world, those who act, and those who are acted upon. Which are you?

Do we act? Do we put the Lord first?

The second part of my studies this week dealt with Light and Truth. We are told that the Lord's power is in all things and through all things. Heavenly Father gives light to all his creations. Through this light we can learn truth. Light and truth are inseparably connected. One begets the other. The more light we receive, the more truth we can learn, the more truth we learn the more light shines in our soul. There are many aspects of this, but it's an eternal round. The Lord's light enlightens our understanding. Truth exists independent of what others think. I read a great quote from Elder Hale's book *Return* today. He quoted President Benson who said, "Popularity is never a test of truth." Truth exists. Truth is. The world can deny truth. The world can declare something popular as true, for example teaching that sleeping around is normal or that "friends with benefits" are a good thing….but that doesn't make it so. The Bible Dictionary defines truth as, "the knowledge of things as they are, as they were, and as they are yet to come."

The light of God enlightens our understanding, enables us to resist temptation, grow in knowledge and power, and learn truth. I liked the way it was explained in my studies this week. Light and truth are dependent on our obedience to God's laws, known as principles of righteousness. Every time we are obedient our light increases enabling us to grow from grace to grace until we will ultimately comprehend all things and gain eternal life. However, every time we make wrong choices our light dims making it easier to make more wrong choices. It is a constant battle; we are never at an equilibrium. We are always, in every moment of every day either gaining light and truth or losing it. When our choices cause us to lose light it becomes more difficult to know right from wrong. I understand this completely, since for a long time I allowed myself to lose light, to not really know the difference, and to really screw up. Thankfully, repentance is always available which has allowed me to gain light and truth, rebuild my understanding and grow my testimony. Light and truth forsake the evil one. Every time we keep the commandments our light will increase again, giving us even more light and more strength the next time we are faced with temptation.

In Doctrine and Covenants 121: 34-43 it states, "Behold, there are many called, but few are chosen. And why are they not chosen? Because their hearts are set so much upon the things of this world, and aspire to the honors of men, that they do not learn this one lesson—that the rights of the priesthood are inseparably connected with the powers of heaven, and that the powers of heaven cannot be controlled nor handled only upon the principles of righteousness. That they may be conferred upon us, it is true; but when we undertake to cover our sins, or to gratify our pride, our vain ambition, or to exercise control or dominion or compulsion upon the souls of the children of men, in any degree of unrighteousness, behold, the heavens withdraw themselves; the spirit of the lord is grieved; and when it is withdrawn, Amen to the priesthood or authority of that man. Behold, ere he is aware he is left unto himself, to kick against the pricks, to persecute the saints, and fight against God. We have learned through sad experience that it is the nature and disposition of almost all men, as soon as they get a little authority, as they suppose, they will immediately begin to exercise unrighteous dominion. Hence many are called, but few are chosen. No power or influence can or ought to be maintained by virtue of the priesthood, only by persuasion, by long-suffering, by gentleness and meekness, and love unfeigned; By kindness and pure knowledge, which shall greatly enlarge the soul without hypocrisy, and without guile-Reproving betimes with sharpness, when moved upon by the Holy Ghost; and then showing an increase of love toward him whom thou hast reproved, lest he esteem thee to be his enemy…."

That's a long scripture to tell us that Light and Truth are inseparably connected and we need to strive to continually gain more light, through meekness, persuasion, long-suffering, love unfeigned…in other words become as a child, for such is the Kingdom of Heaven.

I've learned one lesson above all through all this study and through my time here in Afghanistan. It's the need for patience. In my patriarchal blessing I was told at least five different times to "be patient". I know many of my problems of the past have come from not being patient. When I'm impatient, I'm not meek, full of love, long-suffering. Nope, when I'm impatient…I lose that light, and truth leaves with it…and I'm left to kick against the pricks. But I've been learning patience and long-suffering and I love it. Tiffany is learning patience in dealing with me being gone. I love that woman. She puts up with a lot. Over the last 7 years, I figured out that I'll have been gone for 3 years or more of that time. That's a lot of patience and long-suffering and I know she'll be, and is being blessed because of it. I love the growth that she is going through as well.

How do we get light? The light of Christ is given to all men when they're born. This gives us the ability to understand truth. Acting on truth gives us more light. Not acting on truth takes it away. We gain light and lose it every moment of every day. When we pray our spiritual light increases. The Lord promised that if we pray always He will pour out His Spirit upon us. We should pray morning and night and not just say rote memorized prayers, but we should talk to our Heavenly Father and counsel with Him. When we want to talk to God we pray. Most often when He wants to talk to us, He does it through the scriptures. That is why we're told to "Feast upon the words of Christ". Feasting is more than just reading. It's reading, pondering, praying about what we read…in other words, seeking further light and truth. We should do this with all the scriptures, the Bible, the Book of Mormon, the Doctrine and Covenants, the Pearl of Great Price, and all the words that come out of the mouth of living prophets. We're blessed to have prophets alive today. We ponder the scriptures we read to make the truths we read become part of our every thought and action. The Lord makes known his word to us through personal revelations, often through insights found in our ponderings of the scriptures. The scriptures, though written a couple thousand years ago or more are relevant to our day. They're the road map back to our Heavenly Father.

All in all, this is the crux. Truth exists. Truth is. We need to find out what is true and what isn't. There can't be multiple truths that contradict each other. I testify that there is a prophet on the earth today. I testify that the Book of Mormon, the Bible and other books of Scripture, contain the light and truths given from our Father in Heaven and will lead us back to him. I testify that Joseph Smith restored the Gospel of Jesus Christ to the earth and that the Priesthood was restored. I testify that the world is falling apart, that it denounces truth as lies and rallies behind fiction to make itself feel important. I testify that Heavenly Father is real; that He is the one true God. I testify that He sent His son to atone for our sins, though the mechanics of how His sacrifice on the cross manage to atone for my sins I don't claim to understand, I know that it is so and that He broke the bands of death. I testify that the Church of Jesus Christ was restored to the earth and that there is a living prophet today receiving revelation for the world. I lastly testify that everyone can know for themselves. Light and truth are brought through prayer and the Holy Ghost to testify of truth to each and every one of us if we seek it out.

Chapter 45

IN ITALY AGAIN

You know, this week has been a crazy adventure and bizarre. Last Saturday I was able to depart Kabul, finally getting a break from the insanity and being thrown into a completely new version of the insane. Life is constantly throwing new twists and turns and it sure makes for an interesting ride. That word seems to get used a lot with this program and this scene.

We left Kabul and flew commercially to Dubai, and even though we had a four and a half hour layover, we barely got everything done in time to get to our flight. As odd as that sounds, we got to stand in a lot of lines, and the shortest, fastest one, was the security line. Emirates air was a pretty cool airline, giving lots of perks that you don't see in US airlines anymore, such as in seat personal TV, and for those with international cell phone calling plans, you could actually make calls during the flight. That was the first I'd ever seen something like that on an airliner. But I digress; the security line only took about three minutes. The line for checking in with the airline and getting our seat assignment took almost two hours. They only had three people working that line and it took forever. We finally left Dubai, got to Rome and flew to Naples, where we prepared for a weeklong conference. We were exhausted. By the time I got into the room, finished talking to Tiffany and was able to get to bed, I'd been up and travelling for twenty three hours straight. Needless to say, I was worn out. The next day though I was able to do an amazing thing....sleep! No roommate, no person next door snoring...sleep. It was very nice.

I didn't really do much that first day, other than go do my laundry. I rested. It was needed, since in last week's blog I reported on flying three days and actually attempting to fly five days that week. My body needed the rest. I needed the rest. I took the rest.

This week has been filled with meetings, meetings and more meetings. I've been involved in the Program Management Review, a quarterly review with the company that is building the airplanes that are falling apart in Kabul. Our meetings were all day marathon events and there were a lot of topics covered. The company was hit hard by the fact that the product they're producing is not living up to expectations. One principle and action we had planned for this week and for every aircraft pickup from the factory had been worked out, we thought, the month before by our contracting office that allowed us to do a confidence flight of the airplane before we ferry it into theatre since all the airplanes have had some delaying maintenance issues. Well, this apparently is a sore subject. Now don't get me wrong, the company was all smiles the first day, no problem, no problem, we'll do it on such and such date etc...Yeah right! They don't really like these confidence flights because in my opinion they see it as us telling them we don't have confidence in nor do we trust their declaration that the plane is good to go. The truth is that we don't trust them. They're the company, they make a profit when the plane leaves, the more work done here, the more money they are out of pocket. Even though they were all smiles...the gloves came off and the sparing began.

The plan we had negotiated the month before was for us to do confidence flights on all remaining airplanes. The company brought up the idea that if the plane was used for training, it shouldn't need a confidence flight and our Colonel bought into that, and BOOM! There went our plans and negotiations. From there, we were on an uphill battle and it seemed every time we got ahead and thought we were primed and good to go for our flight on Friday, the company would come up with a new barrier. In the end, Friday came and in the space between 8 PM the night before and 10 AM on the day of the flight, our authorization to fly twisted three or four times and ultimately we were authorized to fly, but only if we could get diplomatic clearances on our own...which takes several days usually! Didn't happen! Therefore, we were only able to take the airplane to the engine run area and just check out what systems we could on the ground. This airplane was used for training. It already had around thirty hours on it. Just in our ground run we found ten things wrong with it, to include a fuel leak in a wing, some gauges that had been cross wired (how that was never caught by their tech adds to the reasons not to trust them!) and a cargo door lock that needed to be realigned. What a crock! It'll be interesting to see what happens when we fly out of here at the end of next week.

The meetings were long. We'd leave the hotel at 0800 and not get back until 1800. I've enjoyed having good internet though and being able to talk and see Tiffany every day for several hours. Have I gone to really see anything? Nope. I've spent my evenings talking to Tip since I don't have a roommate listening in on our conversations and it's been very nice. Wish she was here, but if wishes were fishes we'd all have gelato!

There were so many topics covered, it'll be a while before everything is resolved that was discussed at these meetings, but I'm glad I was there and I didn't just sit and be a wall flower the whole time. I spoke up and put forth my opinion as doctrine, at times to the colonel's chagrin. I had the answers to questions since I'd done the work in developing them for our program the last couple months. I've never been one to keep my mouth shut when things need to be brought up or points made, be it in a boardroom meeting or talking to a General. By the way, The Program Lead, maybe he's the President of the company, is a retired General. "People are people so why should it be..." - Depeche Mode

We should've been leaving the 7th, but due to circumstances that I'm not going to complain about, we got an extra week here. When I get back from this trip I should have exactly two months left. It'll be both quick and slow.

This week has had a difference in my studies, not so much book study as a study of people. Passing through different countries, watching, ever watching, I see people in varying lights. My book study has coincided with my study of people and it's a sad sobering sight. We live in a world that is consumed. It is consumed with itself, with people in leadership roles believing themselves to be above their own laws, with the governed rebelling as we see in Egypt. We live in a world that is constantly searching for answers without finding any. We live in a world that is gradually creating a chasm between good and evil, a world that calls evil good and good evil. It is a sad thing.

Today, as I walked the streets of Naples to go get my gelato--Italian ice cream (It's the best Gelato, Tiffany's and my spot, but definitely the best gelato in Italy) I watched people. People everywhere, shopping like there's no tomorrow, smoking, trying to fill the void you could see in their eyes. When you fill your world with things that are material, it's not fulfilling and you can see the void in the eyes. I watched for that and I could see it everywhere. I was walking through a town with buildings and sculptures hundreds of years old, beautiful in their design, and yet, no one notices. No one notices the trash littering the streets, the graffiti all over the place. This is not just a Naples problem; it's become a world problem. Tiffany was telling me about the town she's in, how she looked at it with the eyes of someone from a different country this week and she was embarrassed by the trash and everything else. How we treat where we live, where we work, and the world around us, in many ways is a reminder or a visual illustration of what's going on inside, maybe not of us, but the community around us.

We only have to look outside, read the newspaper, turn on the TV to see the world is turning away from right ideals and truth and trying to turn them on their heads. What has always been considered wrong, people are making laws to make it right. We're being told that it doesn't matter what someone does, if it doesn't hurt someone else. That's the lie that the world is believing. Sin is being professed to be truth and truth is being called lies. But truth is eternal and sin cannot be voted into a good thing. Our country was founded on principles of righteousness, of the ethos of nobility of spirit, of the absolutes of right and wrong and equality.

Somewhere along the line we've lost that. In the time of Sodom and Gomorrah, in the time of Pompeii (since I'm in Italy it makes for a good comparison) they were civilizations that had become corrupt. Sexual promiscuity was abundant, idleness was the norm, gratifying your pleasures was determined a right, homosexuality was considered normal, all these things were at their heyday in both Sodom and Gomorrah and in the town of Pompeii What do we know happened to those towns? They were destroyed. Not only were they destroyed but they were wiped off the face of the earth. Why? Because they'd offended God with their indolence! They'd gotten so corrupt that they had to be wiped out. Now, this also happened to the people of Noah's time. The people then made fun of Noah as he built the ark...at least until it started raining and wouldn't stop. Do we wait until the rains fall before looking at our own life?

I read in the book of Moses about Enoch. He was shown all the history of the earth. He spoke with God face to face as a man speaketh to his brother. He prophesied and those that listened to him were blessed. His teachings were so powerful, that the people changed in his city so much that they couldn't be kept on the earth. The entire city was taken into Heaven. Contrast that with the people that lived everywhere else. They would not listen to the Gospel. They would not hear. They lived unto themselves, for themselves, and shortly thereafter as the rains fell they died unto themselves. Now, the Lord has sworn that He won't send the flood anymore to wash away the wicked. It's been prophesied that the world will get worse and worse until the Second Coming of Christ. For those who are watchful, this is not a thing to be feared. For those that are doing what they should, this is no cause for alarm. For everyone else, though they don't care....it will be a sad and stressful time.

I remember hearing twenty years ago that the world was already as bad as it was during Noah's time and that it was like unto Sodom and Gomorrah. That was twenty years ago. President Kimball told us that. How much worse has the world gotten in twenty years? I'd say, a lot. Things people do now would have shocked everyone twenty years ago. Things that go on make me shudder to think. The things that kids see on TV and in movies are so much worse than ever. Tiffany told me a week or so ago about how our son Mack's class did a survey about their favorite movies and every kid, except Mack, listed a PG-13 or R-rated movie as their favorite. These are 10-year olds. One kid even listed Nightmare on Elm Street as their favorite. What kind of cracked up crappy society are we becoming?

The only real answer that I have found has been to turn to the Lord. Since Tiffany and I made the changes in our lives, we have found strength that we didn't know we had. We've found peace in the gospel of Jesus Christ. The Church of Jesus Christ is an anchor in a foundering world. The Gospel, the priesthood, the temple, all lead us back to Him and keep us from drowning in a world that is choking on its own glory, ready to split itself asunder, without even realizing it. In Moses, Enoch saw Satan in vision in our day, the last days, holding a chain that veiled the earth in darkness and he, Satan, looked up and laughed. He laughs at us. He laughs as he sees Heavenly Father's children falling into irrecoverable death spirals, never even knowing that that's what they're doing. So sad! Arise and awake. Shake off the chains with which ye are bound. Cast off the evil one. Seek to do that which is good and right. See the light and the glory that are waiting to encompass you. Oh that I could help all to see the joy and the glory that await when darkness is thrust down and light emerges, when we repent of our sins and strive no more to live an unclean life. Give way so that the Holy Ghost can encompass you in healing light and shake off the chains that bind and blind you. Cease to commit whoredoms. Cease to do that which is unlawful. Cease to find fault. I love you all and hope the best for you. I pray for you daily and want you to know that. I am not perfect. I have my faults and work on those daily. "Peace be unto you, my peace I give unto you, not as the world giveth give I unto you..."

Up the spears, at the end of the day, Up the spears come what may; Cross the spears, the devil leers, Cross the spears, we'll make him fear; Up the spears, the battle's joined, Up the spears, your blood it's boiled; Cross the spears, so it begins, Cross the spears, we'll do away with sin; Up the spears, the battle looms, Up the spears, feel the doom; Cross the spears, the devil lies, Cross the spears, this day, the devil dies! – Todd Andrewsen

Chapter 46

BOOM WENT THE DRUM, NOT THE AIRPLANE

Greetings again from Naples

We survived. What do I mean you ask? Well, we departed Naples on Friday and flew to Souda Bay, Crete. We were only supposed to do a gas and go, but we did a gas and an "Oh my, where is that fuel leaking out of!" We thought we had it fixed that night, or at least stopped, but the leak was still there in the morning. We planned on taking the plane back to Italy in order to get it fixed. Well, it only took 8 hours to get the fuel leak capped off so that we could return to Naples and give the airplane back to Alenia. When we arrived in Naples I got an interesting phone call. It's not often that I get to speak to Presidents of a company but he called the international phone that I carry for the flight. He told me he's glad we brought the plane back since he said he'd rather send a good airplane. He was surprised because it was a "training" airplane that had flown 12-15 times prior to our flight. But, especially after hearing all our problems and write ups, he was glad we brought the plane back. In fact, I'm going to recommend all airplane pickups stop at Souda Bay for a gas and go, just in case...that way if there's a problem like what we have (with 15 write ups) you can turn around and give the plane back to the factory to fix...

So for the detailed listing of our problems:

Fuel leak out of the APU (auxiliary power unit) fuel pressure control valve - spraying out in a nice stream, we thought that the problem was at least controlled early today, then as we went to start engines, turned on the boost pumps and it really began spraying. Therefore, we had to find a way to close the shutoff valve, since it was frozen in the open position and this made the gravity weight of the fuel provide a constant drip and when the fuel system was pressurized it just added to the problem. Our maintainer was able to get some fittings, caps and plugs that fit the pressure line. We were able to undo the fuel line, cap it and leak check it. We had the leak taken care of. Finally, four hours after scheduled take off, we got engines started and were ready to go.

Not having an APU found our second main problem...an electrical one. We didn't have the APU generator and found out that the relays between the two generators on the engines were not working right. Each engine was powering its bus, but it wouldn't switch over.

For those of you who think that it's dangerous, it could be, but that's the flying business. Planes break and really a large part of my job in Italy is to fin what's wrong and make sure the company actually stands up for their work and puts out a good product. The plane wasn't dangerous to fly, it just had a lot of issues and that's annoying. I suppose if the fuel leak had caught on fire it would have been dangerous to fly.

The main issues are the fuel leak, which they have to defuel the airplane in order to change out the valves, the fuel problem with the main tank and the SPR (single point refueling valve), the electrical issues (which were pretty weird) and some propeller stuff.

We arrived and spoke with their maintenance representative and they realized it was a bigger job than they'd planned. We're going to try to tow the airplane over to Alenia (or taxi if need be) and they stated they should have it fixed by Tues to depart Wed. That's what we're going to plan for. Crazy, but I'd rather have the factory fix it than limp to Kabul with a broke airplane and end up with another paper weight on the ramp.

Glad we didn't get to do an acceptance flight on this one! (We wanted to but we were denied do to difficulties)....oh wait, we did flight check it, it was a flight to Souda and back! We checked the plane out then ... it failed!

We were unable to do the Acceptance flight, confidence flight, customer flight (call it what you will) due to too many barriers that appeared during and after the week of meetings. We were allowed to do an engine run and ended up finding multiple things (ten pages worth, that's three or four write-ups per page) wrong to include fuel leaking through the wing, seepage through a rivet, Oil leaks from the APU and Hydraulic leaks from under the floor of the aircraft. The list is not full of the details, but is a listing of all the write-ups we've had, from newest to oldest as well as which ones were already repaired by Alenia and the date found. As you can see, we're at 47 total write-ups since our first engine run prior to departure.

For the major issues, we found the Electric issues out when starting engines with an air cart instead of the APU and not having an APU Generator to power all the electrical buses. The Fuel leak was discovered on the walk around after landing in Souda, and finding out that it had been spraying on the APU exhaust. The Prop dipstick and missing chain were discovered either on pre or post flight in Souda in preparation to head back to Naples. One note that isn't highlighted in the Maintenance Summary, but is a QA issue - and personally I think it points at the attention to detail that is NOT being taken on these airplanes hence the aircraft breaking when they depart, and that is - as we took the panel off to get to the fuel leak we found one of the screws on the panel had been broken off and the head GLUED BACK over the hole. If that doesn't point to poor practices, I don't know what does. Over all, most of the leaks, be they oil or hydraulics, all stem from B-nuts not tightened all the way etc...which just seems to be sloppy work. The fuel leak....can't really do much about that one, the part - the shut-off valve, failed open and caused the fuel control to blow its seal which caused it to spray out what I assume is a pressure relief hole - right onto the exhaust. We're lucky we didn't have a fire in flight because of the way it failed, we would NOT have been able to put it out while airborne.

I know I'm belaboring the point about the issues, but it's just to point out that life is never dull around here. For the rest of the week here's a quick rundown of what we did prior to leaving. For one thing, we ran the engines twice finding all the write-ups I talked about previously. I ate pizza and gelato, including eating at the original restaurant that created the Pizza Margherita for the queen a couple years back around 1790. Pretty cool! The history is amazing. I love the elegance and statuesque nature of the buildings. I love the ancient feel. I love the history. I guess that's the simplest way to explain. I wish Tip were here with me. Next time I come to Italy it'll be with her and the kids. I miss not having her here to see stuff with me. Not that I'm touring much looking at stuff. The next couple days I'm pretty sure I'll be overseeing workers trying to fix my airplane. I really dislike it when a job is done half-baked and that's the feeling I get with these airplanes. That the effort is only half there! The sad part is that there are several people that I know working on them that honestly want to put out a good product, but they're only as good as their weakest links and I believe there's a lot of weakest links.

I also had fun going shopping. I received a request from Kabul, from the squadron to purchase a bunch of stuff to enhance the esprit de corps and the morale of the squadron, i.e. food and kitchen supplies to cook for ourselves at times. I had fun and went a little crazy, but we'll be well stocked for a while on some things. When at war, morale is one of the biggest determining factors in how things are going. When morale is high, it doesn't matter, bombs could be falling, craziness could ensue, but everyone would go on about their business and things would get done well. When morale is low…amen to the ability to get anything accomplished well or quickly. That's been one of the biggest problems we face in Afghanistan. Morale has been low due to all the maintenance problems, all the issues with the Afghan pilots that you've read about, and issues with leadership and living conditions. A good chow hall can change morale for the better….apparently our chow hall has gotten worse since I've been gone and it was pretty bad before. It's the little things in life that keep people happy and sane in a war zone. For me, well, I pretty much take things as they come, but I like to be decisive too. Such as deciding to come back to Italy to get fixed, there's a time and a place for everything.

This leads into my study discussion this week. It's been a somewhat spiritual, somewhat inspirational, somewhat empirical studying week. I have several quotes of things that I really liked. Life, after all, is about growth and change and we can take it as it comes. If many of these chapters seem to return to previous topics, it's because I find I always need to relearn lessons. And as I relearn I gain a deeper understanding of things. Take this week for example. I've seen Tiffany stressed out, excited, worn out, happy, and sad, all on different days. She's a trooper and puts up with a lot with me being gone. I'm so proud of what she does. Her attitude ebbs and flows like a tide, and that's to be expected going through the kind of stress she does being a mother, a young women's leader, a building coordinator, etc…very busy and through it all she takes time to look out for others, do things to help others, and even brings a complete cheering section to one of her less active girls' basketball games. She's awesome and I'm a proud husband.

If you haven't figured out I'm talking about attitude. I've learned a lot about attitude. I'm always trying to learn more and I find myself frustrated and upset at times and have a hard time taking my own medicine. Take last night for example. It took us eight hours to finally get off the ground, then three hours to get to Naples. Then we had a couple hours of talking with Maintenance representatives. When we finally were able to head to the hotel there was a problem. We thought we were going to our super nice hotel that we usually stay at. We were told there weren't any rooms at the base billeting, so we stopped by to pick up a "billeting not available" sheet which allows us to stay off base….and they had rooms. I was tired and cranky and we ended up staying on base. The rooms are nice, but they're far from the restaurants and sights of downtown. I'm in Italy; I was whining to myself, I don't want to stay on an American base….so I was grumpy for a bit. I got in my room and actually had a discussion with myself about choosing how to respond to those things that happen to us, taking my own medicine that I dish out at times. I felt much better after that, but here are some of the things I picked up this week that made it an easier pill to swallow.

From the book "Body Fat Solutions" by Tom Venuto (you can learn truths from many places, it's being open to receive it) I read, "Awareness is the starting point of change, because you can't solve a problem if you don't know you have one." While many of these quotes I'm going to write were written to help decide to lose weight and begin a program, I don't and didn't highlight them with that in mind. The following quotes I took out of context and looked at them with spiritual eyes. I hope you can share the view with me. There are a lot of them so don't get too tired of reading.

"Setting a worthy goal for something you want, then pursuing and reaching it through determination, discipline, and hard work changes the very fiber of your being. You become a stronger person, not just physically, but also mentally and emotionally. Work develops your character, strengthens your discipline, and boosts your self-esteem." I have sooo seen this in Tiffany's and my life. This year of change has done exactly that. We've been working towards spiritual growth and it changed us to our core.

"If you're not careful, blaming and excuse-making can become a habitual knee-jerk reaction every time you're confronted with an obstacle or challenge. If you indulge in it's-not-my-fault disease, you're giving up control of your life and playing the victim." I've seen this in my life as I didn't want to accept blame for the screw ups I was involved in and created by my own poor choices. It's-not-my-fault is the building block of the destruction of society that looms because people think that their choices don't affect others, even though they do. We all have tendencies to console ourselves with It's-not-my-fault when things go wrong.

"Many people confuse 'difficult' and 'impossible'. Another definition of responsibility is 'response-ability', which means free will-your ability to choose your response to any situation….Three of the most powerful words in the English language are 'I am responsible'…Taking responsibility for all your results, for better or for worse, is taking back your power to create results in your life." I don't believe I've heard truer words. I am the master of my destiny. If I choose heaven or hell, it's my choices that will lead me there. The Book of Mormon states, "we are saved by grace after all that we can do!" God doesn't turn a blind eye on what our choices are if we only state that we accept Christ as our Savior. We must put action to our words. That is why we are saved by grace AFTER all that we can do. He asks us to be perfect, but knows we won't be. That's when His grace kicks in…when we're striving to live, love and grow to be like Him. It's not just saying the words; it's living His words and striving to find out His will for us, for all things, in all places.

"I also believe that your health is your greatest wealth, and the condition of your body will be about equal to the average of your five closest friends…That is why you must guard yourself against negative people, environments, and influences and build your social network into a fortress of positivity…Your mental and emotional energy is too precious to squander on negative, pessimistic people. Emotional vampires will suck you dry if you let them." True words, very true! I knew a copilot, nice guy, reasonable and pretty cool. He was put on a crew while deployed with three of the bitterest people I've ever had the misfortune of working with. During the 90 days he was with them, he told me later it was the most bitter, angry experience of his life. He was angry twenty-four seven and didn't know why, but we all could see that the happiness was being sucked out of him. It's sad but true that we must guard against pessimism and anger, because it feeds the fire that sucks the life out of us and the Spirit will not strive with man when there is negativity, pessimism, anger etc….

"If you do what you've always done, you'll get what you've always got. If you want a different result, do something different. Or as the humorous Demotivator calendar says: 'Tradition…Just because you've always done it that way doesn't mean it's not incredibly stupid'." I've heard this similar theme often and it sinks in a little more every time. In Eighth grade band class I remember being told, "practice doesn't make perfect, perfect practice makes perfect"...if we do things wrong a thousand times…it'll still be wrong. I'm thankful it only took Tiffany and me 13 years to realize we were being incredibly stupid in our religious non-habits so now we're practicing, not always perfectly but we're working on it, on good spiritual habits and the change has been remarkable in our lives.

"What makes you take action? Where does motivation come from? Why do some people persist and others quit? What triggers impulsive behaviors? What causes someone to sabotage a perfectly good plan? All the answers are in the mind." Everything we do is formed as a thought. Every action is triggered by our conscious or subconscious mind. Everything! That's why our attitude towards our choices, is just that....it's a choice! Whether we make it consciously or subconsciously, we choose how we respond to whatever happens to us.

"Anybody can be positive when the results are good, but successful people choose a positive attitude when it counts the most – in the face of difficulty." I couldn't have said it better myself. I love laughing at challenges. I'm actually really enjoying the challenge that this airplane pickup is presenting. I choose to not be angry about it, though I do get adamant about needing to see results.

"Healthy and successful people have their own vocabulary. They see problems as challenges. They view failure as feedback. Frustration is fascination. Confused means curious. Shoulds become musts. Older means wiser. An injury is an inconvenience. These are all powerful one-word reframes." A simple change of how we speak to ourselves in our mind can change our overall attitude. After all I know you talk to yourself. I talk to myself. We, myself and I, have some great conversations. If you don't talk to yourself about your attitude you're missing out on a great counselor!

"People may say they believe in something, but that's their conscious mind speaking. Behavior is the true expression of what people believe on the unconscious level. People don't always do what they say, but they always do what they believe." I don't think I used to really understand this, but this last year has taught me differently. I didn't always do what I said I believed. Now I strive to make my actions match my statements of belief. How many people do you know that state that they're Christians, but swear like a sailor, drink until they're obnoxious, and do all manner of things that go against what Christ taught? I've been there. I know what I'm talking about. One who is a follower of Christ, doesn't take these things lightly, he/she lets His teachings become a part of EVERY DAY life. I didn't use to understand the catch phrase, as I thought it, 'What would Jesus do?' Now I ask myself. It makes sense. If I want to become like Jesus, I need to not just profess belief, but act on every teaching that has proceeded from His mouth and the mouth of His holy prophets, both ancient and modern. I so look forward to April and October now when The Prophet and Twelve Apostles, living today, talk to us at the semi-annual General Conference of the Church of Jesus Christ. Modern revelation is given. Instruction is passed on to help us get through our day. God watches over us and has prepared prophets and teachers to help us in these last days….if we will but believe and act on that belief.

Last quote and it'll be a long one, but it's so good.

"I don't think you can feel your best if you're not engaged in the journey of self-improvement. Unfulfilled potential inside of you will always call out in the form of a longing, desire, or sense of dissatisfaction. If you're not doing anything, don't be surprised if you feel unworthy of receiving anything. It's the process of improvement and creation that makes you feel good about yourself, more than the end result….Expectation is when you believe that if you follow a strategy or plan, then as sure as the sun will rise tomorrow, you'll get the results you want. You feel expectation as a powerful sense of certainty. When you decisively choose a strategy, and you're confident that your strategy will work, your level of expectancy rises. When you take action and expect success, you almost always achieve it….Although some mental changes take time – and major physical changes always take time – belief change can happen in an instant. You can stop believing in a falsehood the second a truth enters your awareness." Truth will always shine above falsehoods. The truths of the Gospel are there to guide us through this vale of tears, this vale of sorrow and grief. "Yeah though I walk through the valley of the shadow of death I will fear no evil." The Lord is my shepherd, I shall not want! It's taken me a long time to really understand all this. My testimony of the Lord's Gospel and His Church has grown as I've taken this journey of enlightenment.

May all of you choose to live happy, choose to meet challenges, choose to find strength to not only say you believe something, but act on it as well. I challenge all to read the Book of

Mormon and the Bible. Find out for yourself if what I know to be true is true. All I can say is "Choose ye this day whom ye will serve, but as for me and my house, I will serve the Lord."

Life isn't easy. It's full of tough situations and challenges. Sometimes your airplane leaks fuel all over the APU exhaust and thankfully it doesn't' catch on fire because that would've been a very sad day. But Heavenly Father has a plan for each of us and things happen. Life is! I take it as it comes, "Life in every breath" (again quoting the Last Samurai)

Chapter 47

A LOVE STORY

This week has been one of "interesting" events, ideas, expectations, and in all....it's been great so far. As last week let everyone know, we returned to Naples to get fixed. It took two days, ten hour days watching parts being ripped out and replaced followed by engine runs to see if the problems were still there, but finally we managed to get fixed. Of course as soon as we got fixed and were ready to depart...we had a similar electrical problem in the morning which delayed our take off by two hours, but we managed to get up in the air and all the way to Turkey without a hitch. I suspect it had something to do with the fact that almost the entire electrical system was switched out, everything was tightened on the Auxiliary power unit, leaks were fixed and we were airborne.

For all the time I spent in Italy this trip, I only had two days off work and it's been great. I've enjoyed the challenge and the intensity of getting things done and making things happen, being able to depart with a better product than we've had in previous trips....I hope making them fix 47 write-ups, has given us a better airplane. We'll see in the morning when we attempt to depart from here.

This version is going to maybe be a bit shorter, because I haven't done much, but I do want to talk about love. It was

Valentine's Day this week. How can I not talk about love the week of Valentine's Day! I love "Love" stories. I'm a romantic at heart. I bought multiple love story movies this week and have watched them. I cry over love stories. Life is all about love. Our Heavenly Father sent us here out of love. I'm pretty sure I've told Tiffany and my love story before, but indulge me, after all I've missed every holiday for over a year so it's my prerogative to tell stories.

In 1996, as I was hanging out at school, going to college, working on going broke learning to fly, and paying for it myself (only took me six years to repay that loan from Grandpa) I'm sitting there minding my own business when my wonderful younger brother calls me up out of the blue and asks me if I want to come meet my future wife. I was always a flirtatious young man and happily obliged. See, it turns out that Tiffany, having lived with my cousin in Georgia her senior year of High School, was sent off to school in Idaho. While there, my cousin Laura told her she should go visit family down in Utah, mine, and it just so happened that her roommate knew my brother from high school, so off they went. My life was never the same. I obliged my brother and came to my parent's house and met Tiffany. I, of course, was immediately intrigued, after all she was a gorgeous southern red head, and we hit it off instantly...she thought I was weird, a little strange, nutty, but intriguing. I did the best thing I could do...asked her out. We went on our first date and saw the Steel drum ensemble at BYU, and she got to see Rusty and I acting our normal insane selves...it was awesome.

Well, after that, she had to go back to Idaho and I went back to learning to fly. We ended up talking for hours every night on the phone. There's something about talking that really makes couples come together don't you think. Side note...this last year Tiffany and I have gotten closer than we ever have been, and we've been really talking about deep subjects more than ever...spiritual growth will do that and I love it. She really is my soul mate. End of side note...I had to make a cross country solo flight for my private pilot's license and since I was already planning on going to Idaho, I just extended my flight 60 miles and flew to Rexburg. This would be our second date.

It was one of those perfect Sunday afternoons that defy imagination and are just perfect, they leave an indelible memory. Did I say perfect? I flew a little piper Warrior, N8432D - our plane, and she met me at the airport. We spent a wonderful two hours walking around campus, talking and getting to know each other more. I enjoyed trying to make her laugh, since she has the greatest smile and laugh. I did get in trouble though. I found this twenty dollar bill on the ground, and pocketed it to pay for the gas for the plane...she let me know later she was mad that I didn't give the money to her...I've since made up for that by giving her most all of my money. (I keep ten percent back for the Lord) Well, after a magical two hours, I had to leave. She brought me back to the airport, parking behind the airplane, as I got everything ready to go. At that point, I jumped off the wing, pulled her into a nice long kiss, and hopped into the airplane, and flew off into the sunset.

I'd say I've flown off into too many sunsets at this point, having been gone for three out of the last 6.5 years. Ahhh, deployments! Anyways, back to my story. Later that week we were talking and I found out that she was driving back to Georgia and I jokingly, and seriously, offered to help drive back with her, to make sure she got there safe. I knew she liked me when she informed me she'd already looked into the cost of plane tickets for me to fly back to Utah. To make a long story longer, I rode back with her and a roommate, at least I think it was a roommate, I can't remember, I only had eyes for Tip. I was in Georgia for a grand total of a week. At the end of the week I was supposed to fly back to Utah. I planned to return at the end of summer and drive back with her to Idaho. There was only one catch. And that was that the Lord had other plans for us. See, I believe in destiny. I believe that the Lord guides our lives when we let him. I know, my mom said at the time that it was hormones, but I went to the Atlanta Temple and I left knowing exactly what I needed to do.

We went up to Amicalola Falls for a picnic at the end of the week. There, after eating, and while lying there relaxing, I asked her hypothetically what she'd say if I asked her to marry me. With eyes closed, she stated, "I'd probably say yes!" I followed that up with the question, "Will you marry me?" She smiling said yes. About two minutes later she suddenly sat bolt upright and exclaimed, "Did you just say what I think you said?" "Yes," I responded. "And did I say yes?" she asked. Again, I answered yes. She said, "Oh, ok!" and lay back down. Then we went and hawked an old boyfriend's ring to get an engagement ring. We'd officially known each other for 5 weeks.

The rest is history. I love her more now than I did then. We have four wonderful children. We live an insane crazy life at times, but we love each other. Love, it's the fabric that holds everything together. Love sent us to the world. Love sent Jesus to the cross, but even more so, it helped Him resurrect and give us all the opportunity to return to live with our Father in Heaven. Love is magical. Love is truly a gift. Family is a major part of that plan. Without family we are alone. The whole Plan of Salvation hinges on us returning to live with our Heavenly Father, not alone, not as angels, but to live with our spouses, our loved ones. We do our part so He can do His.

The world is trying to destroy family. We're taught that many things don't matter. The world teaches, "It's only sex"! But it's not. Family, Husbands and wives, are meant to be together. He sent Adam and Eve, not Adam and Steve. (I know I'll probably be blasted as a homophobe, I'm not...I've had friends in the past that were gay, but right is right and wrong is wrong.) The world teaches that the family is not necessarily important, but my study this week was all about the family. In Doctrine of Salvation we read about how parents are required to teach the Gospel to their children and will be held accountable for that. If we as parents neglect teaching our children, leaving it up to schools, church, whoever, then, the sins of our children will be answered upon our heads. But, if we do all we can to teach our children truth, and right and wrong, then, if they stray we won't be blamed for the choices of our children.

A home full of love is a beautiful thing. I know this and I miss being there. Only a couple more months, less actually, and I'll be home. Life is short. As I get older, turning 37 this year, I realize how short it really is. I recognize my mortality and that's not a bad thing. I look forward to the time, hopefully many, many, many years from now, when I'll stand before my Father in Heaven, and be welcomed home with open arms. I know I have a long way to go. I'm growing and strengthening and the best part is that Tiffany and I are doing it together. Life isn't easy, but it's worth it. It wasn't easy to tell Tip's dad that I'd proposed to her...on the first day that he met me, but I'm glad to have him as a Father-in-law. Tiffany and I are trying to live and grow together. The changes we've made in our lives are blessedly amazing.

One of the Presidents of the Church of Jesus Christ of Latter Day Saints, I believe it was David O McKay, who our son Mack is named after, stated that, "No success in this life can compensate for failure in the home." We must guard ourselves against that. Working together as help meets to be perfect partners in the business of working towards returning to our Heavenly Father.

One thing that I noticed in the Bible and the Book of Mormon is that there are very few women spoken of. Yet, all the prophets and the apostles had children. We know that they were married, but I like to think that the women are not mentioned out of respect. I'm sure they were cherished and protected. After all, look at how the world treats women for the most parts as sex objects and they are denigrated by crude language and jokes and whatever. I believe that the wives of the prophets and apostles are not discussed in the scriptures to protect them from the repugnance of the world.

I pray that all of you, men and women, will cherish your loved ones. Take this season of love to be extra romantic, show, don't just state, but show, your love. If love has drifted, or you've grown apart, or any of the thousand other things that can happen, take the time to work on yourself and your relationships. After all, life is short. Don't let it pass!!!

Tiffany is my love story and I plan on spending the next several millennia sharing my love to her with her. It's Valentine's Day, I can be sappy ok! Make your own love story come true. More importantly, love your spouse, be the best person you can be. Do what is right. Choose happiness over misery. Be excellent to each other. That's my lesson learned this week.

"Life is the messy bits" (quote from the movie, Letters to Juliet)

"There is nothing worse than a finicky agapanthus" (quote from Bed of Roses)

Chapter 48

THERE ARE DAYS WHEN I LOVE TO LISTEN TO JAZZ MUSIC

In the event of world calamity, stay calm and remember to bring a blanket and an old pair of socks. This week was full. First off, we finally made it back in to Kabul. It was a nice long flight, the wind, which had been our friend up until that point, was not very nice. It decided to drop from a gorgeous tail wind, to a beautiferous crosswind, making us worry about our fuel consumption. Then we had to descend for a couple hours and that didn't help either, making our fuel consumption absolutely ridiculous. With constant recalculations we based our plans on the wind that we had and decided to overfly Kandahar. We landed back at Kabul with just the right amount of gas. When flying there are always a myriad of variables to juggle--from the weather, the wind, the altitude, the power settings, to the path of the flight.

I've spent the rest of the week journeying through the email quagmire. This reality of work is a joke and a pleasure, a joy and a pain. We work with frustration and happiness, stress and intrigue. Sometimes poor decisions are made. Sometimes this program just seems to be plagued by gremlins, surrounded by trolls, unloved by Afghans because we are restricted from doing what they want us to do, which is to fly the snot out of the airplane until we're all glassy eyed zombies, uncaring about safety....that and the fact that our maintenance record has be absurd. The Afghan leadership is not impressed with our airplane. Se la vie!

At least the airplane I brought is sort of working well...it had a minor problem on its first flight that the Instructor turned into a much bigger problem from poor emergency management and that's all I'm going to say about that. The plane is a good plane. It just is like a 1960's Ford Mustang, requires lots of hands on maintenance every day. Oh well!

My gym time has increased dramatically this week. I was a bit of a slacker my entire 22 day trip. Ok, I worked out once while gone, but my body needed the break since I was pretty worn out when I left. Now, however, my goal in the next 6 weeks is to transform my belly to be a bit slimmer....we'll see what happens. Life is interesting how it turns. I got some information about my assignment, basically about my moving to California, since I haven't found out language, or region or any of that yet. They're in the process of deciding where everyone goes and I had to send information about my language abilities and schooling etc. I called and gave them of the information requested and had a nice discussion. Supposedly, unless things change, I'll get to learn another language. I love it. It'll help toward my ultimate goal of speaking 7 languages fluently. Who knows! Maybe someday I will!!!

In all it's been a slow week for stories, but those will be coming again soon. After all, I'm flying several times this week. So stand by, for the next chapter. You'll need to strap yourselves in, keeping hands and legs inside the ride at all times. Should the ride come to a complete stop, then you'll be able to depart, but not until. No standing unless you want to lose your head on a cross beam. And definitely take pictures!

Who am I kidding? I just like acting insane or different for the fun of it. Hence wearing my floppy cap like I was an Aussie or maybe a gay French artist! ☺ There is a distinct shape to my cap and I like it that way. So nyah! (This is me sticking my tongue out at you!) ;0)-

Don't you just love Irish music! Celtic music brings a stir to my soul. Ay layk a good Irish Brogue! Brings a spawkle to me eye it does. I think I like it because it's always fun, even when it shouldn't be. Laughing at sadness, laughing at pain, laughing at the crisis life tends to throw out to us; that's a good Irish tune…and you have to love Riverdance since it's so fast and crazy!

And so I come to the week's study. This conglomeration of subjects and styles, while it may seem a collage, will fall all together and merge into a whole.

I'm a student—a student of life, a student of religion, a student of everything I can get my hands on. I want to KNOW a bit about everything. This is a gift. This is a pleasure. This is also part of the purpose of life. What we learn here on earth will continue with us to the world beyond. I've said it over and over again; this life is a time to prepare. The things we learn in this life, while compared to eternity may not seem like much, are essential to our eternal progression. Our need is clear when we can know that it is more important to learn and have joy in learning in order to be edified instead of just entertained. Elder Robert D. Hales, talking in his book *Return* about viewing education as a process not a destination stated, "We begin to see our education as a lifelong journey. Seen that way, the curriculum outlined by the Lord not only makes sense to us but thrills us 'that we may be instructed more perfectly in theory, in principle, in doctrine, in the law of the gospel, in all things that pertain unto the kingdom of God,…of things both in heaven and in the earth, and under the earth; things which have been, things which are, things which must shortly come to pass; things which are at home, things which are abroad; the wars and the perplexities of the nations, and the judgments which are on the land; and a knowledge of countries and kingdoms'(D&C 88:78-79)" (sounds kind of like my new job description doesn't it!)

Elder Hales continues talking about education, about lifetime learners. He discusses attributes of someone that makes a lifetime of learning—courage, faithful desire and curiosity, humility and patience, communication because lifetime learners are teachers at heart.

Why are we asked to study the scriptures every day? The obvious answers are the primary answers. One, it opens our souls and our eyes to our Heavenly Father so He can instruct us. Two, it makes us more aware of what learning is important and what isn't. Three, most importantly it increases our spiritual learning and yearning. Spiritual learning accumulates exponentially. It is a fact that as we learn line upon line, precept on precept, our knowledge grows in leaps and bounds. I've seen this working in me over the last year. I used to think I knew the Gospel…I was wrong. I'm still learning and will continue for a lifetime. Interestingly enough one of the quotes I really like from the same chapter states that "earning a master's degree in theology is far less valuable than the degree of knowledge we obtain from the simple teachings of the Master Himself." Our learning and study really only profits us if it produces the mighty change of heart that King Benjamin's people had in the Book of Mosiah in the Book of Mormon. They felt such a stirring and change in their hearts that they had "no more disposition to do evil". That is a massive change that only comes through exponential spiritual growth that comes through daily study.

Proverbs 4:7 states, "Wisdom is the principal thing; therefore get wisdom: and with all thy getting, get understanding." Wisdom comes through study, but with wisdom we need to understand the purpose of life. If we don't gain that understanding all our study is for naught.

Shifting focus a little, one of the main things that frustrates me about the Afghans is how idle, lazy and indolent they can be. They prefer to have us do everything for them and always take the easy, slack way out. And guess what? We Americans are not that different. True, I'm exaggerating a little or stereotyping a little, but that's the way I see it at times. Look at how many people are on perpetual welfare. Look at how our society has become a generation of "I deserve its". Our society has devolved into the haves and the have not's. Keeping up with the Joneses is a way of life. Debt is rampant because we don't have the patience of our parents to wait until we can afford things. We think we deserve everything. I look at our society and I see the Nephites, or the Jews, before the slaughter and destruction of their civilizations. In short, we've forgotten what it means to work (as a society, not as individuals). Here are some things I read. From our lesson in Gospel Principles page158 we read, "The Lord is not pleased with those who are lazy or idle. He said ,'the idler shall not have place in the church, except he repent and mend his ways' (D&C 75:29)….From the earliest days of the Church, the prophets have taught Latter-day Saints to be independent and self-sustaining and to avoid idleness. True Latter-day Saints will not voluntarily shift from themselves the burden of their own support. So long as they are able, they will supply themselves and their families with the necessities of life. Our attitude toward work is very important. Not all of us can choose the kind of work we do. Some of us labor for long hours for the bare necessities. It is difficult to enjoy such work. Yet the happiest people have learned to enjoy their work, WHATEVER IT IS." (emphasis added)

We have opportunities to share, grow, work and help others. When we share our time and talents to help others, all are blessed. The Lord said, "When ye have done it unto the least of these my brethren ye have done it unto me."

Ahhh, ain't life grand. We have the opportunity to do much, if we think beyond ourselves.

I am reminded of the Primary Song "Row, Row, Row Your Boat". The song is simple, a round, that goes. "Row, Row, Row your boat, Gently down the stream, Merrily, merrily, Merrily, merrily, life is but a dream." Now I don't know how many of you have either rowed a boat or been on a rowing machine, but I have. I've done both. And you know what? IT'S WORK! I spent 15 minutes on the rowing machine this week at the gym and it was painful. Man it hurts. It's tiring. But, if we look at the song, it's the attitude towards the work that changes everything. I hurt as I rowed, I didn't have fun, but I was happy because I felt good working out. I was doing something productive and helping my body and though it hurt in the moment, I felt much better for it. All worthwhile work is like that. Our attitude can make the worst kind of job or duty a blessing and we can have a happy life and continue learning.

There are days when I love to listen to jazz music. It's an amazing drawn out feeling, pulling emotion and verve out of oneself. There's a free-flowing spirit about it. An emotion pulled from the depths of a soul. The music, pulled from the player, can be wild or mellow, deep or unseen, carefree now callous, dripping and finally, lustrous.

How is emotion expressed in your life? How do you react when things don't go your way? How do you treat those around you? Is life full, or half empty? Do you see the shiny side or the dark? Where is your little I AM?

Life is a mystery wrapped in an enigma, drunk on the pressure of its own glory. Be yourself. Choose who you are! Be free from the self-induced pressures to conform to society's vagaries. Believe in what you know to be true and act on it. That's how the Gospel works. We choose to follow, or not. Life is full of tough choices. Patience and virtue, patience and joy, patience and strife all combine into a kaleidoscope of paradoxes.

Music has a way of helping, hindering, sharing, enabling, growing and ensuring that our souls either expand or contract as we let it in. You see different types of music and feel the way they affect you for good or ill. Music is a compilation of sounds that tear at us deep inside and wraps itself around our mind and heart. We can either feel the Spirit more intensely through music or feel it literally run away from the negativity that some types of music engender.

Love is a feeling that grows in our heart. Ask any couple and they have a song or two that is "their" song. Tiffany and I have several. Each has its own special memory; like "Somebody". I was sitting in my cousin's garage playing it for her for the first time when we were young and barely knew each other, yet to this day it is still "our song". We have several others, but we'll keep those personal. I know I sometimes go overboard on the personal data, but we need to have at least a little kept for just us.

Friends can also have songs that epitomize their friendship or their time together. Rusty and I will forever be known for the insanity that would commence whenever we cranked up Roxette's

"Joyride". Even deployed there are songs that stir the heart. When I was deployed to Bosnia we were a small group and had our own camp. Literally, the Green Day song "Time of your Life" became our camp theme song. We grew that bond that only comes when you work together in a war setting AND your hearts and minds are in the same place.

Some music transports us back in time or transcends whatever mood we're in. When I'm down, and at home alone, I just crank up some 80's music and dance like I was 15 again, until I notice Tip watching me shaking her head at her silly man. But, that's the whole point. Life is about growing, learning, being who you want to be, not who you think the world thinks you should be. Life is about finding out what's important and what's not. There's a book called "Don't Sweat the Small Stuff, and it's all Small Stuff", the title says everything. Life is short. You blink and your kids are teenagers. You blink again and you've been married 15 years, only a wonderful eternity to go. You blink again and you're no longer a young punk, but an old punk with a belly and a head full of ideas about what you'd still like to do.

Love stories are the bomb! Life is too short to not romance your better half. Time, money, things, words, emotions, feelings, flowers, poetry whether it's in life or in song, it's a rocket fueled passion of outstanding glory. Am I describing insanity? Nope. It's a beautiful metaphor for life and love. Love is an emotion we don't always share; we don't give of ourselves openly to the most cherished people in our lives. We trap our feelings inside and ensure that we'll have frustrations and deep unmet expectations which lead to our immutable defense mechanisms kicking in. That just leads to further unmet expectations and frustration. I love it when I do just the right thing for Tip, but I don't always get it right and I've screwed up more often than not. Women tend to think that men are knowledgeable. The truth is that we are stumbling in the dark and unless we're told what you're thinking we just don't get it. Dr. John Lund puts it best telling us to own our expectations, to stop expecting others to read our minds and to say what we mean and mean what we say.

Life continues, life moves on, every day, every minute. What do we do with it? Do we ignore the signals we send our mates? Do we ignore the passing of time? Every so often, do we ask, who am I? Why am I here? Is life this insane game of chance? No, it's not. I just love answering my own questions. I'm kind of a functionally delusional misfit at times. There's a sort of joy and liberty in asking questions. If you don't ask questions you can never get answers. Life's just that way. Ask many questions, get many answers. Life revolves around learning. Heavenly Father sent us here to learn. Step by step, learning minute by minute evolving into years of growth and maturing, line upon line precept on precept….that's the goal of this life. The Book of Mormon teaches us that this life is the time to prepare to meet God. In this momentary existence in the grand scheme of eternity, we have a true opportunity to grow into people destined for greatness, if we but learn what is important and what is not.

Tip is my inspiration. As we've grown together our desire for learning and our romance has increased, our closeness has grown as we've opened ourselves up to each other and followed Dr. John Lund's advice to own our words and our expectations. Romance, what a great thing! It's a joy to romance my wife, surprise her. Life is that we might have joy. We're given this time of life to prepare, and how much better is it when we can prepare to meet God with the one's we love. So cool! The Plan of Salvation is so awesome it's hard to imagine a more perfect plan. You can't tell me it doesn't answer the age old questions of the meaning of life, because it does in a full and complete way. From pre-mortal existence to life in the spirit world following death to judgment and finally to a kingdom of glory, our questions are answered. Simple and complex at the same time, kind of like my mind and the way it works, it is a kaleidoscope of joy wrapped in a pretzel spitting out my ideals.

All in all, I must say that life is full of opportunities, if we but take the time to search, learn, grow, seek out…In other words, life is to be lived; life is an action verb.

There was a Spanish song that was pretty good, even though it was making fun of almost all religions and their propensities to spout off one thing and do another. The song was called, "Jesus is a verb, not a noun". While it was part joke, the message at the same time was not. It meant that our actions speak louder than our words. If I say all these things in this book but don't continue to live them, I am nothing more than a hypocrite. I've been the hypocrite and refuse to be one any longer. This year has taken Tiffany and I and forged us in a refiner's fire and may the Lord bless us to continue in our growth as I return home. Action, not sublimation. Action not static. Verbo no sustantivo.

Chapter 49

SOME TIMES WE FEEL LIKE A NUT, SOMETIMES WE DON'T

Sometimes it's easier to not start something than it is to start something; though starting brings great fancy and fun with all new projects. Flying - a sport of kings, a journey of splendor, a flash of pleasure, and a conundrum of chaos. I promised a roller coaster ride last week and by jove, I am about to deliver. In only two flights, I managed to collect an assortment of experiences to knock the socks off a grown man, all done in the safest way possible.

Put on your parachute, strap in and enjoy the ride. (Of course we don't carry parachutes on our plane so you'll have to find your own.)

First flight of the week we went on a normal training mission. Went up to Mazar and while the weather wasn't great it wasn't horrible. In fact, we had a fairly decent flight, doing instrument work first and then proceeding to normal pattern work. Normal pattern work entails a certain je ne se qua and a practice of emergency procedures. My student flew fairly well, with his standard problems, but it wasn't until we began to work on emergency procedures that the issues emerged. Sometimes when simulating emergencies I don't like to preface it with the words simulated. We don't have a simulator so any emergency training is done on the airplane through simulations….or something really fails.

I began moving one of the throttles back and forth, while the student was attempting to give his briefing for a normal approach. As I moved the throttle, obviously the power would cycle back and forth on that prop. My student wasn't getting it, even when I asked the loadmaster if he saw a problem on one of the engines. He agreed with me that a cycling prop was bad, but the copilot just didn't understand. His method of understanding was to try to squeeze the throttles and not let me move the one I was moving. I'm stronger than he is so I kept up the movement. He refused to acknowledge that I was doing something so I kept it up for almost two minutes as we kept trucking along in the air. When he called for flaps down and gear down, I pulled the throttle to idle and informed him his engine had simulated failing because he wouldn't acknowledge the issues it was having. That threw him for a loop and he attempted to correct. He performed the correct procedure, but didn't realize that he couldn't keep up his airspeed or his altitude with the configuration he had set up. I allowed him to slow down, and slow down and slow down, until he was ten knots slow…Then I took the airplane away from him. I proceeded to demonstrate how to properly fly a single engine approach, missed approach and go around…..then made him do it again, this time he had a lot better control and didn't let his airspeed get away from him.

My mind is trapped in a cyclone of blahhhhhhh, as I sit here on the edge of a sniffle. The flight ended, the mission complete, life moved on as normal. All was well, until my next flight.

There's an interesting thing about lightning. It's unique, it lances out of a sky turned cold and dark and unforgiving. It screams through the air shattering sound and rumbling walls. The historic significance of each storm is lost in its own tiny memory, devoid of thought for that instance of chaos and cacophony. My next flight was scheduled, the airplane was ready, and we boarded with a suitable weather report. As we started the engines we could see some weather brewing to the southwest and had no desire to go that direction. Lucky for us our path was to take us to the north and west. We ran through our checks, taxied to the runway and by the time we got there we were ready for takeoff. I informed tower of our readiness to depart and they informed us that lightning had been seen to the southwest. I told them to let us know if it got within five miles of the airport. I could see the storm blowing our direction and knew we needed to get going soon or we'd be stuck there indefinitely. Tower cleared us for takeoff and off we went into the wild black yonder…

The storm was making its way across the tarmac as we accelerated down the runway. Liftoff! Our gear came up, our flaps came up and we were into the clouds. We hadn't been in the clouds for but two seconds it seemed when there was a loud boom, a flash of light, just below the nose and the airplane rocked as we continued to climb. I hurriedly checked all the instruments and it appeared that everything was fine, nothing had been fried. It's quite safe in the airplane if we were to be struck by lightning, with special lightning wicks on the wings to funnel the electricity off the airplane. Amazingly we weren't hit in that boom. Our cohorts on the ground had watched us takeoff, disappear into the dark cloud and then a large bolt of lightning struck somewhere nearby on the base. From the flight deck we continued our climb and we had wind and turbulence and rain and suddenly right before our eyes flashed a beautiful burst of lightning maybe a hundred feet in front of us. It burst from right to left across the window screen and forked, one fork heading for the ground the other across the sky in a brilliant sheen of blue-green light. It was pretty cool, but flying in thunderstorms is not something we're supposed to be doing. Taking off into weather and having it turn out to be an imbedded thunderstorm--not cool!

At that point I was pretty much done with thunderstorms because for one thing, it's not someplace you want to be and for another, lightning while it won't cause the airplane to explode, can cause extensive damage if it strikes and fries your electronics. Thank goodness for old 1970's technology right…not too worried about things frying. Anyways, at that point we'd reached our turn point, all of this occurring in about thirty seconds time, and we turned right and were out of the storm in seconds, having only been on the very edge. We were a little annoyed with the tower controllers for not letting us know that the storm was within the five mile ring, because they shut down all traffic then. But we were out and we went on our merry way to do our training.

I must say it was fun, but alas there's more to the story. I was in the right seat as the instructor. We were in the clouds the whole time, at least until we were above 17 thousand feet. We were told to maintain 13,000 feet. My Afghan pilot was struggling with the controls and while I was on the radio and double checking things he blew right through our altitude which caused air traffic control to yell at us. I grabbed the yoke and shoved the nose down to get us back on altitude and away from traffic that was being called out to us. The pilot was drifting left like he was having a bit of the leans and I helped correct him. He got a bit perturbed and threw his hands up and said, "If you want to fly the plane you fly it." Obviously, I calmed him down and explained the situation. It was just his stress showing. We broke out for a second and the traffic that had been called out to us passed overhead between 500-1000 feet above us. Ahh, the joys of instructing and dealing with weather! I was actually having a great time. It was fun, it was difficult and I felt like laughing. My Afghan pilot—not so much!

We finally got on our way and had no more issues for the rest of the training flight. We flew to Bagram after an hour at Mazar i Sharif and stopped to drop off a pallet, pick up a crew member and get a good dinner. Following dinner we loaded back up (did I mention I got a delicious bowl of mint chocolate ice cream…yummy!!!!) and proceeded back to Kabul. The only problem was that our nice forecast weather….didn't appear. We were almost to the Instrument approach when we were told the weather not only was below minimums, but it was way below minimums. We had something like 500 feet visibility, fog, and an indefinite ceiling. Ummmmm, not the best weather and not even legal to attempt an approach for us! We went to hold, pulling the power back and settling in to wait. A foreign aircraft attempted the approach and landed at their own risk and we requested a PIREP (pilot report) on the weather. All we needed was a mile visibility to be able to land. The punks reported the lights at ¾ of a mile. We were bummed. If they'd given us the mile visibility we could have attempted the approach. Tower even queried them, knowing that's what we needed for the attempt. They stuck to their guns. Oh well, we had held for half an hour. At that point we were informed that the visibility was not forecast to get any better until 3 AM. We definitely didn't have gas nor crew day for that so we returned to Bagram with our tail between our legs and decided to call it a night.

We called for gas, but it took them over an hour to get a gas truck to us. We also called for a crew bus, letting our leadership know we were done. Just before the gas got there though I decided to check the weather, and found it within limits to attempt the approach. After talking with the crew, and having an hour and a half of duty day left, we decided to attempt it. We got engines running, got ready…and the crew bus showed up, nearly two hours after our request. We sent him away and went to Kabul and had no problems. We landed at Kabul literally to the minute of our crew duty day. It was awesome and turned out to be a fun interesting albeit harrowing day at points.

There're my stories for the week. It's been a good week and full of intriguing adventures that you ask yourself later, "did that really happen?" Or the statement, "You just can't make this stuff up!" That's a common phrase here, though most people use other terminology. That brings me to my study topics this week. My studies have been seriously influenced by events that are occurring in my family and in my studies. Let me tell you another story, this one is a little sad.

Emma, my darling daughter, has been plagued in her time at her school with friends that are not true friends. They formed a club and created positions like president etc. Emma and another girl wanted the same job so they did rock, paper, scissors for it. Emma continuously won….but they kept going until the other girl won and they immediately gave the other girl the position. Emma they declared as "Congress" then held a meeting in which "Congress" was not allowed to attend. The next day they also had the gall to tell her that she could still be in their group if she wore "cuter" outfits the next day. They made fun of her for reading so much and I felt very bad for her. She's a trouper though, and such a good kid. She understands that they aren't true friends and she finds her friends in her family and in her books right now. But, this story made me think and it really made me concentrate on what I'd been reading this week in both the scriptures and in other writings.

How do we treat others? Are we civil? Or do we live a crude, haphazard lifestyle that begets wanton abuse of others just because they're different? I've been reading the chapters in the Book of Mormon that are termed the war years. I've been circling all the times that the word contention is mentioned and it's a lot. There was one verse that stuck out to me. It says in Alma 51:16, "For it was his first care to put an end to such contentions and dissensions among the people; for behold, this had been hitherto a cause of all their destruction..." Dissention, contention, it's everywhere a cause of sadness and pain. Contention is of the devil. He incites men and women to look down on others, to backbite, to stab, to criticize, to humiliate, and to say all manner of accusations against them.

In the movie Hoosiers, Gene Hackman's character suffered from a past and he was filled with regret because of it and was looking for a new start in a different town. But, the people didn't want to give him a chance. He was different and did things different than what they were used to and they tried to run him out of town. It wasn't until the people's attitude changed that the mood changed and he could be accepted. It's difficult for all of us to know what's going on with others.

President Gordon B. Hinckley wrote in his book *Standing for Something* the following statement, "It is appalling. It is alarming. And when all is said and done, the cost can be attributed almost entirely to human greed, to uncontrolled passion, to a total disregard for the rights of others—in other words, to a lack of civility. As one writer has said, 'People might think of a civilized community as one in which there is a refined culture. Not necessarily; first and foremost it is one in which the mass of people subdue their selfish instincts in favor of the common well-being.' The writer continued, 'In recent years the media have raised boorishness to an art form. The hip heroes of movies today deliver gratuitous put-downs to ridicule and belittle anyone who gets in their way. Bad manners, apparently, make a saleable commodity. Television situation comedies wallow in vulgarity, stand-up comedians base their acts on insults to their audiences, and talk show hosts become rich and famous by snarling at callers and heckling guests.'

All of this speaks of anything but refinement. It speaks of anything but courtesy. It speaks of anything but civility and tolerance. Rather, it speaks of rudeness and crudeness and an utter insensitivity to the feelings and rights of others."

And continuing he wrote, "Those who routinely take the name of God in vain and resort to filthy, crude language only advertise the poverty of their vocabularies, a glaring paucity in their powers of expression, and a flaw in their moral makeup. Civility invites the ability to speak, to converse, to communicate effectively. It is a tremendous asset."

I read this and it makes me think. I've noticed for a long time that the world is growing darker and less civil. Even as I write this my roommate is watching a television show that in the last thirty seconds characters insulted each other for humor at least 15 times. It's insane to think that the Spirit will strive with man when he spends his time in base concepts and insults. One thing I dislike about the military is that so many people in the military are not civil. They believe that being a soldier or airman gives them license to act, speak and converse in extremely crude and rude manners. I am appalled because I know I've joined in, in times past, and made fun of someone at another's expense and I feel ashamed because of it, especially with the changes I've made in the last year. I can't go five minutes or most days even one minute at work without hearing f-bombs and all manner of vulgarity being spouted by coworkers. I'm not trying to demean anyone I work with, just stating facts. To me it's embarrassing. Another thing that is embarrassing is the fact that as I have watched others over the years, when someplace, among people of other cultures, the first thing they want to learn is how to curse and take the Lord's name in vain in the foreign language. That has always annoyed me.

What is annoying is the hypocrisy in it. Many of those spouting off vulgarities are "Christians" or it doesn't really matter does it. They espouse a belief in God the Father and then turn around and basically curse God with their lips. President Hinckley stated, "How can one profane the name of God and then kneel before Him in prayer? Profanity separates us from Him who has supreme power to help us. Profanity wounds the spirit and demeans the soul."

It used to be that civility was honored. Humility was respected. Meekness was rewarded. Not so today! Today Hollywood profanes the very word civility as "old fashioned". We're taught that humor is best at someone's expense and we never are shown the side of the story of the person being made fun of. I've been there. My daughter is going through it. My wonderful wife went through it for years growing up, hating herself because she didn't measure up physically to her sisters. Her self-esteem was low or non-existent and it wasn't until she turned to the Lord and really found herself that she began to like herself and realize that she is a wonderful daughter of God, an amazing woman, an excellent mother, and my best friend.

In line with civility is humility. The Lord taught us that, "And whosoever will be chief among you, let him be your servant." (Matt 20:27) He also stated in Matt 18:4, "Whosoever therefore shall humble himself as this little child, the same is greatest in the kingdom of heaven." What does it mean to be humble? It means teachable. It means civil. It means looking after others rather than ourselves. It leads us to exclaim as Christ did, "Not as I will, but as thou wilt." When we humble ourselves before the Lord and are penitent, sorrowing for our sins and indiscretions, we're teachable and we can accept the will of the Lord for us, rather than attempt to tell him what we think we need to do.

So, how do we treat others? How do we treat our significant others? Elder Hales in his book *Return* states, "Our Savior knows our hearts—each one…..When our suffering wounds us spiritually, or physically, our first reaction may be to retreat into the dark shadows of depression, to shut out the impulses of hope and joy, and to give up on the light of life, which comes when we try to live the commandments of our Father in Heaven….How do we get out of this? We too, as the Savior, can focus our concern on caring for the needs of others. Reaching out to help others can quickly dispel feelings of loneliness and imperfection—and replace them with feelings of hope, love and encouragement." This will allow us to develop that humility of spirit that will allow the Savior to guide us through these troubled times. We are not meant to endure alone. We are not meant to suffer in silence. We are meant to support and strengthen one another, to be civil, to be courteous, and to build each other up.

I feel for my daughter as she struggles through this period of life. The world can be a coarse, mean place and it is going to become more so. Let's not be part of the crowd. Let us stand like a city set on a hill and be a shining example to those around us.

I want to end this with the parable of the Sower in Mark 4:3-20. Humor me for a minute please because it all ties in. "Behold, there went out a sower to sow: And it came to pass, as he sowed some fell by the way side, and the fowls of the air came and devoured it up. And some fell on stony ground, where it had not much earth; and immediately it sprang up, because it had no depth of earth: But when the sun was up, it was scorched; and because it had no root, it withered away. And some fell among thorns, and the thorns grew up, and choked it, and it yielded no fruit. And other fell on good ground and did yield fruit that sprang up and increased; and brought forth, some thirty, and some sixty, and some an hundred.... And when he was alone, they that were about him with the twelve asked of him the parable. And he said unto them, Unto you it is given to know the mystery of the kingdom of God: but unto them that are without, all these things are done in parables: That seeing they may see, and not perceive; and hearing they may hear, and not understand; lest at any time they should be converted....and he said unto them, Know ye not this parable? And how then will ye know all parables? The sower soweth the word. And these are they by the wayside, where the word is sown; but when they have heard, Satan cometh immediately, and taketh away the word that was sown in their hearts. And these are they likewise which are sown on stony ground; who when they have heard the word, immediately receive it with gladness; and have no root in themselves and so endure but for a time: afterward, when affliction or persecution ariseth for the word's sake immediately they are offended. And these are they which are sown among thorns; such as hear the word, and the cares of this world, and the deceitfulness of riches, and the lusts of other things entering in choke the word, and it becomes unfruitful. And these are they which are sown on good ground; such as hear the word, and receive it, and bring forth fruit, some thirtyfold, some sixty, and some an hundred"

By this I just want to emphasize that our actions are seen by everyone. What we say and do are of paramount importance. Are we going to be doers and true followers of Christ, or are we going to be those seeds that fall in stony ground? I hope each day to continue to be one of those that bring forth fruit thirty, sixty or a hundred fold. The Lord loves us and helps us grow, but only if we let him in. How we treat others, if we're civil, if we're humble, if we're teachable, then we'll be able to grow and develop those traits that emulate the master.

From Longfellow, "Trust no Future, howe'er pleasant! Let the dead Past bury its dead! Act,--act in the living present! Heart within, and God o'erhead! Let us then be up and doing, With a heart for any fate; Still achieving, still pursuing Learn to labor and to wait."

Chapter 50

OH, WHAT A BEAUTIFUL MORNING

What a week! I had two very different experiences this week. In the first, I put my foot in my mouth, figuratively speaking by leaning too far forward to get a mission done, and in the second I validated a student's inability to learn. I've had a certain focus this week. I'm finally to a point where I've got a month to go and it's time to ensure that there is a strong foundation for our departure.

Last Sunday it was a wonderful day to fly. Snow was falling off and on, it was nice and cold and the weather was expected to be amazing when we got back….in other words, completely rotten. Our departure went smoothly at least as far as departures go. I had a mission that was thrown on me at the last minute on Saturday. It doesn't seem to matter at times that things go directly against the way we attempt to teach the Afghans to schedule things. Oh well, such is life. We can't seem to teach an old dog new tricks!

Okay, so the mission was set, we did our thing and made the mission happen. We departed, picking up some icing along the way but without any problems. Breaking out into clear sky is a beautiful thing and we flew along serenely all the way to Shindand. While descending into the airfield we attempted to start our Auxiliary power unit, but it wouldn't start. It acted really weird. That wasn't too bad. We landed. Taxiing in to drop off our passengers we got rid of them and then attempted again to start the APU. This didn't work out so well. I sent my loadmaster out to look and he found ice filling the opening for the vent. This caused the valve to break because it couldn't turn to open with the snow and ice there. At this point we had a problem. I had to go to Kandahar to get gas, and I needed to shut down engines to do so. One problem with this was the fact that without the APU we wouldn't be able to start the engines. I called back to the squadron and had them coordinate to get an air cart at Kandahar ready for us. This worked only so well. I made the mistake of not ensuring they notified the Director of Operations…so I got in a little bit of trouble when I got back. We flew down to Kandahar and got gas, got started and flew back. We made it back no problem…

The second flight this week was just yesterday. It was my opportunity to fly with our worst student on a phase check for instrument work. He didn't do so well. In fact, he bombed…He bombed….he BOMBED. It was not a good flight. In the world of problems when flying, you can get by with making a few mistakes. In fact, usually, things are very forgiving…but when you make mistake after mistake after mistake, such that the instructor … me … has to take the airplane away from you because you have no idea whatever about where you are or what you're supposed to be doing … that compounds an already difficult situation. The sad thing is he's a nice guy. He's just not cut out for flying, at least not flying the way we're teaching which is to be day/night/all-weather capable pilots. Needless to say I can't even list all the problems he had. For one thing each time we did an approach, the approach controller in the tower gave us alternate missed approach instructions. Each time we fly an approach there are written instructions for what to do if you can't land or can't see the airport. The controller has the option to give us alternate instructions.

That's standard practice. Yet when my student was flying he didn't hear the instructions, nor my reply concerning the instructions and when I sent him around without landing he had no clue what he was supposed to be doing and was just trucking off into the wild blue yonder clueless until I'd tell him where to go. Ahhh, some people just aren't meant to be pilots. He definitely is one of them. At this point he has over a hundred hours in the airplane and still doesn't remember the information he's supposed to be looking at during an engine start. Sad, but at least he didn't try to crash me into a mountain. He was too high on his altitudes for that, but at least the Loadmaster and I knew where we were and what we were doing.

I don't mind being the one that sends him to possible elimination. I was tough but fair with him during the flight. I was objective. I didn't go into the flight thinking I'm going to give him an unsatisfactory score. I hoped he would do well. He didn't. It's part of the nature of the business to have to call a spade a spade sometimes, even when it won't be taken well. My brother Kurt knows all about this, having had to fire people a lot in his line of work. I don't envy him that responsibility at all.

Well, our student has a chance tomorrow to see if he can pull it together. I hope that he can. And I suspect that he won't. If he does, you'll all be the first to know.

"I'm just so tired, won't you sing me to sleep and fly through my dreams so I can hitch a ride with you tonight. And get away from this place, have a new name and face; I just ain't the same without you in my life. Late night drives, all alone in my car, I can't help but start singing lines from all our favorite songs, and melodies in the air, saying life just ain't fair, sometimes I just can't believe you're gone, and I know the view from heaven, beats the heck out of mine here, and if we all believe in heaven, maybe we'll make it through one more year down here…." It would be nice if everyone believed in heaven wouldn't it. Those are the lyrics from Yellowcard's "View from Heaven". I love the chorus. That part where he sings "and if we all believe in Heaven maybe we'll make it through one more year." I tell you what; it's been my belief in Heaven and my knowledge and study of the Gospel that has gotten me through this past year. The reason for the Gospel, for all of this life, is so we can learn. If we're not learning, what are we doing?

I just am having a great day. It's been one of those days where everything goes deliciously sweet. I got to talk to Tip first thing in the morning, and that always makes my day go well. I went in to work and found my taxes had come in and I was able to spend some time this morning doing something I've been working toward for a long time. I scheduled and paid my credit card and loan debt. By the end of next week when everything goes through I will only be beholden to the banks that own the loans on the cars and the house, but I'll have paid off my loans and credit debt. For years the church and our leaders have taught that we need to get out of debt. Tiffany and I are on that trip, we're on that road, and we're making the goal happen. I love it. It feels soooooo good and like a load is ripped off my shoulders. Obviously, I'm in a very good mood and have been all day. Even when working out at the gym, killing myself with running and stair machine since today was my cardio makeup day for the week. I feel good. Mentally, spiritually, physically, all aspects are in line to dictate a great mood.

Columbus once said, "God gave me the faith, and afterward the courage." This is such a profound statement. We learn and grow through our efforts. If we sit and rest and wait for things to change, they won't. Sure the world may change and things may change around us, but if we don't make efforts we are stuck in a rut and possibly going backwards. The message of the Gospel is such that we develop faith unto repentance, as that faith grows we repent of the sins of the world that we've accrued over the years, then we wash those away through baptism and covenant to take upon us the name of Christ since He suffered so that we won't have to suffer if we endure to the end. After receiving the gift of the Holy Ghost we have the requirement to endure to the end.

What does that mean? This has been the topic of much of my study this week – enduring to the end! Conversion, true conversion, brings a mighty change of heart. A true convert seeks to be the person that the Lord would have them be. A true convert wants to become the person the Lord would have them become. True conversion isn't in words only. True conversion isn't in a one-time statement of faith and feeling. True conversion is shown daily in the acts and words of the convert. What we do, say, think daily are testimonies of our mighty change of heart. It doesn't mean we'll be perfect, because we won't be. We'll fail if we think that it's completely black and white. The Lord knows we'll sin, but that's why He's prepared the fullness of the gospel to teach us, faith unto repentance.

J. Golden Kimball used to be a character as a General Authority of the church. One comment that is attributed to him was something to the fact that the devil couldn't have him because he repented too often every day. Whether that truly was a comment he made, I don't know, but it has truth in it. We pray and repent and change and grow every day so that Satan has no hold over us and can't dictate the terms of our life. Enduring to the end is a process that continues forever. Life is to be lived and endured and enjoyed. By enjoyment I'm not referring to the world's definition. I'm referring to the joy and hope and fun that can be found in the freedom of obedience to the commandments. Obedience to the laws that our Heavenly Father prepared doesn't bind us down as the world espouses, instead we are MORE free, more happy, and more prepared to thoroughly ENJOY life than those that don't abide by God's laws.

During one of the conference talks in 2005 the speaker stated, "If we pray to know his (meaning God's) will and submit ourselves to it, spiritual healing can come and will come in his way and time." Our Heavenly Father answers our prayers, though not always as we expect, or in the way we want. Another speaker, Elder Won Yong Ko, stated, "Do not be afraid of sacrifice. Occasionally there is a time gap between sacrifice and blessings. Don't worry about it. We are following council." This applies because maybe if we sacrifice some of our time, money, or things, we'll end up being the answer to someone else's prayer. Most often I've found that prayers are answered through others. In Alabama, Tiffany has had many prayers answered by the thoughtful concern of our friend Teresa. She's helped Tiffany in so many ways, and always when Tiffany needed the support or the kick in the butt, and had a hard time asking for it. This has really been a year of a refiner's fire. I'm so thankful for the opportunities and lessons that we've learned in the last year. I've sacrificed time away from my family, but ohh, what blessings we've received this year.

In the Gospel of St. Mark, chapter 8 verses 34 to 36 Christ stated, "Whosoever will come after me, let him deny himself, and take up his cross, and follow me. For whosoever will save his life shall lose it; but whosoever shall lose his life for my sake and the gospel's, the same shall save it. For what shall it profit a man, if he shall gain the whole world, and lose his own soul." When we change and grow and turn to the Gospel, we are blessed and when we lose our life, meaning we cut off our worldly desires and get rid of the chains with which Satan binds us, then, we find our life and the freedom that exists in obedience to the Gospel. I finally understand this scripture. I didn't really understand it before. I thought a lot of things, but until I realized that I couldn't have one foot in the world and one in the Gospel and put both feet on the path of the Gospel, that was when I found the freedom and the hope and the light that infuses the soul that is doing what the Lord would have them do.

Christ explained the conditions of men that we see today. Again in Mark 7:21-23 he states, "For from within, out of the heart of man, proceed evil thoughts, adulteries, fornications, murders, Thefts, covetousness, wickedness, deceit, lasciviousness, an evil eye, blasphemy, pride, foolishness: All these things come from within and defile man." In that same vein King Benjamin taught in the Book of Mormon, "For the natural man is an enemy to God, and has been from the fall of Adam, and will be, forever and ever, unless he yields to the enticings of the Holy Spirit, and putteth off the natural man and becometh a saint through the atonement of Christ the Lord, and becometh as a child, submissive, meek, humble, patient, full of love, willing to submit to all things which the Lord seeth fit to inflict upon him, even as a child doth submit to his father."

We can become as children, as directed by King Benjamin. It takes effort every day. It takes humility to realize that without the Lord's help, we can't make it. It takes realizing that there are things such as right and wrong, black and white, good and evil. We can't have one foot in the world and one in the Gospel. Doesn't work! I know, I tried it for years and it just doesn't provide for happiness, security, strength, or anything good. I love working with Tip together every day, even though it's over the phone, to grow together in the gospel and as parents. We are charged to teach the Lord's Gospel to our children. We are responsible for what happens to our children. We are responsible to teach and to live as an example to them. If we say one thing and live another, we're just hypocrites and kids see right through that. I've found out that kids aren't dumb. They see through things that parents think they're hiding. In fact, kids see more than we know. That's because they are open canvasses on which our teachings, whether good or ill, are being written every day.

I've been reading the war years in the book of Alma in the Book of Mormon. There are many lessons I'm supposed to learn, but there's a couple I learned this week that I want to share. The first is regarding the sons of Helaman. Two thousand sons of the Anti-Nephi-Lehi's covenanted to help their brethren the Nephites fight the wars that were thrust upon them. They were young, but their faith in Christ was unshakeable. In Alma 53:20-21 it states, "…and they were exceedingly valiant for courage, and also for strength and activity; but behold, this was not all—they were men who were true at all times in whatsoever thing they were entrusted. Yea they were men of truth and soberness, for they had been TAUGHT (emphasis added) to keep the commandments of God and to walk uprightly before him." Later, we are told in Alma 56:47-48 that, "Now they never had fought, yet they did not fear death; and they did think more upon the liberty of their fathers than they did upon their own lives; yea they had been taught by their mothers, that if they did not doubt, God would deliver them. And they rehearsed unto me the words of their mothers, saying: We do not doubt our mothers knew it."

These sons never perished in battle. They fought in many battles, but not one of them was lost while thousands around them died. This faith came from the teachings they learned in their youth at home. THAT is how important the example and teachings we as parents have towards our children. If we don't have children, THAT is how important it is that our INTERACTION with children, be we teachers or friends, show a perfect example of living righteously.

The second inspiration I received from these chapters so far was this, and I wrote it in my journal to not forget it. We make weaknesses strengths by being victorious over self and other wins to build stronger defenses against temptation. That's the lesson learned from Captain Moroni, who I like to think of as a friend, a perfect upright soldier and commander. He overcame large armies of the Lamanites and then used those prisoners to build the walls and fortifications which enabled them to defend themselves from further attack. In the same way, as we overcome habits, bad choices, worldly desires, etc., then we use that victory to build a stronger wall, a greater defensive perimeter around our soul protecting us from the fiery darts of the adversary. Life isn't meant to be easy. All the answers won't be given to us. In fact, part of this life is for us to learn to make correct choices and if everything and every answer is given to us, we won't grow.

I just finished watching a very cool movie called Charlie St Cloud. One of the things the younger brother asks Charlie to promise is that they'll always be brothers, come Hell or high water. I liken that to the Gospel because, if we LIVE the gospel, receive the ordinances in the temple, do what we are supposed to and endure to the end we're guaranteed that family relations will continue in the eternities. I look forward to spending the next eternity with Tiffany by my side, my kids and their future spouses and children in a line all the way forward to the future and also all the way back, tied together so that we have that promise. If we DON'T live, grow, choose, receive, we have no promise. We'll have resurrection because that's promised to everyone, but without the fullness of the Gospel, we won't be able to have eternal life, to become as our Heavenly Father and continue to have eternal offspring ourselves.

I love this Gospel. I love my wife. I love my kids. I love my savior. I love the Afghan people. I love the strange twists life takes, especially mine. I love looking to the future and seeing it very bright.

Isn't it funny? I talk about how we react to things that happen to us and how we choose to respond, at least I've talked about it in many chapters....and right as I finish this one and attempt to log on to the internet, my computer won't log in, yet my roommate ten feet away is logged on and enjoying a strong signal. What a crazy life we live!

Chapter 51

WHAT A DIFFERENCE DOES A DAY MAKE?

What a difference does a week make? What stresses, conglomerations, fun, frivolousness, freak accidents, frustrations, and just plain weird happenings can transpire during the course of a week? What insanity can be stressed? What knowledge can be gained? What idiocy can be demonstrated? Lastly, what enables us to focus when conflicts arise, fires are stoked and people's ire is awakened?

I'll tell you what, weeks like this come and go and leave a trail of surprising frustration and pathological blah-ness over the week. If you haven't figured out from the tone, this has been a weird week. I flew twice and each flight was unique. Flying adventures first, but the true story is in the personnel story in the squadron. Maybe it's because so many people are getting ready to go home; maybe it's because so many people are A-type personalities; maybe it's because everyone is PMSing even though we're a bunch of guys; all I know is there's been a lot of tension in the squadron this week and I tend to be one of the ones that people vent to, or on. Maybe it's because I listen; maybe it's because I'm happy-go-lucky a majority of the time; maybe it's because I see into the issues…I don't know, but it makes for an interesting week.

First flight this week was scheduled but never materialized. We went to the plane and got it ready and as we were getting it ready the wind came. Now I'm not talking about a nice northerly breeze. I'm not talking about a calm little fluff of air. Nope, I'm talking about winds 90 degrees across the runway gusting to over 30 knots (more like 35 Miles an hour) and forecast to get worse. There were airplanes flying, but we have a wind limitation on our airplane of 25 knots for crosswind and this was exceeding it. We sat there for an hour and a half and finally called it a day since the winds weren't supposed to get better until the next morning. The winds didn't die down until nighttime so we made a good call cancelling that portion.

Second scheduled flight, and the first to get off the ground this week, was with one of our qualified pilots. We got to go fly a training practice sortie, and those are always fun because, since he's already supposedly qualified, I can make things a little more challenging for him. We got to the area and began to do our training and really, I don't have anything bad to say about his flying. It wasn't great, but it wasn't bad. There were some things he needed to work on, like not descending too early on approach, and not following the needles in his instruments 100% correctly, but that's ok, it was a fun flight and a good training flight. It's nice to be able to report on the good flights. I know, I know, you probably think that since all I do is talk about the bad craziness of their flying that they are not good. The reality is that they're OK. They're not great, but they're not bad either. They have a long way to go before I'll trust them to fly without an American Instructor on board, but that's life. We play the cards we're dealt.

Finally, I flew with our favorite long term student, you could almost say our permanent student, and flew a challenging ride with him. I'll start this adventure story by saying that the ride was good. He did well and has progressed a lot from where he was a couple flights ago when I had to mark him down for unsatisfactory performance. He's improving and hopefully he continues. However, the ride was not without its adventures and since I make it a point to try to scare you, make you airsick, ensure you're appalled, and paint an accurate adventure picture at the same time, I hope you won't be disappointed because there were definitely those times. I really only had to mark him down for safety for the ride, though overall it was a good ride. "What?" you say! "How can it be a good ride and be unsafe?" Well, it was a "Safe" ride, but he did some things that if I weren't there watching him, would be considered unsafe. We flew into the area and began our instrument work. I like to begin with that because it's the hardest, especially when you're simulating failed engines. Actually, let's back up. Enroute from Kabul we had an hour of time to practice different things. We entered the clouds right above the highest peaks along the route. (They go up to 18,000 feet at that point, and we were only flying at 20,000 feet) I began questioning the crew on what we would do if we lost an engine at that point. First, on average on one engine we can hold about 14,000 feet of altitude. I would obviously consider that a problem because at that point it would put us 4,000 feet below ground. The tall peaks don't last long and what I wanted to see was if he'd analyze where we were at, and what the terrain is like ahead of and behind us. He didn't. He stated we'd turn around and return to the nearest airfield, Bagram. This obviously generated some discussion about the smarts of turning around, while descending in the clouds into terrain that could be and probably is, only 2,000 feet below us. Ahead, though the airfield is further away, the terrain rapidly drops to about 10,000 feet or less in front of us and I eventually talked him into seeing that the closest place may not always be the best. We broke out of the clouds and I must say I love beautiful cloud formations over the mountains, even when I have to fly through them, as long as they're not thunderstorms.

Continuing on the flight, I simulated the crew entrance door coming unlocked in flight. We all put our oxygen masks on and he did a good job of remembering things from our pre-brief. It was definitely eye opening for both he and our Afghan Loadmaster to try and communicate with the oxygen mask on. They saw the difficulty of going through language barrier problems (the loadmaster didn't speak any English and we had to have an interpreter the whole time), and the confusion that occurs since there were glitches with the system, and the radios weren't connected right. It brought out a lot of deficiencies that you only see through practicing this stuff. All in all I thought it was fun and quite entertaining, though my American Instructor loadmaster didn't think so. However, we got some good Emergency Procedures training out of it, not just for my pilot trainee but for the Loadmaster as well. It was a little funny from my end watching the loadmaster struggle with the microphone on his oxygen mask since he plugged it into itself….Kind of hard to hear anyone when you're plugged in a loop and not into the system.

Well, after that debacle was finished and emergency training complete, we arrived and I was pleased to see my student had improved a lot. There were the usual problems in the Instrument patterns where he would lose track of his altitude and I had to correct him, or he lost track of his course, but for the most part he did fairly well…until I started pulling engines on him. That's when things got interesting again! On one approach, using the translator, I started moving the propeller RPM back and forth and asked the loadmaster if he noticed anything wrong…he didn't so I had to repeat the action, meanwhile the translator's translating, my Afghan copilot is floundering as the plane yaws left and right, and I'm sitting there thinking, "Uhhhh, anyone gonna figure this out anytime soon!" I made it obvious the second time and pointed to the needle that, instead of being steady, was now oscillating back and forth. They declared it a problem (good call on their part) and simulated an engine shutdown. Ahh, the joys of flying a pig in the sky with only one good engine!

My student sort of forgot about altitudes and began to go right through his altitude. I stopped him after a couple hundred feet and told him to climb back up…he found climbing single engine doesn't work so well, especially when you're heavy weight like we were. I wouldn't let him do some things until he got back to his altitude, or at least was making a good effort. After all, it's hard to make a pig fly. We made our turn and he flew a decent approach after that. At least he did until I told him that we didn't have the runway in sight and he had to go-around without landing. Oh my! He's got a lot of hours, and it was ugly. Good rudder control, horrible wing/power/flap or gear control! Nothing was done in the right order. Then, to make things even more fun, as we were on downwind going to land visually, he was so worried about another plane that was on final to land that he kept pulling his power back to slow down. The problem with that was that we were already at our slowest speed I was comfortable with and he wasn't paying attention. After I told him "NO!", and "Stop that!" and made sure he kept power and speed … he did it again. I ended up yelling. For me yelling is not really yelling per se, but being very adamant. Three times in a row he did this in the space of one minute.

At that point, I really got onto him. I had fun with it. We were flying over some hills, so I told him his actions were going to crash us into those hills and he'd be strewn all over the place. I told him he'd make a widow of his wife and she'd come get what was left of him for doing that to her. I asked him if he wanted to die because that's what his actions would lead to if I wasn't watching him. Needless to say, he got the point. We did two more single engine go-arounds. The second was as bad as the first. The third, after a few more lectures about death and all his friends, he did it right. The funny thing is, his instrument work gets better and his normal flying suffers, but his landings are always good and THAT is important. We'll see how he continues. I'm flying with him tomorrow and I suspect he's going to have a LOT, a lot a lot a lot of engine problems. In fact, I bet he simulates shutting it down enough that his leg will be very, very tired from pushing on the rudder pedal.

In continuation of my discussion last week, my studies have branched into similar themes and similar topics. A little background; last week I talked about my being sick of the "f" word and other such things, talking about how we need to treat others. This is a similar discussion and it comes from what I've seen the last few days. Negativism, pessimism, frustration and other issues cause problems not just for the person that is festering in their own supposed wounds, but for everyone around them. I mentioned at the beginning several questions. And the truth is that our actions affect others. Even those actions we think are only affecting ourselves, they affect someone, somehow.

There've been several issues going on at work. As the stress of us leaving mounts, people's tension ratchets up and emotions get involved and people say things, or do things and instead of accepting responsibility for things they might or might not have done wrong, they point the finger at others. Instead of coming up with solutions to problems, they throw problems out on the table, but don't offer solutions, thereby causing others' tension to increase because pessimism and anger breed pessimism and anger. It's a negative double-edged sword. It's a negative outlook. It's a sad state of affairs when we reach that point. I've tended to be people's sounding boards on all sides of all issues. I don't know what it is about me, but I tend to be a receiver of venting. The truth is that I don't mind. I'm always a counselor at heart and always have been. I remember being counselor to all my friends in high school. I was counselor to all my friends in college. I've been counselor to my wife and kids and coworkers. I enjoy listening and being a part of everything. I don't always know the answer, but sometimes the answer is just that someone needs someone to listen to them. So, I've ended up listening a lot this week.

Since I love sharing, here's something I found out that goes along with this counselor bone in me. I was reading through my patriarchal blessing the other day while I was talking to Tip and it was so cool to share with her a comment in it that I'd read a hundred times, but only just understood. It says, "In the pre-existence you mingled with the great and noble and were a part there in *supporting and teaching* the plan of salvation. You *added strength to the spirit sons and daughters of God...* (italics added) That hit me. Even in the pre-existence I was a counselor. I added strength to others. I supported and taught. What do I love to do? I love to teach and support and help others. I love to listen and "be in touch with my feminine side" as people say to support others when they need the strength. I've always been an optimist. Sometimes I'm an optimistic pessimist, but that's just my chaotic brain. In Luke 10:25-29 it says, "And, behold, a certain lawyer stood up, and tempted him, saying, Master, what shall I do to inherit eternal life? He said unto him, What is written in the law? How readest thou? And he answering said, Thou shalt love the Lord thy God with all thy heart, and with all thy soul, and with all thy strength, and with all thy mind; and thy neighbor as thyself. And he said unto him, Thou hast answered right: this do, and thou shalt live. But he, willing to justify himself, said unto Jesus, And who is my neighbor?"

Who is my neighbor? Good question. It's everyone. It's the coworker that bothers me. It's the crazy member of the family. It's the person I don't know on the street. It's my friends, my family, and everyone I come in contact with. In reality, being a good neighbor is often a struggle. But, I find it's listening and being there when we're needed. We can't be the good neighbor when we're not acting in the spirit of love. President Hinckley commented in his book *Standing For Something* (and yes, there will be several quotes again), "The snide remark, the sarcastic jibe, the cutting down of associates—these too often are the essence of our conversation….Criticism is the forerunner of divorce, the cultivator of rebellion, the catalyst that accelerates to failure….But, if we will turn our time and talents away from vituperative criticism, away from constantly looking for evil, and will emphasize instead the greater good, America will continue to go forward with the blessing of the Almighty and stand as an ensign of strength and peace and generosity to all the world."

These are the words of a prophet of the Lord. He's not only asking us, but directing us in what we should do. He adds, "My plea is that we stop seeking out the storms and enjoy more fully the sunlight. I am suggesting that as we go through life, we 'accentuate the positive.' I am asking that we look a little deeper for the good, that we still our voices of insult and sarcasm, that we more generously compliment and endorse virtue and effort….What I am asking is that we turn from the negativism that so permeates our culture and look for the remarkable good in the land and times in which we live; that we speak of one another's virtues more than we speak of one another's faults; that optimism replace pessimism; that uncertainty and worry be pushed aside by and enduring feeling of hope."

Now a comment was made asking if my changes over the last year were real or staged; if I am really changed or if this is all just a big game; if I really am a new person. To that comment and to all who have seen my changes I say, I am a different person; the changes are real and not skin deep; I have a faith and hope that allow me to look with optimism to the future that Tiffany and I are creating with all the experiences of life that we're going through. This really has been a refiner's fire. I appreciate the concern, but with the strength of the Lord, all things are possible and I am firm in my faith and convictions and have developed good habits to take with me as I go home. Will things be different at home. You betcha, but it will be a good different because Tiffany and I have grown so much over the last year that we'll be working together on personal and family goals that will culminate after our enduring to the end in Eternal Life…that's the true ultimate goal isn't it, for all of us.

I can't help but quote Winston Churchill, as did Pres. Hinckley, regarding the dark days Great Britain faced during World War II, "Do not let us speak of darker days; let us speak rather of sterner days. These are not dark days: these are great days—the greatest days our country has ever lived; and we must all thank God that we have been allowed, each of us according to our stations, to play a part in making these days memorable in the history of our race." Does that sound like a spirit of pessimism? NO! Does that sound negative? NO! The point is that in these last days, there will be darkness and chaos, sin and evil all around, and we can either succumb to the negativity that is spouted all around us, or we can see the sunlight through the clouds. We must resist the spirit of negativity. I love seeing the bright side of life. I love seeing the fun in the challenges. Sometimes it gets people looking at me funny, but that's just life. I enjoy it and it allows me to be ready to support and listen when others need it.

We can only develop this kind of optimism through faith. "Faith in something greater than ourselves enables us to do what we have said we'll do, to press forward when we are tired or hurt or afraid, to keep going when the challenge seems overwhelming and the course is entirely uncertain….Faith and willingness to believe will chase pessimism away and replace it with hope and confidence. It is a source of immense personal comfort and peace of mind to have the knowledge that God is with us, and that even when there is no way—perhaps particularly when there appears to be no way—He will open the way." How do we develop this faith that President Hinckley talks about? We develop it through study and prayer. We develop it through our personal relationship with God. He quotes a writer who stated something to the effect of: as the United States removes God and Christianity from schools and forbids the use of Christian values, the Russians are inviting him (God) in. The Russians have invited Christian teachers to come and bring Christian values to their schools to teach their students values that have been missing from 50 years of atheistic rule. Apparently, the Russians learned something from us, but we didn't learn anything from the Russians….Sad isn't it.

As we pray, and I am so thankful for prayer, we can talk with our Heavenly Father. The amazing thing is He listens. I've felt and heard Him respond to me many times this year. He's informed me of where I stand and what I need to do. I haven't heard him audibly, but the still small voice that whispers through the Spirit has often answered my prayers. I used to say prayers and that was it. I didn't listen for a response…but prayer is our communication with our Father. He wants to talk to us and guide us and help us. The bonus is, He's there for everyone. It doesn't matter our color, creed, religion, race. It doesn't matter. He's there to listen….and respond, if we listen. As we listen, our faith grows. That's why I know that my changes are real and deep. I've felt the Spirit. I've felt the answers to many of my questions. And I've seen fulfillment of personal revelation over the last year. Tiffany and I have been extremely blessed and I'm thankful that together with our children we are able to make these changes.

How often do we read in the scriptures, "Ask and it shall be given, seek and ye shall find, knock and it shall be opened?" He's there and He's waiting. One last thing, that came across during our lesson is that we can't survive without honesty. One of Satan's favorite tools is to get us to lie to ourselves thereby making it so that we can't understand right or wrong because we can't tell the difference. He starts us out slow. Then he builds us to bigger and bigger lies. Afghanistan is a perfect example. The people don't even realize the extent of the dishonesty and corruption in their society. Everyone thinks only of themselves or their families and they don't think about how their actions affect others. I've come full circle. Corruption, lies, pessimism, negativism, they all breed upon themselves and the only person happy in that instance is the devil as he carefully leads everyone down to hell.

Take the prophets advice. Heck, take my advice, or take Bill and Ted's advice and "Be excellent to each other." And "Party on dudes" (meaning enjoy this crazy life and see the sunlight through the clouds and rain).

"Life is change, Growth is optional, choose wisely!" – Karen Kaiser Clark

"We can't control whether we win or lose, but we can control ourselves." – Lisa Fernandez

"Optimism is the faith that leads to achievement. Nothing can be done without hope and confidence." – HELEN KELLER

I have one long addition to make. My wonderful wife is a trooper. In the kids schools they have watched an amazing amount of movies that I can't believe they'd allow kids to watch. Rather than me say more I'm going to include the letter Tip sent to the superintendent and a whole bunch of board members and teachers. It's appalling and I am soooo proud of Tip. She is awesome.

She wrote:

"I am completely appalled at this school system! We have been here just over a year and this is the worst system we have ever been in! My children have been in eight school systems now around the country because we are military. I have let so many things slide because we will be moving in a few months! What ticks me off the most is that there is NO communication from the school to me about what my children are being exposed too! I am strict and we have very high standards so the movies and programs that my children are having to take a part in watching, without my permission, really makes me upset. I have four children in this school system and all of them come home telling me what (inappropriate) show they watched today or what they talked about in there "counseling" class, without my knowledge. What's next???? Are they going to show them how to put on a condom??? Thank goodness we are very open with our children and they are comfortable coming to us! I have wonderful, smart children that have to suffer because other parents use public education as a babysitter!! I would love to come in and chat!! My husband will be back from Afghanistan in three weeks and I would rather wait for him to get home before I come in!!

My fourth grader watched Saving Private Ryan today! This movie (edited) is maybe a PG-13 at best and I do not allow them to watch these kinds of movies! This is a long list of some of the shows they have been allowed to watch, edited of course!

Troy; The Boy in the Striped Pajamas; Braveheart; Black Hawk Down; Flowers for Algernon; We Were Soldiers; The Odyssey; The Man in the Iron Mask; Fly Boys; Caesar; Clash of the Titans; Myth Busters; Flags of Our Fathers; The Blue and the Grey;

These are some of the movies and shows that my children have watched this year!! I know that there are more but my younger kids are in bed! I am sending this note to everyone I feel needs to know about it because we are doing a huge disservice to the future leaders of this great nation! I am considering pulling my children out because of these issues and others! I am very concerned about my children's education!

Thanks! Tiffany Andrewsen"

Chapter 52

THE VALUE OF WORK

In a week's time I will finally be leaving Kabul and beginning my trek home. Home, such a good word and a wonderful place! Those who haven't ventured far from home or for lengthy periods of time just don't understand the joy that that one word evokes. It evokes a love of wife and children, security of soul and refuge from the chaos of life. Even with the family chaos, it's a blessing to be able to return. There are many people in this war that do not get that opportunity, except in a box. I've carried my fair share of those brave men and women home over the years. Home is a feeling, regardless of where the house may be, home is where the heart is, where the family is, where we can truly be ourselves without fear of recriminations or judgment. I'm thankful for a wonderful wife, family, kids, and home. And I'm ecstatic to be heading there soon.

This week has been full of adventure, and paperwork. After all, as Assistant Director of Operations, I get to assist and deal with the issues that come up and this week there were a lot of things that came up. As a unit, for the first time we broke three hundred flying hours in one month. Half of that occurred in the last week and a half. It's been an adventure. The airplanes have been working better, coming up on line as the parts arrived and we've been working them hard. In fact, two days in a row we flew six lines each day. The weather hasn't helped us with thunderstorms building every afternoon, winds blowing in and rain enjoying falling. Half of the airplanes have anti-icing problems so even though we had airplanes that worked we cancelled a lot of missions due to the weather needing anti-icing on the airplane. I cancelled at least once this week for that.

I flew twice this week and one of them gave impetus for parts of my discussion later. I'll start with the second flight, move to the first and then skip around to what I learned. The second flight was flown today. It was a normal training flight for our struggling student. He has improved a lot and it was an interesting flight. I'm impressed with his desire to work hard and learn. The sad thing is that it took his almost failing to get to this point. Now, he is working hard to not mess up the same things that he messed up during previous flights. When he messes up, he drops something out of his cross check. Today's flight was no different. Last week, I talked about his issues with single engine procedures etc. Today, he didn't have any problems with his single engine procedures, but his pilot not flying duties during my portion of the flight, were not up to par. I only took the airplane once from him when he descended through his altitude assigned, and didn't make a move to correct it. I pushed him hard today. I want him prepared for when he takes his check ride. He is getting better, but still needs work. I was tired at the end of the flight. I had to yell at him a few times due to the fact that he was NOT doing what he was supposed to in order to back me up when I was flying. He got behind the airplane, but then when we flew back to Kabul, he did just fine. The problem is that he doesn't understand the German controllers when they speak English. Therefore, he seems to ignore them. That doesn't work so well, since they talk directly to us…

I flew the approach back in to the airport at Kabul today because the winds were at our maximum crosswind component. I love that. Why? You ask! Because, I love the challenge and the opportunity to show my student that with practice, even when the wind is blowing crazy, you can still put the airplane down smoothly on centerline on the spot you plan on landing on. (Insert self-gratifying praise here!)

The first flight that caused me to ponder a bunch of things this week happened earlier in the week. I flew my first operational mission in a long time. I've spent so much time doing training flights that I've only flown one or two operational missions in the last six months. I really enjoy the training so it hasn't bothered me. I flew this line and it was a long, long day. In fact my butt was sore from sitting on the plane from it being such a long day. We literally did a complete circle of Afghanistan. Most of the flight was uneventful, aside from the length of the flight. We picked up 6,000lbs of tents, interestingly enough made in Iran, while at Herat. The Afghans tend to not palletize things so it was all hand loaded onto the airplane. Flying to Faizabad the weather was difficult. We overflew the city and couldn't see anything, looked socked in. But, we're nevertheless trepidacious so we turned and found a hole a few miles away in the cloud and descended to a safe altitude, where we could see that we could get in under the cloud deck.

The runway there is interesting. It's basically corrugated steel plates linked together and it was a unique experience to land on. It was one of those places that you just say to yourself…You just can't make this stuff up. Anyways, the Afghan Army was taking its slow sweet time getting there to help unload the cargo. Daylight was quickly fading. This wasn't good because the runway sits in the middle of this bowl, a tiny valley and it's a day visual only field. Literally, we were right next to a road. People would drive by and gawk at the airplane sitting there. So, I gave an ultimatum, either they showed up soon or I was hauling everything off the plane and leaving it in a pile behind the airplane. My timeline expired and the Army hadn't shown up yet. Therefore, my loadmasters and I, along with a couple people that were there and our one passenger that was continuing on to Kabul, began to unload the tents. We unloaded about 3,000lbs worth by the time the Army showed up. I was sweaty, dirty and annoyed at that point.

This is where my study came in. I was annoyed because I had an Afghan Lt Col copilot that I've taught since the beginning.

And while we, including a passenger, unloaded the plane, he just stood and watched us. He was either too good for work, or too lazy and that bothered me. It bothered me because I was the aircraft commander, though he outranked me. I was busting my butt and enjoying it. It was fun, ok, it was work, but I was having fun and he just sat there and didn't want to get his hands dirty. It wasn't the first time I'd seen it.

That brings me to my studies. It's now almost three o'clock in the morning. I just finished listening to the first day of the General Conference of the Church of Jesus Christ of Latter Day Saints. There was an overriding theme that I noticed. The theme was one of service and work. What's awesome is that is exactly what I'd been studying this week, or thinking about, since most of my studies have been strictly scripture. But, work; work is one of those things we take for granted yet, when I see laziness, it bothers me. I'm too tired to finish this tonight because I have a lot of thoughts I want to share and I'm really tired, so I'll continue this in the morning.

It's a new day, and it all feels good. It's a good life, that's what I'm told. Ok, really, I'm back, a little mental, but back. Finished with work and ready to relax, eat, watch conference, finish this chapter and have a good evening. Tomorrow I've got my second to last flight here. In fact, it could end up being my second to last flight in a long time because of the training and assignment that I'll be going to. We'll see what happens. I found out that I'll be learning Italian. Yep, Italian!! Them crazy Italians can't get rid of me apparently. I'm looking forward to that. My goal will be to leave school and training completely fluent. It helps that I can already read it. I can hear a lot and understand and I can speak somewhat, so I'll sort of have an unfair advantage over many people in my class. We'll see what happens.

Back to what I was stating earlier, as in last night, I despise laziness. I have watched people for all my life. I'm a people watcher. I also learned at an early age the value of work. Thanks dad and mom! Tiffany is doing a great job while I'm gone of teaching it to our kids. If everyone doesn't help someone else has to shoulder the burdens. So, people that are lazy tend to bother me. I just commented on the Afghan Lt Col that watched the rest of us work. It's sad really. While work can hurt physically at times, it's been proven that it stimulates our sense of self-worth and helps us feel better especially when we're working towards something we want.

In the Bible, in Luke chapter 19, Christ shares with us the parable of the nobleman who gave unto his servants and then went away for a while. He returned and wanted to see what they had done with the money he'd given. This is very much in line with the parable of the Talents and means the same. The servant, who'd received 10 talents, had doubled its worth and was given control of ten cities. He with five had done the same and received his reward. The one that had received one had hidden it in the earth, done nothing with it, and returned it back to his Lord. The Nobleman then took that away from him and delivered it unto him who had ten. Quoting verse 26, "For I say unto you, that unto every one which hath shall be given, and from him that hath not, even that he hath shall be taken away from him." This statement, when aligned with the previous story makes sense. The Lord gives us talents, abilities, challenges, etc. We are on this earth to be tested. As we are tested, we grow and increase our talents, abilities, and strength to face challenges, working to become better. Those that don't use what the Lord has given them….lose it!

In another parable, that of the husbandmen, when the wicked husbandmen cast out the owners servants and eventually slew his son, because they didn't want to serve or give to the rightful owner, we're told, "He shall come and destroy these husbandmen, and shall give the vineyard to others." Luke 20:16. This was a type of the church and Gospel that Christ was teaching. The Son of God was rejected of men, and killed on the cross. The Gospel, which was the vineyard, was given to others to preach and care for. We have the opportunity to either be the good or the wicked husbandmen. It's our choice. Everything is a choice. I've said it once, and I'm sure I'll say it a thousand times. We choose that which we want, for good or ill, life is a choice.

Now back to my complaint about laziness and people that don't work. We've all seen it, the epidemic that sweeps across our country, people wanting something for nothing. Entitlement feelings abound. Work dispels those feelings and imparts true self-worth. One of the talks yesterday that I loved talked about desire. He stated, "Desire dictates our priorities, our priorities shape our choices, our choices dictate our actions and our actions determine who and what we'll become." Where our heart is, there will our actions take us. That's why in the Book of Mormon we read, "Before ye seek for riches, seek ye the kingdom of god, then if ye desire riches, ye will receive them with a desire to do good…" If we get our priorities straight we'll be blessed. As we're blessed and keep our priorities straight, we'll use our excess to help others. The best part of all the talks, in my opinion, was how they each related to helping others.

We have the opportunity to share what we have, our time, our talents, our energy, our compassion, our religion, our money, our goods, our spirit, our feelings, our worth, our friendship, our open arms with others whether they be of our faith or not. This opportunity comes and enables us to feel good, to be enveloped by the spirit and to do as stated before: comfort those that need comfort, mourn with those that mourn etc. Ours is a wonderful opportunity, to be more, to grow more, to not just be us, to not just think about ourselves.

Real quick I just want to put down some key notes that I took.

"The atonement covers all conditions and purposes of mortality." – Kent F. Richards of the Seventy

"Christ chose to experience pain and afflictions to understand us. He chose to learn by his own experience and not just through revelation so that he can succor us." – Kent F. Richards of the Seventy.

"The principles of helping are eternal. Take opportunity to help whenever and wherever…Everyone is happier when they can provide for themselves and others…Way to have a surplus is to spend less than we earn…When you give service, you 're abundantly blessed…First prepare yourself and those you lead because you can only see a goal clearly when you see it spiritually…draw on the feelings of unity…Work, service is a work of love." – President Henry B. Eyering of the First Presidency

"How do we obtain revelation? When we've listened, read, studied and pondered, then we ask God if it's true…sincerely asking gets answers."

Lastly,

"The Gospel is simple. We need to keep it and our lives simple. We need to keep focused on those things that matter…simple sublime principles of the gospel can be summarized by love the Lord they God with all thy heart with all thy soul and with all thy strength and love thy neighbor as thyself. Christ stated Love one another as I have loved you, by this shall men know, ye are my disciples, if ye have love, one to another….Charity begins at home….each of us can do something for someone….we need to seek the gift of charity." – Elder M. Russell Ballard.

Thanks for listening and I hope we can all work, and not be lazy whether it is in our personal lives, professional lives or our spiritual lives. This life is a test. It's a good race and we're running it. How we do depends on our decisions, our abilities, our choices, and our convictions. Where we put our desire, there will be our actions.

"If every choice was weighed independently on a moral basis-that is to say, without claiming justification like justice, revenge or necessary ruthlessness—then far less evil would be done in the world." – Raymond E. Feist in Exile's return page199.

Flying at the top of the world, final flight in C-27

Chapter 53

FINI FLIGHT FINAL FUNCTION FINITO

This is the last chapter of this deployment. This is it. This is the last. It's almost over, just a few more days. It's unreal. It's amazing. It's time! What a week to end on too! It's been a crazy week and I've thoroughly enjoyed it. In all, it's been surreal.

I want to tell a story. This is a true story. For arguments sake, I'll be the protagonist and hero of this story. Hey, it's my story after all, I'm entitled. Fifteen months ago, I left home. When I left, I wasn't the best person. I had my issues. I had my faults. Some would be characterized as major. You've all taken a journey with me, a journey of discovery and change. While I didn't enjoy being gone from home, especially for such a long time, it was a necessary step in my life and I have been blessed because of it. I have worked with and met some of the most interesting, strange and messed up people in the world…and that's just the Americans! Really though it's been a grand adventure full of growth and discipline, change and courage, admission of faults and uplifting of heart. I've said it before that this year was a refiner's fire and that's the only way to truly describe it.

This week, as all weeks, I begin with some flying adventure. Buckle up and hold on! Per my request I flew my second to last flight with the most dedicated troubled student ever. He's been our struggling student, but I've had the opportunity to work closely with him. If there's one way to describe him, it's all heart. He has great desires to achieve, but struggles as a slower learner. Repetition has made him better and I've thoroughly enjoyed getting to know him. He's tenacious and has been hanging on by the fingernails, clawing his way up the lessons and succeeding, slowly but surely. He's improved. It's a testament to determination and hope and tenacity in the face of overwhelming difficulty. You've all read the stories lately when I've had to take the airplane away from him. But that's only a portion of the story. I've had to take the plane from every Afghan I've flown with. It's the nature of the way they learn that sometimes they're just plain dangerous.

For the first flight we went to our training base and flew a normal mission trainer. I didn't make it easy on him. In fact, I made it a point to make it difficult so that hopefully, when he's flying with someone else, it'll seem easier to him. We flew and he did well. Approaches, Engine failures, simulated fires, simulated problems….he did fairly well and I only took the airplane once, but not for getting slow which used to be the problem. I was impressed. It still wasn't a great ride, but for him, it was! Slowly, but surely, he's getting it and I am proud!

Second flight of the week turned out to be a flight to behold, a flight to dream of, a wonder and a pleasure. We started out early, too early in my opinion since I'm a night owl not a morning person, arriving at the squadron at 0600 on the day of the flight. Then we planned. This was to be our fini-flight, our last mission in the C-27 so we were taking two airplanes and flying formation. We hadn't done this in a while but we had great aspirations and it turns out that we had a beautiful day. We all came from the world of formation flying and we prepared well for our flight. The Lord was watching out for us, granting us a crystal clear day for flying. Taxiing out, we began our operation, taking the runway together and departing with minimum spacing. The pigs of the air, (the two heaviest airplanes we have) were actually climbing well in the crisp morning air. We moved into position a couple hundred feet or less from the other aircraft tucked into their wing position. It was perfect and challenging. I got to do a lot of the flying since the other American I was with wanted to take pictures. We climbed into the sun and got higher and higher until we could clear the mountains, then began our trek north.

The north eastern section of Afghanistan is a mess of mountains that drive into the highest mountain in the world. We proceeded to this rugged area and maintained our formation spacing. If you look at a map there is a finger that juts off to the east at the very northern tip of Afghanistan. We cancelled our IFR flight plan and proceeded VFR. Like I said, the day was perfect and crystal clear. The winds at altitude were calm and the air was smooth like my wife's legs after shaving! Love you tip! We proceeded to flow up the valleys, staying around the crests of the mountains and passing such mountains as K2 and others. But, the truth is that it cannot be described; the utter starkness and beauty of that mountain range. Snowcapped mountain peaks, glacial valleys and herds of Marco Polo (a type of mountain goat) along with people dwelling in little villages at 13,000 feet above sea level. It was, in a word, amazing. We flowed over mountains, along valleys, skirting knife edge ridges and driving over glacial water flow. Beauty and stark reality contrast in a surprising gleam. We continued along this route, waving to Pakistan on the one hand and Tajikistan on the other until we reached the end of the road on the map. Upon coming up one side of the claw shaped end of Afghanistan, we said hello to china, which was just on the other side of the ridge and turned around.

We chased the Marco Polo as we swung in a wide turn in the valley, three hundred feet off the ground and racing along at a good clip. Lead was a ways ahead of us and for the second part we were going to switch lead. We stayed low and accelerated to catch up. Lead had climbed and was a good 500-1000 feet above us. Directing him to make a hard right followed by a hard left it put him in position to drop down onto our six and take the number two position in the formation. Many pictures were taken. The flight proceeded uneventfully, but it was surrounded by the surreal. Not only was it a perfect day, we also were realizing it was our last flight in the C-27 and in cases like mine, could be my last flight for several years due to the job I'm going to. The mission was both surreal and sublime. We proceeded to Mazar e Sharif, getting there just in time to order snitzel from the German Snitzel haus. After a delicious lunch, we flew back to Kabul.

Arriving back in Kabul, we proceeded for a formation landing. Lead aircraft at the time got a little confused and turned early for the airfield which put us WAAAAAAAYYYYYY high. We configured and proceeded on a formation drop like a rock approach. Lead made his touchdown with us following a few seconds behind. We taxied to parking and were met by the rest of the squadron. Before disembarking from the plane we made sure to remove things from pockets we wanted to protect. As I got off the plane, as we got off the plane, the squadron hit us with the fire hose from the Fire truck they had called. Normally, you'd like to use plain water…the Afghans don't always understand that, so we got foamed! The stream hit me full in the side of the face, knocking my sunglasses off and then went for my chest, trying to knock me down. It was fun. As soon as the water stopped, we did the best thing we knew how…we went and hugged everyone that looked dry! We got the squadron commander pretty good and shook hands with everybody. What a great day! Many pictures were taken and we had a great time.

It all seems a bit surreal as I've stated previously. I'm almost done. I leave tomorrow to begin the trek home. It's always a long process to travel with the military but it's effective and we get there. I'm looking forward to going home. I will miss the Afghans and the craziness that ensues whenever they get involved in anything, and I will miss the flying, but I will not miss Afghanistan. I am thankful for the lessons I've learned here. I'm thankful that I had the opportunity to serve. I know that what I did here will have a lasting impression and I'm certain that things will continue on as we trained them, at least until the US and NATO pull out then they'll go back to doing things the way they want to anyways.

I want to grow a little introspective. I've served my country here for over a year. I've dealt with many issues and believe I've become a better man through my service and my learning. I've grown in ways I never expected when beginning this journey and I am excited and ready for the future. I can't wait to get home to Tiffany and the kids. They are the light of my life and I'm looking forward to being able to spend quality time with them. Seems like life just keeps trucking on, while everyone has changed through the course of this year. The kids have grown and matured. Tiffany has developed and grown. As I've shared more than once and will continue to share, she is the greatest wife, lover, mother, and friend that I could possibly be blessed with.

Friendship…It's rare for me to share close friendships. I'm quiet, except when I'm not, and I hold friendship as something to be prized. I cherish my friends and I thank you all for listening and learning with me. It doesn't matter what material possessions I accumulate in this life. It doesn't matter where I live. What does matter is what I do with my life and how I act and how I treat others and what kind of man, husband, father, and friend I become.

Life is full of options and different roads that we may travel. Life is a challenge and a path full of growth, if we accept it. As I walked late last night from the office back to the dorm, through the Afghan base, back to my room, I didn't walk alone. I figuratively turned to my friend Captain Moroni, and talked about Afghanistan and how it doesn't matter where we are, it doesn't matter when we live, it doesn't matter what part of the world we come from, and we're all Heavenly Father's children. I felt protected walking through those dark streets. I imagined a legion of stripling warriors surrounding me as I walked. I could picture their armor, their swords buckled on their sides, carrying spears with their head plates and breastplates girded about them. I imagined Capt. Moroni walking by me and talking with me, and I held a mini conversation with him about life, and the Plan of Salvation.

The time that he came from, living in America a hundred years before Christ, was a terrible time, and a good time. It wasn't all that different from our day. Wars were constantly raging. Men in their own country's hearts were failing them. People were looking for other things besides God to fill their lives. Many wanted a king. Many wanted power. Many just wanted riches and to be seen of the world. They justified all their actions, assuming themselves better than others because of their costly apparel or their new chariots or their fine linens. Is this any different than our world today? At the time, there was a set enemy, the Lamanites. They were stirred up to anger against their brethren the Nephites because dissenters from the Nephites wanted power and authority over everyone. They get everyone angry at those that followed the Gospel of Christ. And thousands upon thousands died.

Religious zealotry (and I'm stealing this idea from another talk I read today) has been the cause of great heartache and death throughout the ages. A preacher burns the Koran in the US and more than 20 people have been killed in Afghanistan and 90 others wounded because of it. We preach and teach, but we MUST NOT belittle or demean other's beliefs. I may not agree with my friends' beliefs, but I respect them. I have friends that are Evangelical, Wiccan, Catholic, Muslim, Buddhist, and probably Atheists as well. Does this mean I'm going to demean their religion just because I believe differently? NO! I love to share my religion and have done so frequently, because I know and believe it to be truth, having received a witness for myself, and I offer that same opportunity to all. But, I will never, and if it seems that I have I apologize, belittle or fight with you about your religion. "We claim the privilege of worshiping Almighty God according to the dictates of our own conscience, and allow all men the same privilege, let them worship how, where, or what they may." We believe the admonition of Paul. "We believe all things, we hope all things, we have endured many things, and hope to be able to endure all things. If there is anything virtuous, lovely, or of good report or praiseworthy, we seek after these things."

Let me think for a moment. This life isn't easy. It wasn't meant to be. There was a story told in a conference address that I love and is applicable. It tells the story of a gardener who was going to end up as an Apostle in the Council of twelve Apostles, Elder Hugh B. Brown, going about in his field and I think it best to tell in his own words the story. I thought a lot about this story this week as I thought about my life and this last year. I quote, "I was living up in Canada. I had purchased a farm. It was run-down. I went out one morning and saw a currant bush. It had grown up over six feet high. It was going all to wood. There were no blossoms and no currants. I was raised on a fruit farm in Salt Lake before we went to Canada, and I knew what ought to happen to that currant bush. So I got some pruning shears and went after it, and I cut it down, and pruned it, and clipped it back until there was nothing left but a little clump of stumps. It was just coming daylight, and I thought I saw on top of each of these little stumps what appeared to be a tear, and I thought the currant bush was crying. I was kind of simpleminded (and I haven't entirely gotten over it), and I looked at it, and smiled, and said, "What are you crying about?" You know, I thought I heard that currant bush talk. And I thought I heard it say this: "How could you do this to me? I was making such wonderful growth. I was almost as big as the shade tree and the fruit tree that are inside the fence, and now you have cut me down. Every plant in the garden will look down on me, because I didn't make what I should have made. How *could* you do this to me? I thought you were the gardener here." That's what I thought I heard the currant bush say, and I thought it so much that I answered. I said, "Look, little currant bush, I *am* the gardener here, and I know what I want you to be. I didn't intend you to be a fruit tree or a shade tree. I want you to be a currant bush, and some day, little currant bush, when you are laden with fruit, you are going to say, 'Thank you, Mr. Gardener, for loving me enough to cut me down, for caring enough about me to hurt me. Thank you, Mr. Gardener.'"

Time passed. Years passed, and I found myself in England. I was in command of a cavalry unit in the Canadian Army. I had made rather rapid progress as far as promotions are concerned, and I held the rank of field officer in the British Canadian Army. And I was proud of my position. And there was an opportunity for me to become a general. I had taken all the examinations. I had the seniority. There was just one man between me and that which for ten years I had hoped to get, the office of general in the British Army. I swelled up with pride. And this one man became a casualty, and I received a telegram from London. It said: "Be in my office tomorrow morning at 10:00," signed by General Turner in charge of all Canadian forces. I called in my valet, my personal servant. I told him to polish my buttons, to brush my hat and my boots, and to make me look like a general because that is what I was going to be. He did the best he could with what he had to work on, and I went up to London. I walked smartly into the office of the General, and I saluted him smartly, and he gave me the same kind of a salute a senior officer usually gives—a sort of "Get out of the way, worm!" He said, "Sit down, Brown." Then he said, "I'm sorry I cannot make the appointment. You are entitled to it. You have passed all the examinations. You have the seniority. You've been a good officer, but I can't make the appointment. You are to return to Canada and become a training officer and a transport officer. Someone else will be made a general." That for which I had been hoping and praying for ten years suddenly slipped out of my fingers.

Then he went into the other room to answer the telephone, and I took a soldier's privilege of looking on his desk. I saw my personal history sheet. Right across the bottom of it in bold, block-type letters was written, "THIS MAN IS A MORMON." We were not very well liked in those days. When I saw that, I knew why I had not been appointed. I already held the highest rank of any Mormon in the British Army. He came back and said, "That's all, Brown." I saluted him again, but not quite as smartly. I saluted out of duty and went out. I got on the train and started back to my town, 120 miles away, with a broken heart, with bitterness in my soul. And every click of the wheels on the rails seemed to say, "You are a failure. You will be called a coward when you get home. You raised all those Mormon boys to join the army, then you sneak off home." I knew what I was going to get, and when I got to my tent, I was so bitter that I threw my cap and my saddle brown belt on the cot. I clinched my fists and I shook them at heaven. I said, "How could you do this to me, God? I have done everything I could do to measure up. There is nothing that I could have done—that I should have done—that I haven't done. How could you do this to me?" I was as bitter as gall.

And then I heard a voice, and I recognized the tone of this voice. It was my own voice, and the voice said, "I am the gardener here. I know what I want you to do." The bitterness went out of my soul, and I fell on my knees by the cot to ask forgiveness for my ungratefulness and my bitterness. While kneeling there I heard a song being sung in an adjoining tent. A number of Mormon boys met regularly every Tuesday night. I usually met with them. We would sit on the floor and have a Mutual Improvement Association. As I was kneeling there, praying for forgiveness, I heard their voices singing:

"It may not be on the mountain height

Or over the stormy sea;

It may not be at the battle's front

My Lord will have need of me;

But if, by a still, small voice he calls

To paths that I do not know,

I'll answer, dear Lord, with my hand in thine:

I'll go where you want me to go."

(*Hymns,* no. 75.)

I arose from my knees a humble man. And now, almost fifty years later, I look up to him and say, "Thank you, Mr. Gardener, for cutting me down, for loving me enough to hurt me.""

I look back at this year and I say unto my Heavenly Father, Thank you Mr. Gardener, for cutting me down, for loving me enough to make me change, to make me become the person you would have me be. I'm still a long way from where I need to be and I love that I am on the road to become what he wants of me. This is the point. This is life!!!!!

That's the whole point of life. We are here to learn to become what the Lord wants us to become. I've mentioned many times that this life is part of a plan, the Plan of Salvation, also known as the Plan of Happiness. We were sent here to learn, to be tested, to "see if we'll do all things the Lord our God commandeth us to do." We are literally children of our Heavenly Father. We are his offspring. He is the father of our spirits and sent us here to gain a body, gain knowledge, and use our agency to choose right or wrong, good or evil…to become like him. When Adam and Eve were tempted in the Garden of Eden, Satan the great serpent, the liar, used his standard method of telling partial truths. He told them that by partaking of the fruit of the Tree of Knowledge, that they'd been commanded not to partake of, they wouldn't die but become as the Gods, knowing good and evil. Dissecting this a little bit we can see his partial truths and lies.

The truths were that they would learn good and evil, which would make them closer to being like God. The truth was they wouldn't die….right then, though death entered into the world when they partook. They made the choice to partake so that they could progress and become as their Heavenly Father. He knew this would happen and planned for it. Man, having fallen from his presence couldn't redeem himself, so he sent his son Jesus Christ to Atone for all our sins, our infirmities, to take upon him our afflictions, but not without cost. Reading the Beatitudes we read about all the blessings promised to the peacemakers, the poor in spirit, the meek…which deal with what we need to "BE" then He gets into what we need to "DO" ultimately telling us that we need to become perfect even as our Father in Heaven is perfect. The Gospel is a Gospel of action. It is a Gospel of striving to become perfect…and it won't end with death. After our life is over, our spirit will continue to strive and grow in the spirit world until at the resurrection we'll have the opportunity to be judged and receive our final estate, at which point, we'll still continue to strive and grow in that estate to become, ultimately like our Heavenly Father.

Think of the trials of your own life as opportunities to grow. Maybe you're going through serious reflection, maybe your life is struggling to find purpose, and maybe you're suffering through others' actions, and if you are, think of yourself as the currant bush. It has brought me good thoughts and great consolation as I reflect. Hopefully we can all say at the end of the day, "Thank you Mr. Gardener!"

This year hasn't been easy. It's been difficult, and frustrating, dangerous at times and absolute fun at others. May all of you enjoy your lives and the challenges that come! After all, we're here to learn. I hope that I've never insulted, belittled, degraded, or demeaned you or your religion. I say what I believe and that which I know to be true. I've not always known it, because I've not always done what I should, but I know that the things I've learned and the things that I've told in these Blog emails are true. I know it and you can know it. Every truth can be found through study, pondering and prayer. Ask and ye shall receive, seek and ye shall find, knock and it shall be opened unto you. For him that asketh receiveth, he that seeketh findeth and to him who knocketh it is opened.

"Friends, Romans, countrymen, lend me your ears!" I thank you all for listening/reading, etc.

Stay safe, stay sane, stay good…

The time has passed

It's been and gone

The darkness fell upon

The day as the long redoubt did end

And the presence felt did grow

For while gone, twas gone

And grew within

Spirit developing digging out of sin

And growing to be

The man I should

A year of time

Is not that much

To turn a life around

But thankful, am I that it was

An opportunity of mine

For now, past wars and circumstance

I grow, I live, I learn

And with Tiffany at my side

Eternity awaits!

Chapter 54

THE BREAK ENDS

It's been a long time since I last wrote. And frankly, I've been busy and haven't had the time or the impetus to write. In reality, I have had some time and I've had a lot of impetus. In fact, I've written part of this message several times over the last couple weeks. This has been an interesting and a challenging month. For starters, it's amazing and awesome to be back with my family. Of course as I write this I'm sitting in NC while they're in Alabama, but that seems to be life at times. At least, for us, since I had to finally go back to work. The good thing is that this is temporary. I'll be finishing at Pope in just over 6 weeks and we'll be moving and finally be together as a family, almost two years later!!!

It's been wonderful being home. It was everything and more than I could hope for. Tiffany surprised me the day I got home by taking me to the same mountain retreat that we went to on our honeymoon and it really was like a honeymoon, I'd been gone so long. Tiffany's family was nice enough to watch the kids so we could have those couple days together. It was wonderful and fun and we totally missed the chaotic storms that were all around us. Apparently, shortly after we drove through Sanford, a massive tornado hit town and demolished the Lowe's and people's houses etc. We never even hit rain. Then we were in our cabin and it was a little rainy, but nothing out of the ordinary and as we were driving home on Saturday, everyone was asking us if we'd been hit by tornadoes where we'd been. Weird, because we didn't have any sort of storm like that...of course we didn't venture outdoors much those two days. It was just soooo nice to just be together and not only able to see each other via Skype.

This became even more poignant a little over a week later, on the 27th of April, when storms and tornadoes slammed the south, with towns being destroyed all around us, three tornadoes passing by us not too far away and causing a lot of destruction in the south. Not only were Tiffany, and I, happy that I was home during this crazy situation during which we spent most of the day hidden in the closet.

But, that was the same day we found out that nine people I worked with in Afghanistan were killed by an angry Afghan helicopter pilot. While I only knew two of them well, it was difficult to realize that those guys and one girl were not finishing their deployment, but were coming home for their last farewell. It was sad. It was hard. Especially when thinking that the meeting where this took place was a meeting I used to attend. It could've been me, but it wasn't. There is a time and a place and a reason for everything. I'm certain of that. The scriptures tell us that our time is known and our days will not be counted less. This doesn't make it any easier on the families though that had to have the men in blue arrive at their door with that horrific news.

One thing that got lost in the deadliest day of tornadoes was this story. It made the news for very little time because of the massive tornado outbreak. Sad that something so heart wrenching is lost amid further destruction. It is made worse because so many hundreds lost their lives in the tornadoes that day as well. It became a day of mourning, a day of sadness and a day of insanity. I'm sure more will come.

I'm not morbid. I'm not heartless. I'm realistic. We're told that before the second coming of the Lord the signs and wonders (most of which involve destruction) will get more and more extreme. The world is going to become one crazy place. But, we don't need to lose heart. We don't need to lose faith because the closer we are to the Lord, the more peace we'll feel when all the world is turning upside down and things that happen just don't make sense or pass the sanity check. (Take our gov't debt snowball that just gets bigger and bigger and bigger...yet REAL cuts are almost impossible for politicians to make) Anyways, that's a different subject.

How can we have peace when there is death and destruction all around? "Where can I turn for peace? Where is my solace? When other sources cease to make me whole? When, with a wounded heart, anger, or malice I draw myself apart searching my soul? Where, when my aching grows? Where, when I languish? Where, in my need to know? Where can I run? Where is the quiet hand to calm my anguish? Who, who can understand? He, only One.

He answers privately. Reaches my reaching. In my Gethsemane, Savior, and friend. Gentle, the peace He finds for my beseeching. Constant He is, and kind. Love without end." I love the words to this hymn. It's gentle, it's peaceful, and it's true. When anger or malice or frustration or despair threatens to weigh us down, we can turn to him for peace. He is the one that calms our heart and helps me realize that "OZ" (Major Jeff Ausborn - C-27 instructor I worked with killed in Kabul) is going to be all right. After all, death has been overcome. I've talked the Plan of Salvation many times, but this is where it really makes sense. Death is not the end. I just saw an article where Stephen Hawking (famous scientist etc...) claims there is no heaven and that at death there is nothing. How sad! I know for a fact that death is not the end that we were all alive as spirits before we were born, chose to come to earth to gain a body and be tested and then die, our spirits returning to the spirit world to await judgment. But through Christ, the bands of death were broken, and though the body die, it will be reunited with the spirit eventually and we'll receive one of three degrees of glory. That's the glorious truth of the Gospel, that we will live again, that we are being tested and that we can see our loved ones again after they die.

Oz's was the first funeral I've been to in a very, very long time. It was a stark reminder of life. A funeral is a good place to contemplate eternity and our place in it? Am I doing everything I can to live worthily to be with my family again? Am I exercising my faith? If today were my last day, how would I be judged? Too often we get so focused on life that we don't' realize we're living it, or we don't understand the necessity to live it right, right now! For some, tomorrow doesn't come. Two weeks before those murders in Kabul, I was sitting with OZ talking about the plans for the program and what they were going to do...two weeks later, those plans were thrown out the window by an angry man with a gun. Stupid! But, at the same time, it could be anything. It could be illness, or car accident. I'm not trying to paint a negative picture, I'm just saying that life is short and while we want to live it, we NEED to live it correctly so that when we meet our maker He can say, "well done though good and faithful servant."

Life is chaotic and beautiful. I hate having to leave each Sunday to return to work in North Carolina when I go home to Alabama on the weekend. But, I know it's necessary to provide for my family. Necessity and duty. Honor and responsibility. More and more I wish the world would go back to olden days where a man's word meant something. Where, if someone said they'd do something, they'd do it and you wouldn't have to worry about it. But that's not the case anymore. Too often, a man's word isn't worth the breath they use to speak it. We've lost some of that honor and integrity in the world and it's sad. But, each of us can make the decision, as I have, as Tiffany has, to say what we mean and mean what we say; to do what we say we'll do. That's the world I want to grow up in.

Look around you and be happy with life. It goes and it's here to be enjoyed, but not overindulged. Adam fell that men might be and men are that they might have joy. May the Lord bless you with joy in your lives every day!

EPILOGUE

Finally officially, we're back together as a family! This summer has been amazing, though stressful due to travelling and moving and travelling for two straight months before we finally emerged from our long separation and moved in to the home we're renting while I go through school.

We've been doubly blessed by the Lord. First, we had decided to not look for houses anymore until we arrived in California, but then, the next day the Lord showed us the house we were to rent. It's perfect, exactly what we need. Not only that, but we are in a ward that welcomed us with open arms. There are sure to be many more trials and struggles as we progress, but for now we are happy to be together. Spending so much time apart is difficult, but the growth that we went through is worth it.

I close with a wish that all who read this can learn from it. I've been changed in ways I never understood over a year ago when I began writing. We've grown as a family and are even homeschooling this year. Our trials and our challenges, our weaknesses even, are becoming our strengths as we are promised in Ether 12:27, "that our weak things will be made strong". I love my family. I love the Lord. I love the Gospel. I love the opportunities that have been afforded me and I know that, as I follow the guidance of the Holy Spirit, I will be blessed along with my family. Be good. Be excellent in what you try and what you do. Lastly, be the person you know that our Heavenly Father wants you to be. No gimmicks, no shortcuts, no excuses. We are all sons and daughters of our Heavenly Father and He wants the best for us.

Patience – By Todd Andrewsen

Take a stroll down memory lane;

You didn't get here fast;

Look inside and feel no pain;

As you look back at your past;

Decisions made are long past gone;

Just a flashpoint in your mind;

You made some choices right or wrong;

No choices left behind;

Now as you stroll down life's sweet path;

Roads go left and right;

With patience, faith and holiness;

We go on in life's high flight;

We waste time doing so many things;

Unknown when in our doubt;

The miracle of what life brings;

Do you know what I'm talking about?

Have patience friends and struggle on;

Don't give in to your doubt;

Patience helps you write the song;

That brings hope out and about.

Hope, the winter solstice brings;

Hope gives us the strength;

Hope will help a poor heart sing;

Hope makes life a bank…a bank of peace;

Life full of wisdom;

Life full of song;

Words teach bits of knowledge;

Words give you peace!

In memory of Jeff "Oz" Ausborn and others killed 27 April 2011 at Kabul International Airport

- Remember, death is not the end. Through Christ we will live again.

BIBLIOGRAPHY

1.Tom Venuto, *The Body Fat Solution,* New York, NY: Penguin Group (USA) Inc., 2009

2. Robert D. Hales, *Return: Four Phases of Our Mortal Journey Home*, Salt Lake City, UT: Deseret Book, Publishers Printing, 2010

3. Gordon B. Hinckley, *Standing For Something*, New York, NY: Times Books, 2000

4. Victor Hugo, *Les Miserables*, New York, NY: The Modern Library, 2009

5. James L. Ferrell, *The Peacegiver*, Salt Lake City, UT: Deseret Book, 2004

6. Anita Stansfield, *A Distant Prayer*, American Fork, UT: Covenant Communications, Inc., 2008

7. Anita Stansfield, *The Sound of the Rain*, American Fork, UT: Covenant Communications, Inc., 2008

8. Anita Stansfield, *Shelter From the Storm*, American Fork, UT: Covenant Communications, Inc., 2009

9. Anita Stansfield, *Winds of Hope*, American Fork, UT: Covenant Communications, Inc., 2009

10. Gerald N. Lund, *The Kingdom of the Crown – Fishers of Men*, Salt Lake City, UT: Shadow Mountain, 2000

11. Gerald N. Lund, *The Kingdom of the Crown – Come Unto Me*, Salt Lake City, UT: Shadow Mountain, 2001

12. Gerald N. Lund, *The Kingdom of the Crown – Behold the Man*, Salt Lake City, UT: Shadow Mountain, 2002

13. The Church of Jesus Christ of Latter Day Saints – *Preach My Gospel*, The United States of America: Intellectual Reserve, Inc., 2004

14. http://www.pilotpsy.com/flights/3.html

15. LeRoi C. Snow, Improvement Era, June 1919, p. 656.

16. Teachings of the Prophet Joseph Smith, sel. Joseph Fielding Smith, Salt Lake City: Deseret Book, 1938, pp. 345–46

17. Eliza R. Snow, pp. 46–47; italics added. Brigham Young was President of the Quorum of the Twelve at the time

18. Eliza R. Snow, Biography and Family Record of Lorenzo Snow, Salt Lake City: Deseret News Co., 1884, pp. 9–10

19. Gerald N. Lund, "I Have a Question," Ensign, Feb. 1982, 39–40

20. PROCLAMATION TO THE WORLD ON THE FAMILY, THE CHURCH OF JESUS CHRIST OF LATTER DAY SAINTS

21. M. RUSSELL BALLARD, Let Our Voices Be Heard - Ensign, Nov 2003

ABOUT THE AUTHOR

Major Andrewsen is an avid pilot, having begun flying in Cessna's and Pipers before he could drive. His Air Force career began as an enlisted military linguist. After completing his degree, he was accepted into officer and pilot training and chose the C-130 path upon completing basic pilot qualification, eventually becoming an Instructor Pilot in the C-130 Hercules. Over the years he's compiled over a thousand combat hours in both the C-130 and the C-27. The deployment to Afghanistan that this book is about was his ninth deployment. He and Tiffany, along with their four children, are overjoyed to share these stories and this message of growth, healing, and change.

Made in the USA
Charleston, SC
18 June 2012